IMAGES
of America

MILLEDGEVILLE

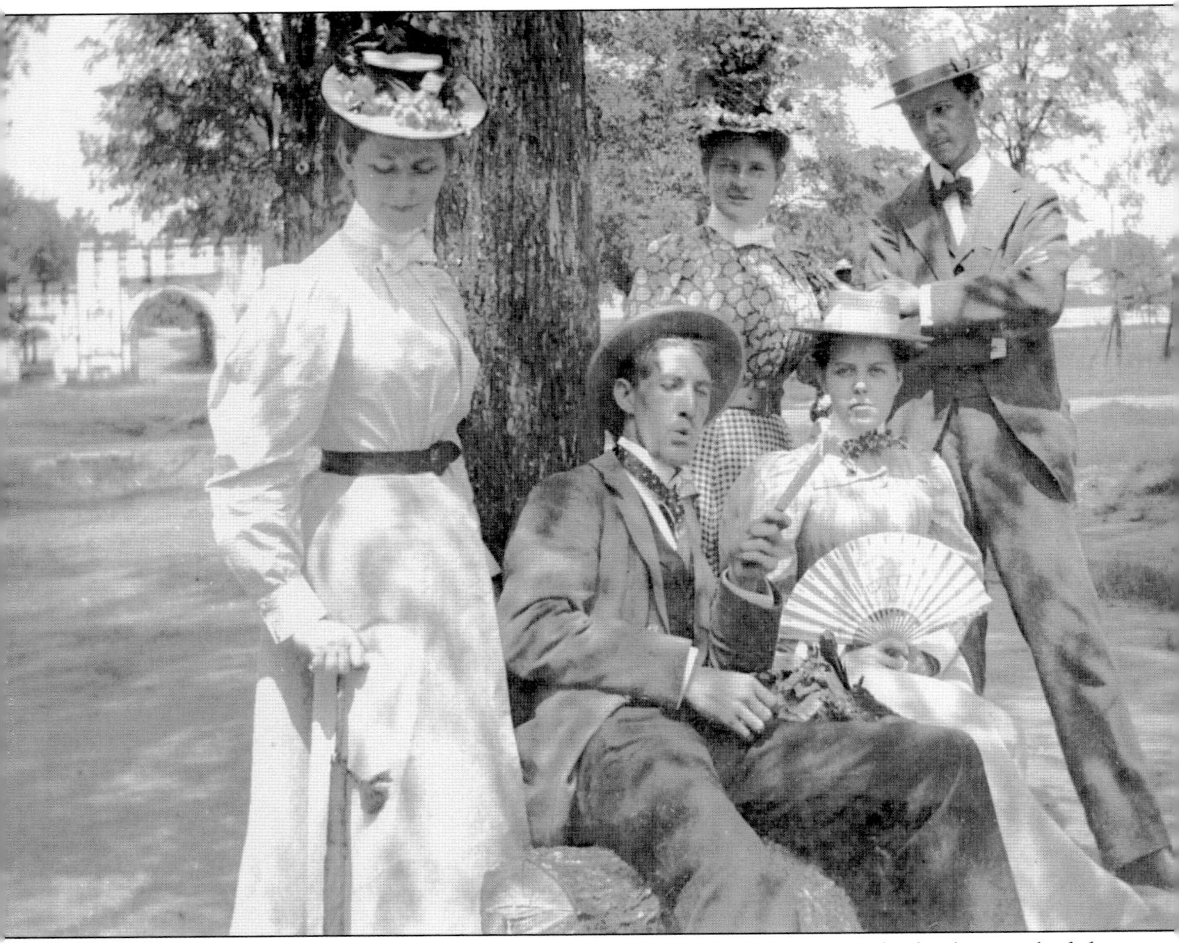

The easily recognizable Gothic Revival statehouse gates are visible in the background of this photograph of an unidentified group of youths in the early 1900s. (Courtesy of Charles Smith.)

On The Cover: In a 1934 photograph, these women pose in front of the Colonial Theatre. The Colonial opened its doors on October 8, 1914, and was managed by Edmund Reid. It was billed as the new wordless playhouse. It also featured a soda fountain as well as a candy, cigar, and cigarette stand. (Courtesy of the Georgia Archives, Vanishing Georgia, bal-116.)

IMAGES
of America

MILLEDGEVILLE

Amy E. Clark-Davis

ARCADIA
PUBLISHING

ISBN 978-0-7385-8793-6

Published by Arcadia Publishing
Charleston, South Carolina

Printed in the United States of America

Library of Congress Control Number: 2011925289

For all general information, please contact Arcadia Publishing:
Telephone 843-853-2070
Fax 843-853-0044
E-mail sales@arcadiapublishing.com
For customer service and orders:
Toll-Free 1-888-313-2665

Visit us on the Internet at www.arcadiapublishing.com

To my husband John and my children Savannah and Evan, thank you for your abundant support that allowed me time that was needed to write this book.

Contents

ACKNOWLEDGMENTS

The process of writing and compiling the material for this book proved to be exciting and a great privilege as well as a greater challenge than I had anticipated. I have a deeper appreciation for the individuals who have given their time to study, document, and share history for its preservation. First of all, I must thank my acquisitions editor, Brinkley Taliaferro. Being completely knowledgeable about guidelines and layouts, always available to answer my multitude of questions, and having patience to let me develop and deliver quality work, she was an integral part of this endeavor. Many contacts were made to find the photographs I needed to document the history of Milledgeville as I wanted it presented, and I appreciate all of the individuals who were gracious in sharing their personal photographs with me to preserve and share Milledgeville's history with readers.

With deep appreciation and indebtedness, I thank Dr. Bob Wilson for sharing his time to review my work. His expertise in history through years of study and considerable time spent for my benefit helped to achieve an accurate finished product. I also extend many thanks to Dr. Tom Toney and Randy Cannon, who shared my enthusiasm for my photographic finds and contributed to my research by discussing local history with me and comparing observations. My family and friends have been incredibly supportive and encouraging and, for that, I consider myself fortunate and am eternally grateful.

What started as a seemingly simple plan to gather photographs and write history was additionally an unexpected and rewarding restoration and archiving project. It was exhilarating to find images, which, in many cases, had not been seen in more than a century. I extend my deepest gratitude to Charles Smith, who allowed me access to a treasure of Milledgeville's history on film. He placed great confidence and trust in me by allowing me to take possession of his priceless and fragile photograph negatives for preservation and use in the completion of this book. Unless otherwise noted, all the images in this book appear courtesy of Charles Smith.

Introduction

Uncommon to the way most cities are founded, Milledgeville, Georgia, was conceived of and planned with a definitive purpose. Milledgeville, like Washington, DC, was founded with the purpose of being a capital city. In 1803, a commission was appointed by a joint session of the Georgia General Assembly to survey an acceptable site for a permanent state capital. A location within the already established Baldwin County was chosen for the future city, and it was named for then governor John Milledge. Milledgeville was the capital of Georgia from 1804 to 1868, after which time the capital was moved to Atlanta, where it remains. The economy of Milledgeville during the antebellum years was largely agricultural and, to some extent, industrial. Milledgeville's economic system became driven by cotton production and gave rise to textile mills for its manufacturing as well as improved transportation for its distribution.

The Civil War changed conditions in Milledgeville from a time of expansion and prosperity to the city being immersed in economic, structural, and societal recovery after loss of the state capital and the residual effects of the war. The reasons the war was fought involved large, complicated, and interrelated factors. Emancipation was a result of war, not a cause. Confederate currency and bonds were worthless after the war, and financial institutions were especially hard-hit. In a process known as the crop-lien system, farmers borrowed against the anticipated value of their crops and depended on the harvest bringing enough profit to cover the cost owed on everything from seed and planting materials to basic necessities such as food. Owners of general stores often charged interest and raised prices on the goods sold. In this cycle of debt and profit, the local economy was nearly destroyed in the early 1900s by infestations of the boll weevil, an insect that decimated cotton crops. The economic hardships faced by Milledgeville, as a result of the Civil War and agricultural losses, were further compounded by business closings, job losses, and individual financial distress. Milledgeville has faced the challenges of women's suffrage, civil rights, changes in industry, two world wars, the Korean and the Vietnam Wars, and both social and political upheavals. The city has been home to numerous figures of wide-ranging influence and interests, including author Flannery O'Connor, Congressman Carl Vinson, Dr. Benjamin Judson Simmons, comedian Oliver Hardy, and chemist Charles Holmes Herty, just to name a few.

Specific locations also came to be associated with and define Milledgeville. Central State Hospital is one of these sites. As a result of society's progression toward social reform, a law was enacted in Georgia in 1837 to establish the first "lunatic asylum" for the state in Milledgeville. Upon the building's completion, admittance was open for patients on December 15, 1842. Later, the name was changed to reflect revised attitudes toward mental health. First, the institution became Georgia State Sanitarium, then Milledgeville State Hospital, and finally Central State Hospital, the name it has today. By the 1960s, Central State Hospital had become the largest mental health facility in the United States. The colleges located in Milledgeville are also major defining locations. Georgia Normal and Industrial College, which became Georgia State College for Women, was later renamed Georgia College. The college began as an institute to prepare women with the knowledge and educational tools necessary in an increasingly industrialized society. The school's structure changed with the transitions in women's roles and attitudes toward women in society. Another institution of learning having instrumental impact on Milledgeville's development was Middle Georgia Military and Agricultural College. Founded in 1879, it accepted both male and female students and began at primary school grades. The name of the school was later changed to Georgia Military College. In part, Milledgeville has been built on and influenced by these two institutions of learning.

Milledgeville has triumphed at its height as the capital of Georgia and endured through economic and societal hardships. It is a testament to the determination and perseverance of the people who built the foundations and framework of this city that elements of who they were and what they did are evident more than 200 years later. Whether or not past events or persons are a complement to the place and time from which they come, the enduring fact is that each of us can use those experiences to improve the history presently being created. It is crucial to recognize history as a tool to learn and to create productive opportunities rather than it being a defining principle.

To think that every small detail of history could be included in this one book greatly underestimates the vast amount of valuable past events and people that have shaped the course of Milledgeville. While great effort went into gathering information and researching facts, some records in history have been lost, events not well documented during the time period in which they occurred, or difficulty encountered obtaining photographs. Consequently, preserving history should be of vital importance and every effort made to ensure that information passed on is accurate and representative of every facet and viewpoint making up the rich and diverse city of Milledgeville, Georgia.

One

The Development and Growth of a City

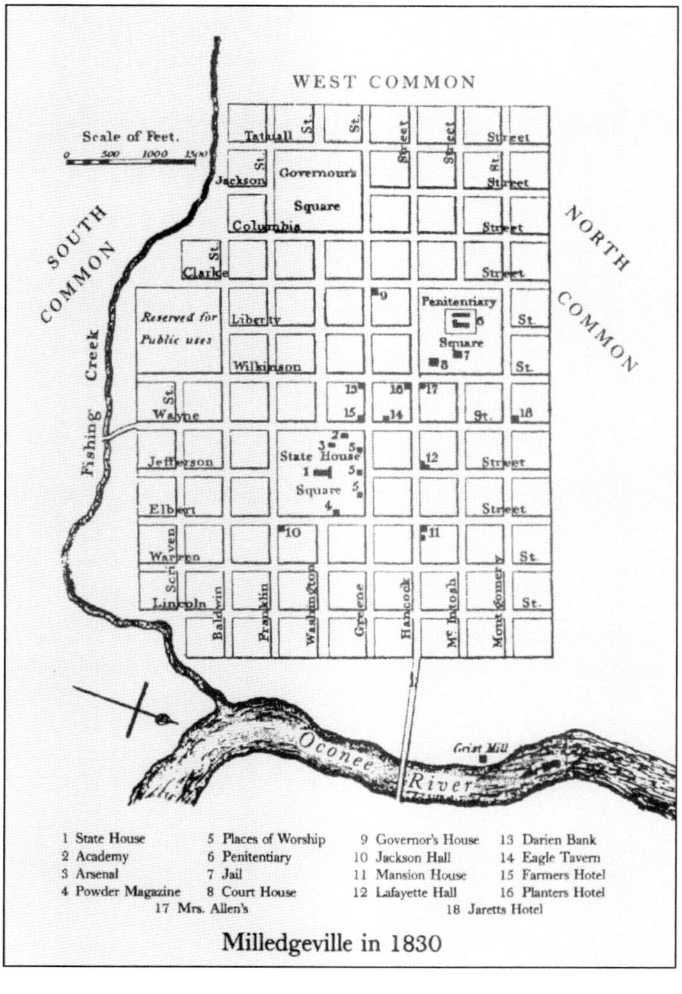

Milledgeville, like Washington, DC, is a city that was planned and designed with the primary purpose of being a capital. Previously, the site was occupied by Fort Wilkinson, which protected the Indian border, on the west side of the Oconee River three miles south of town. Prior to Milledgeville becoming the capital city of Georgia, Savannah, Augusta, and Louisville served as state capitals. (Courtesy of Allied Arts.)

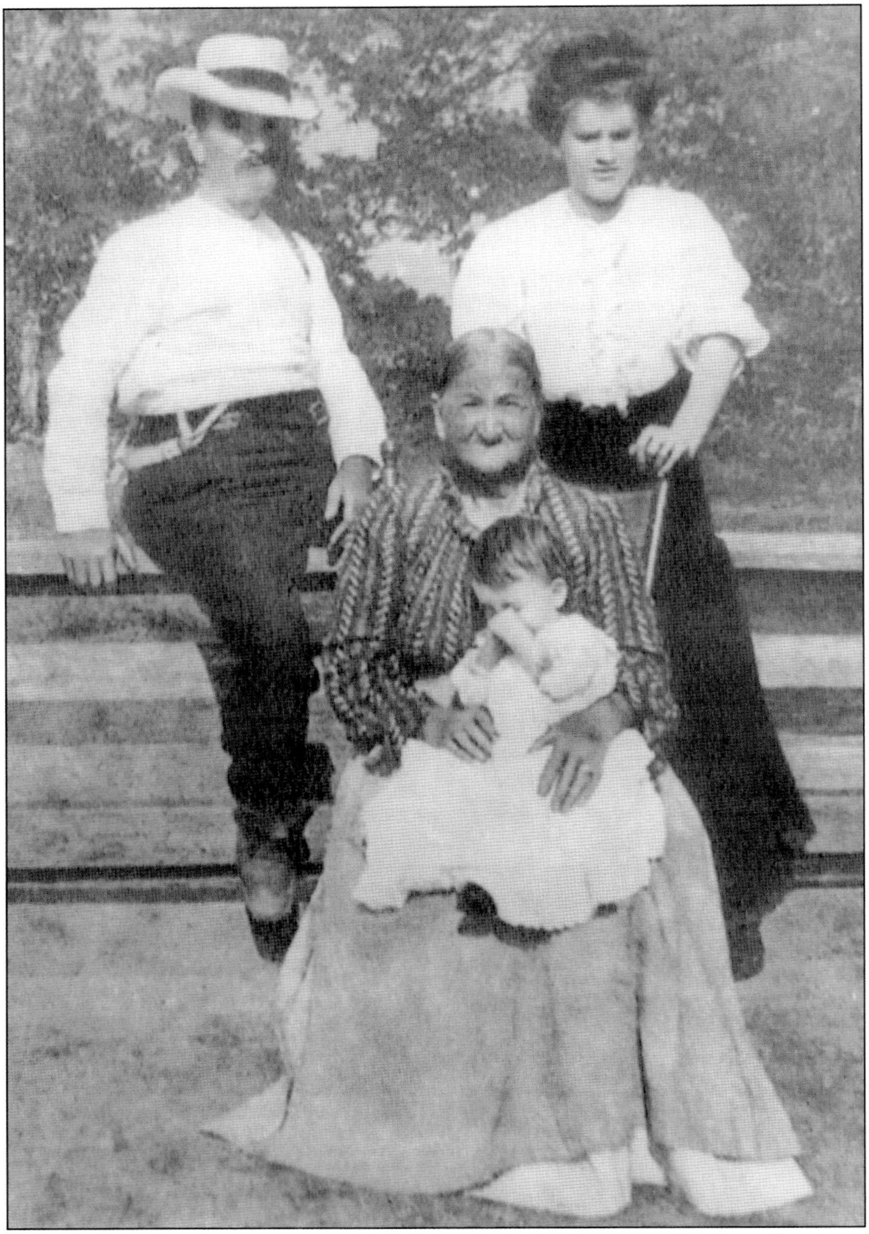

Cultural ties developed between natives and newcomers in Georgia as a result of established trading of goods and slaves. Native Americans adopted Anglo American practices in an attempt to deter hostilities. Intermarriage between Creek women and foreign trading partners was common. Traders took up residence with the Creek and married Creek women. The bicultural children of such marriages often became tribal leaders as adults because of their understanding of both the Creek and Anglo American cultures. Taken in the late 1800s, this photograph shows Louisa Ray Gilmore (seated), a Creek Indian, with her family. Standing are Jessie Gilmore (left) and Myrtle Gilmore. Louisa Ray is holding infant Sarah Gilmore. The Gilmore family descendants reside today on the same land that was appropriated in the 1880s through a land grant. (Courtesy of Stacey Gilmore and the Gilmore family.)

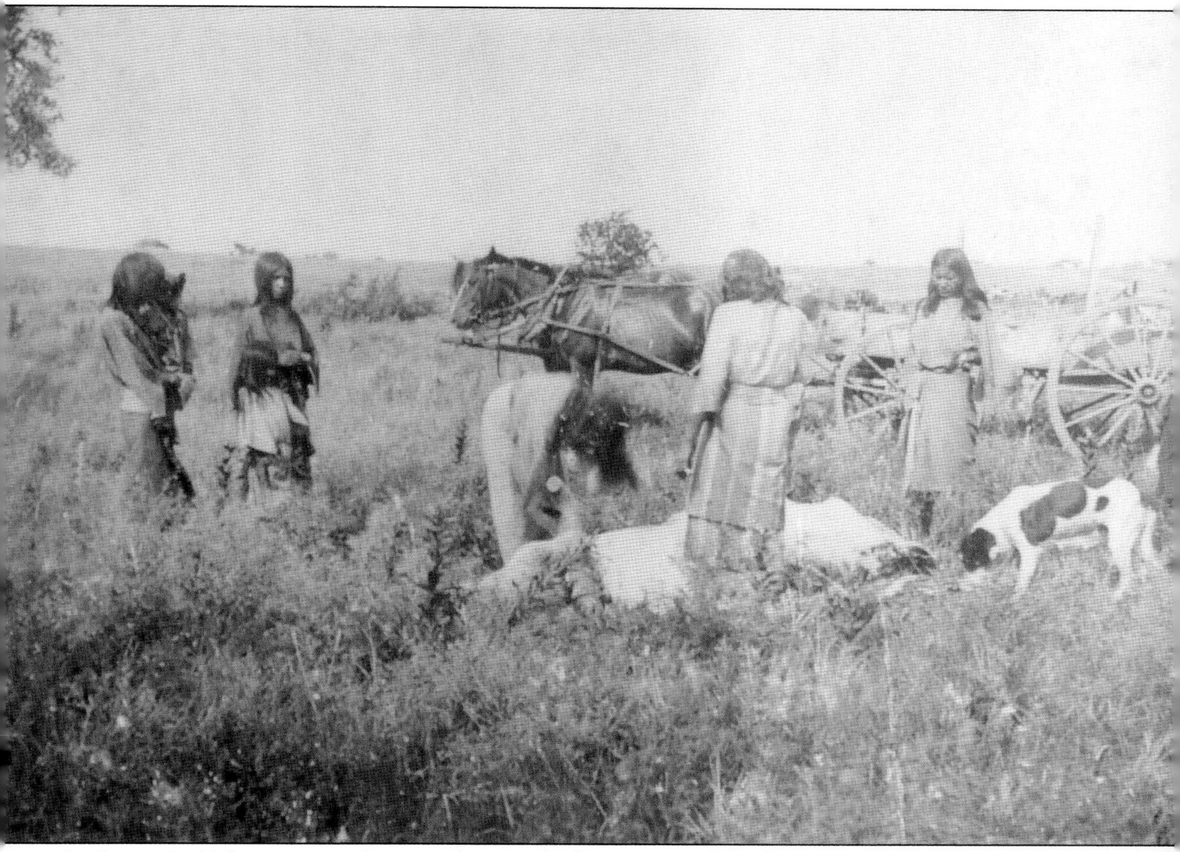

In the early 19th century, white settlers saw Indians as an obstacle to expansion and progress. Between the late 1700s and 1830s, the Creeks signed several treaties ceding property in Georgia in the hope of retaining some of their land. In 1832, they signed a treaty agreeing to relocate to lands in the west, designated as Indian Territory and later known as Oklahoma. The relocation of several Native American nations from the Southeastern states to reservations was part of what would later be known as the Trail of Tears. It was so named because of the devastation of famine, exhaustion, and disease that killed about one-third of Indians making the journey. This photograph, taken between 1880 and 1894, documents Indians hunting on the reservation in Indian Territory. (Courtesy of the Georgia Archives, Vanishing Georgia, usa0006.)

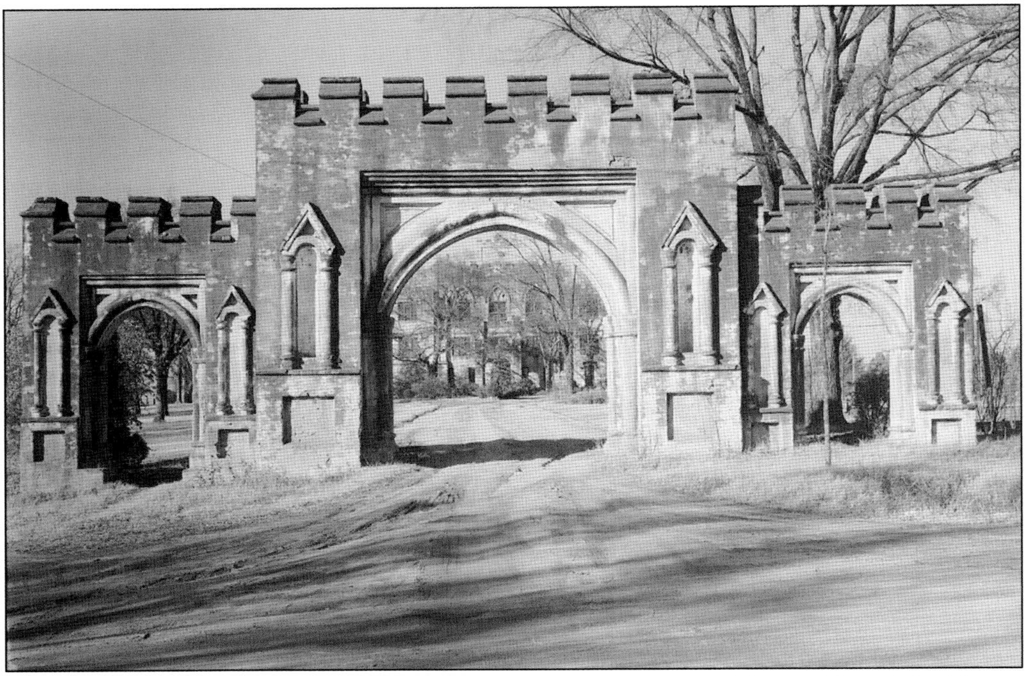

After a survey of the land during the previous year, an act was passed by the Georgia legislature on December 2, 1804, to move state capital from Louisville and build a new capital in Baldwin County. The push of settlers desiring more land, newly ceded land from the Creek Indians, a more geographically central location in the state, a site on the Oconee River, and abundant natural springs were all factors that contributed to relocating the state capital. This photograph of the statehouse gates was taken in 1939. (Courtesy of the Library of Congress, Carnegie Survey, LC-J7-GA-1434.)

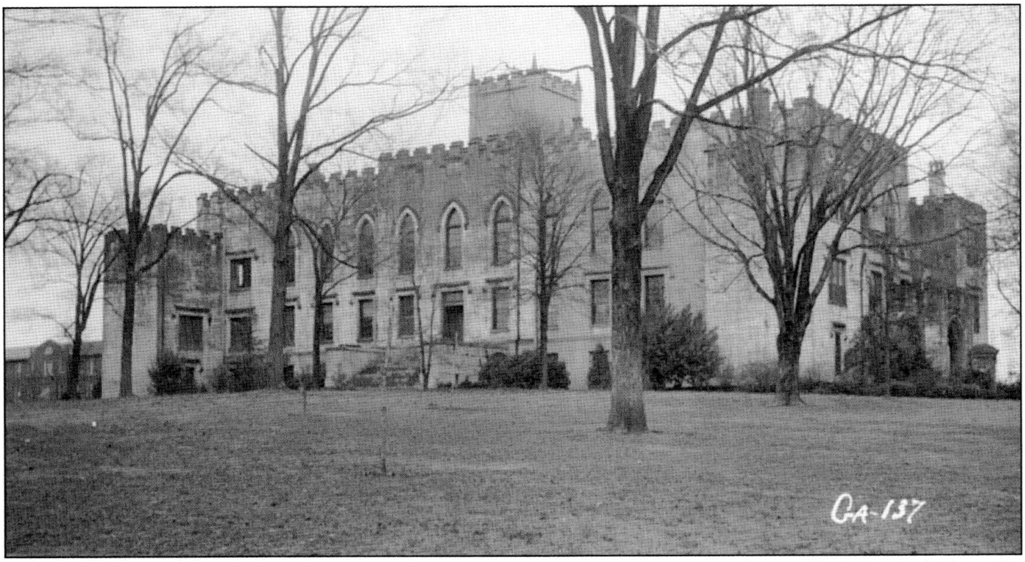

The new capital city was named in honor of Georgia's then governor John Milledge. Milledgeville served as the state's capital from 1804 to 1868. The former Georgia State House, shown here, was the location of the 1861 Secession Convention, at which Georgia officially seceded from the Union. (Courtesy of the Library of Congress, HABS-GA-137.)

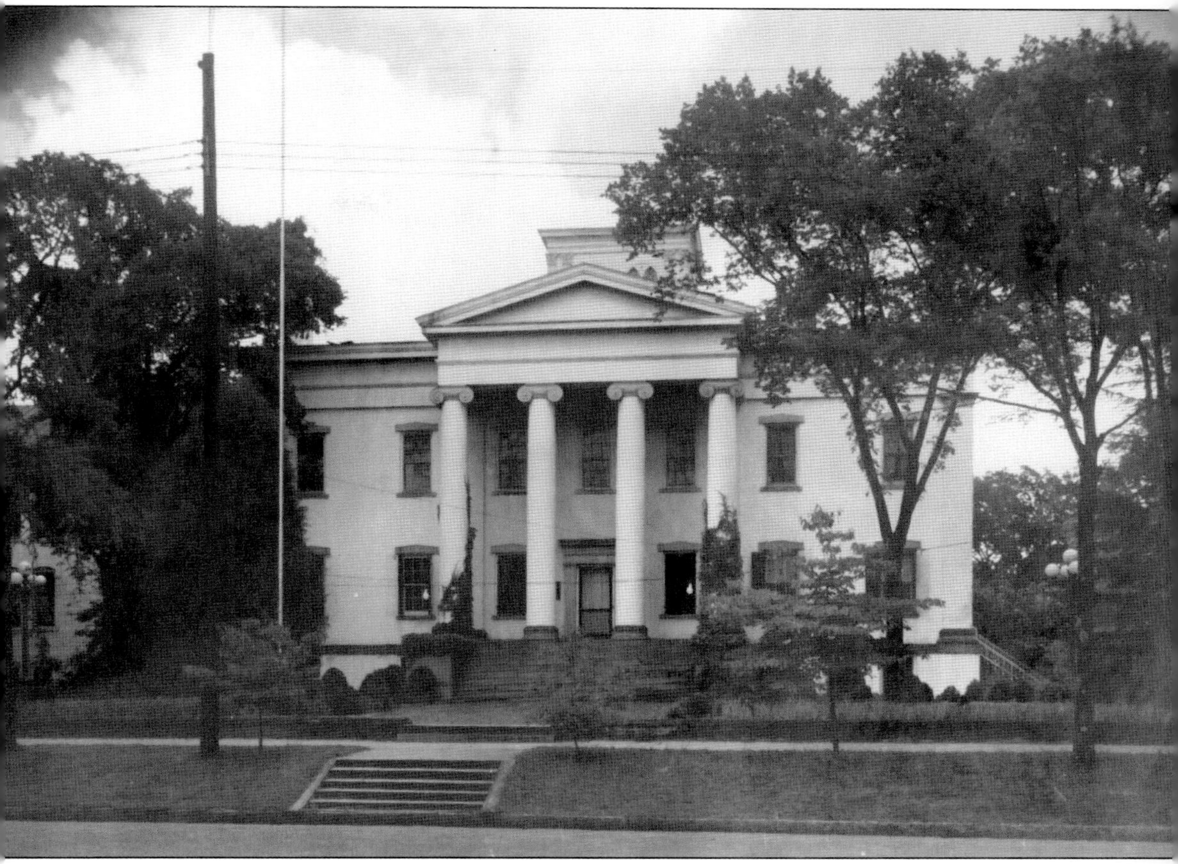

After a resolution by Georgia's legislature in 1835 to build a new residence for the governor, construction began in 1836. The home was completed between 1838 and 1839. The historic Old Governor's Mansion in Milledgeville housed 10 Georgia governors. The state's seat of government resided in the old capitol. The Secession Convention was held there on January 16, 1861, and the Secession Act was passed three days later by a vote of 208 to 89, making Georgia the fifth state to secede from the Union. Georgia's secession was not a single determinant for the Civil War but a contributing factor. The mansion has been a primary witness to key historical events such as the Georgia Platform Convention on the Compromise of 1850, the occupation by Gen. Sherman's troops during the Civil War, and the beginning of the Reconstruction era. During their occupation of Milledgeville, Union troops gathered in the state capitol building and held a mock trial repealing Georgia's secession from the Union. (Courtesy of the Library of Congress, LC-J7-GA-1432.)

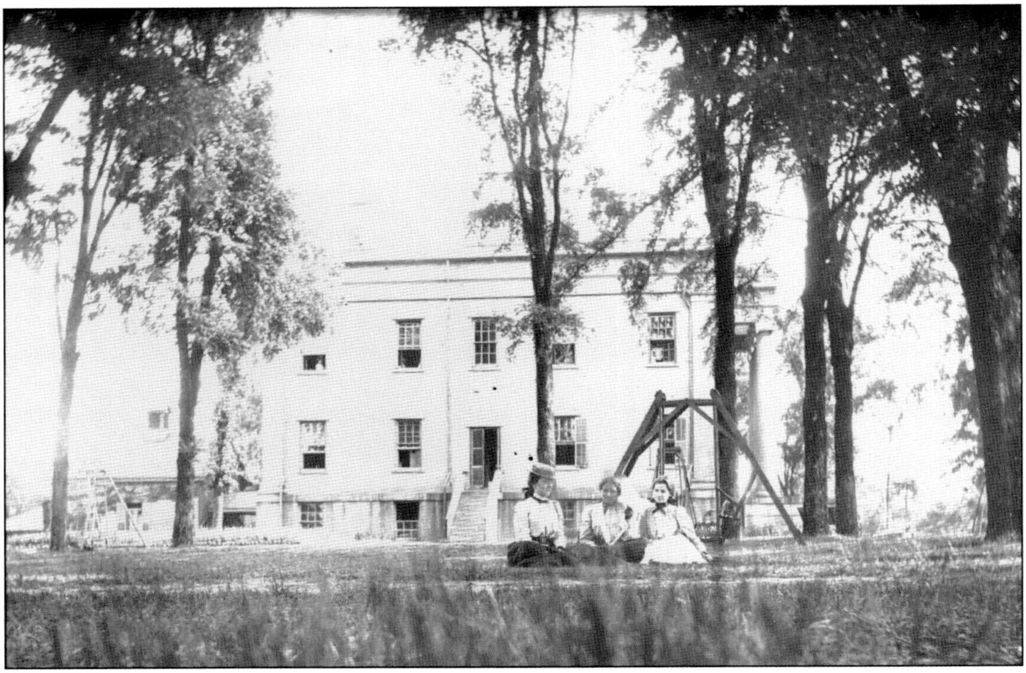

Irish architect Charles Clusky designed the mansion in the Greek Revival style of architecture, with stucco over brick and Ionic columns. The popularity of the style in the mid-1800s resulted in it also being called National style. (Courtesy of the Library of Congress, Carnegie Survey, LC-J7-GA-1432.)

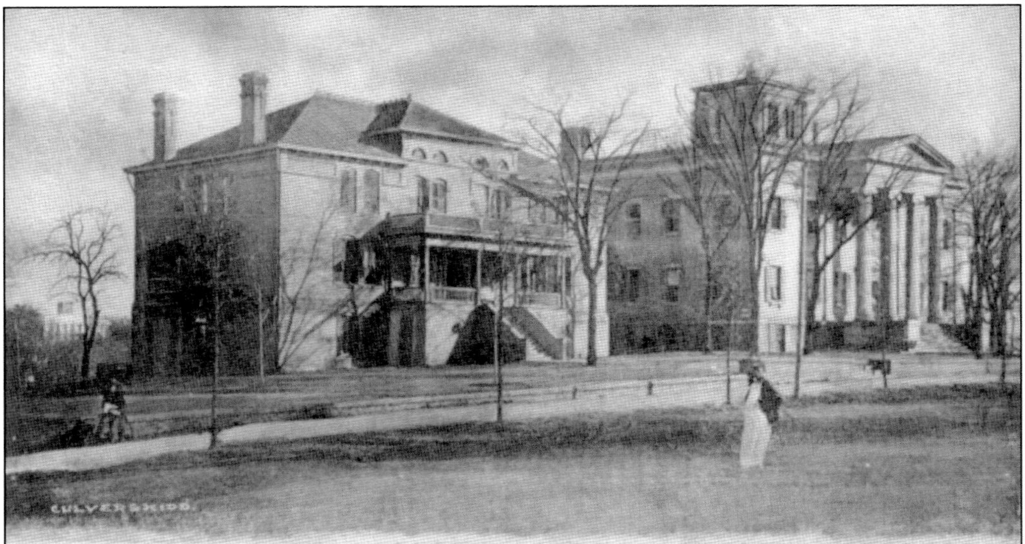

After Georgia's state capital was moved from Milledgeville to Atlanta in 1868, the city's colleges replaced government institutions. The Governor's Mansion was used in later years as cadet barracks for Middle Georgia Military and Agricultural College and then as housing for presidents of Georgia College until the mid-1980s. Students at Georgia College were housed in the annex of the mansion. (Courtesy of Bo Edmonds.)

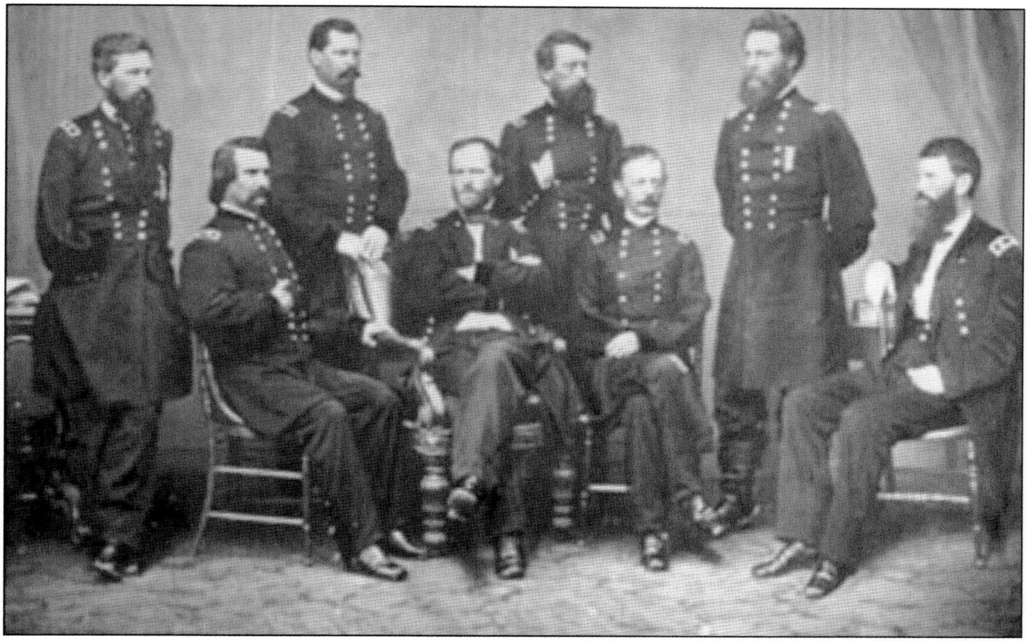

The original negative of this 1865 image was marred by a protruding, out-of-focus element on the left side of the frame. It was later retouched by eliminating the blurred form on the left, and a seated figure of General Blair was inserted on the right. Seen here are, from left to right, Major General Blair, Major General Howard, Major General Logan, Maj. Gen. William Tecumseh Sherman, Maj. Gen. Jefferson Davis, Major General Slocum, Major General Mower, and Major General Blair (seen twice in this doctored image). (Courtesy of the Chicago Public Library, Special Collections and Preservation Division.)

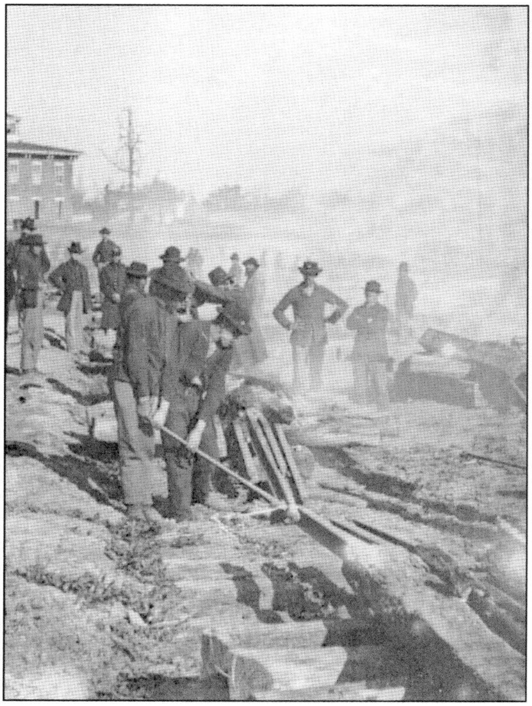

In 1864, contributing to the bleak outlook for Milledgeville after the war, railroads were destroyed by Sherman's troops on his March to the Sea. Pillaging of homes was widespread as the troops moved through the city, and grain and livestock needed to sustain troops during the winter were taken. Called Sherman's neckties and Sherman's hairpins, railway bars were heated and bent out of shape, preventing them from being fixed and reused. (Courtesy of author.)

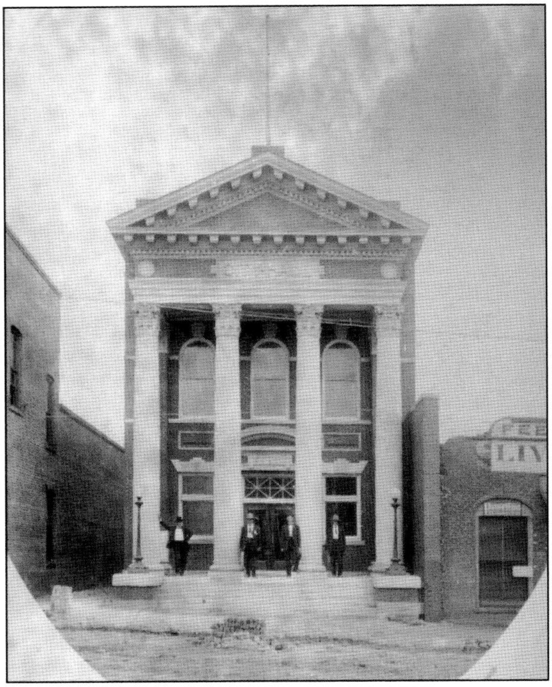

Law enforcement officers are shown in front of city hall, which was constructed between 1907 and 1908. Chief Lawrence is second from left. He was also responsible for collecting business-license and street taxes. Other pictured, in unknown order, are Captain Roberts, Night Officer Ivey, and Special Officer Wilson. Wilson regulated blind tiger ordinances. As stated in the code of ordinances at the time, a blind tiger was any house, storeroom, or other place in which beer, wine, liquor, or other intoxicants was kept illegally or for the purpose of illegal sale or other dispensing.

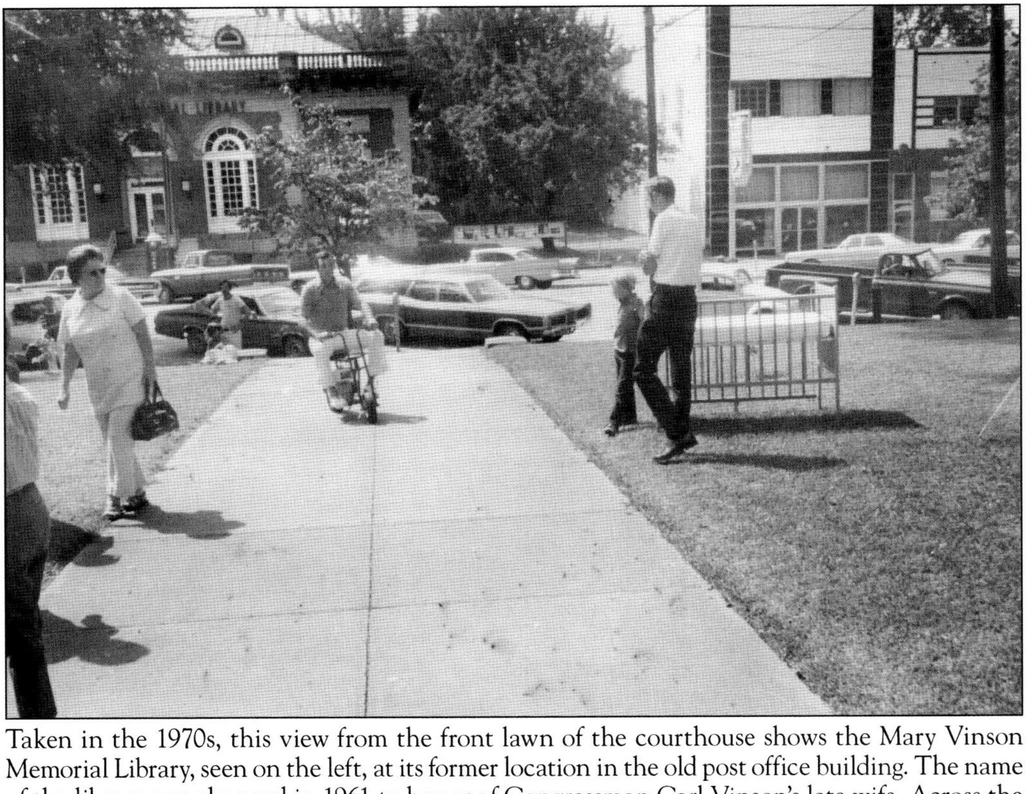

Taken in the 1970s, this view from the front lawn of the courthouse shows the Mary Vinson Memorial Library, seen on the left, at its former location in the old post office building. The name of the library was changed in 1961 to honor of Congressman Carl Vinson's late wife. Across the street on the right is the Exchange Bank. The Exchange Bank first began operation in 1903 and was located at 120 West Hancock Street. (Courtesy of John Milledge Academy.)

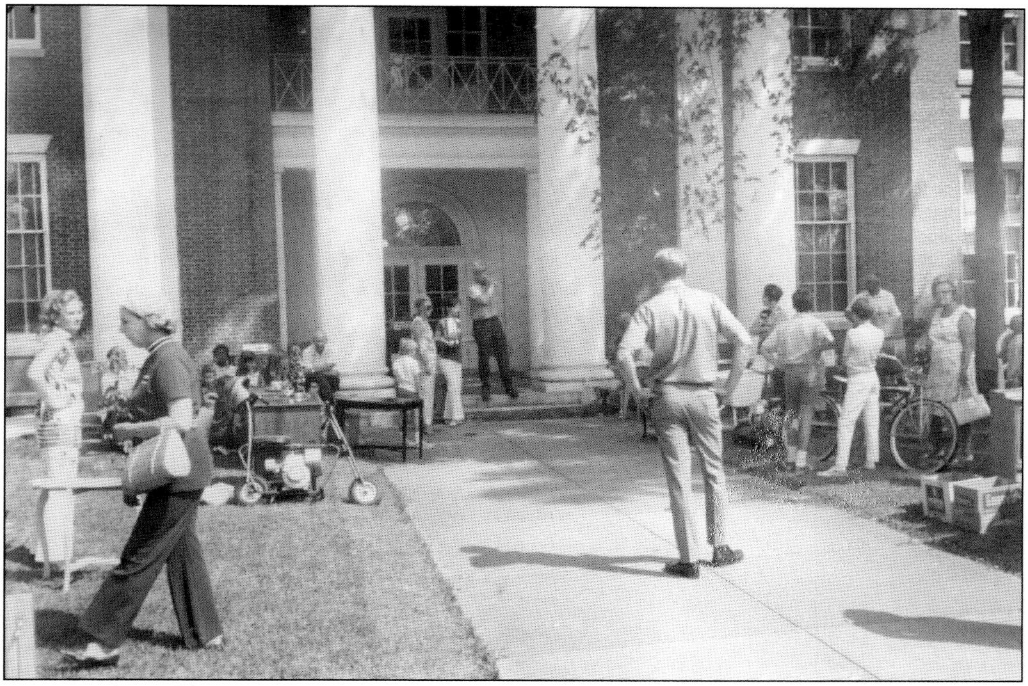

In 1887, the Baldwin County Courthouse, shown here, was built on the site of the original courthouse, which burned in 1861. During the years before construction of replacement courthouse, sessions of court were held in the Masonic lodge, in both chambers of the state capitol, and at the opera house. (Courtesy of John Milledge Academy.)

All persons in this photograph taken in early 1900s are unidentified, but the man on the far right is evidently in law enforcement, as suggested by the badge he is wearing. It is not known if he is a police officer or a sheriff's deputy; both departments operated simultaneously in Milledgeville by 1896. Peter Cline's Dry Goods Store is shown in the left background.

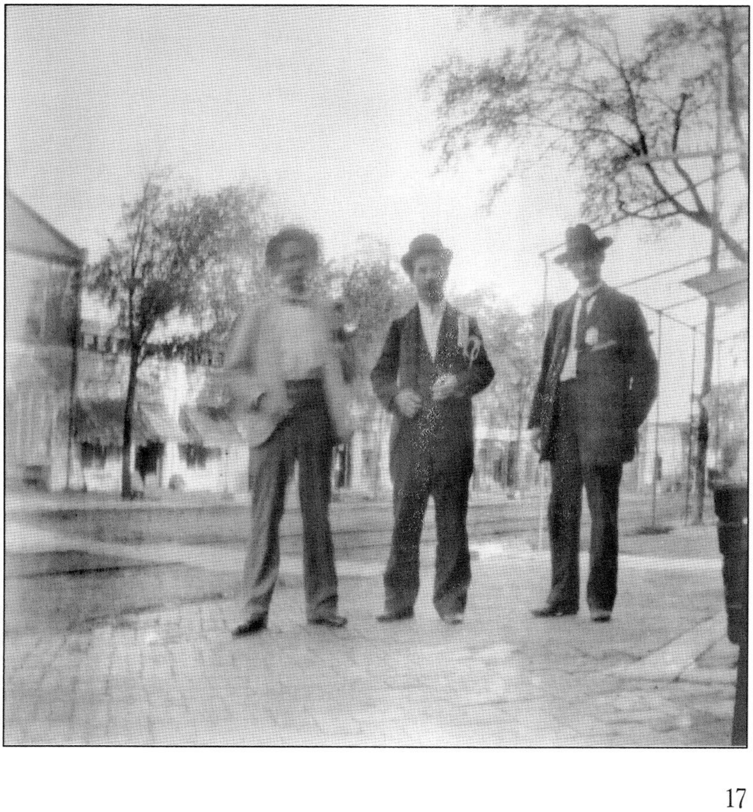

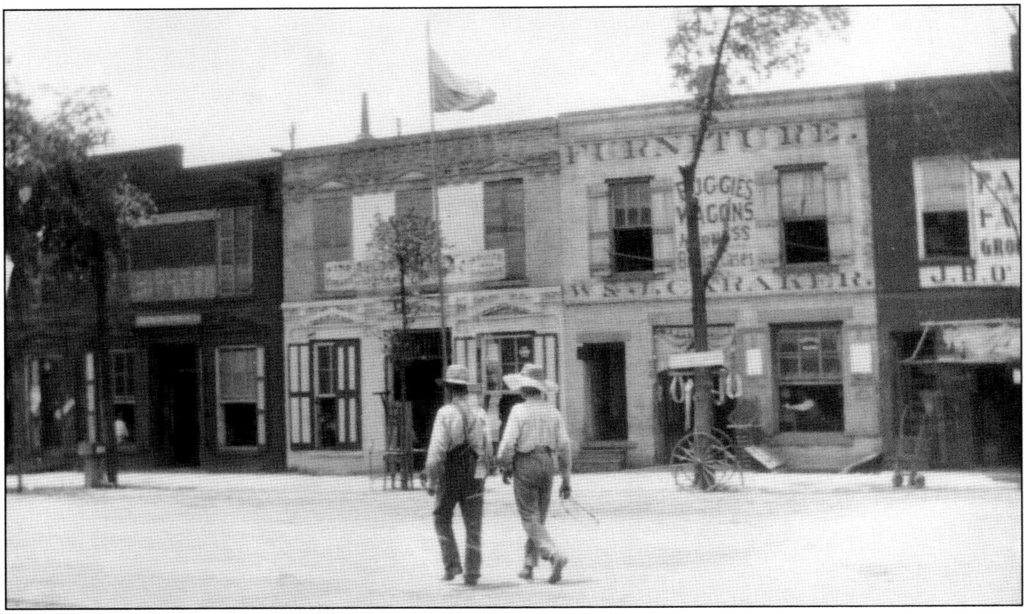

This photograph was taken in the 1890s on South Wayne Street. The businesses, from left to right, are R.A. Stembridge's Liquor and Beer, Finney's Pure Food Groceries, Caraker's Furniture, and Pace and O'Quinn's Fancy and Family Grocery. The two men photographed are unidentified. One of them is carrying a bridle.

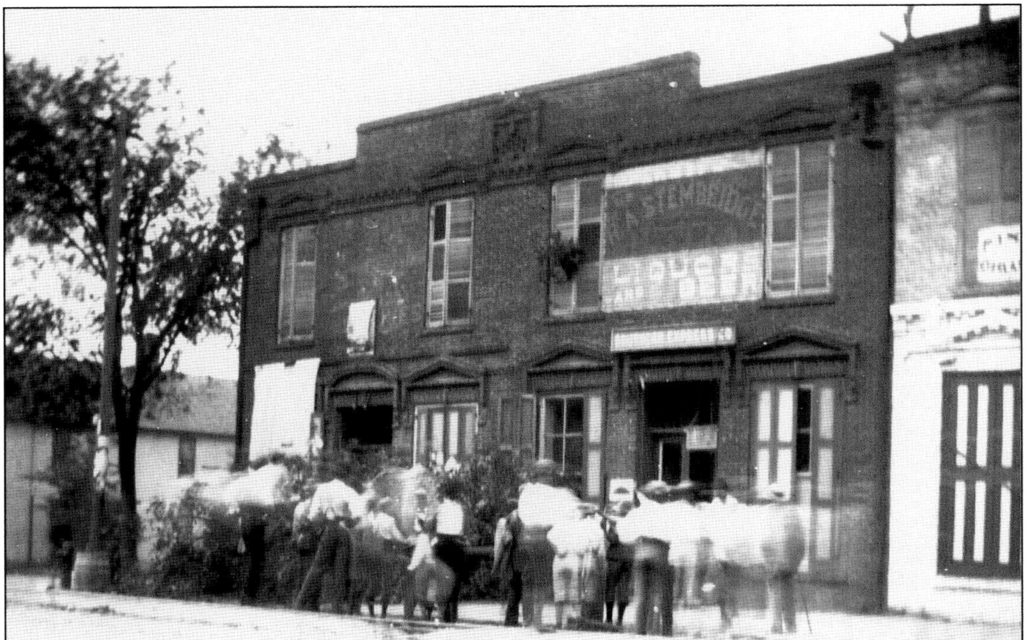

A crowd gathers in front of the business on Wayne Street known as the new Brown's building, next door to Finney's grocery. On the right is the Lindrom Sisters' Dress Shop; and the old Farmer's Hotel is in the far left background. This photograph was taken in the late 1800s on Wayne Street, at the current location of Century Bank and Trust.

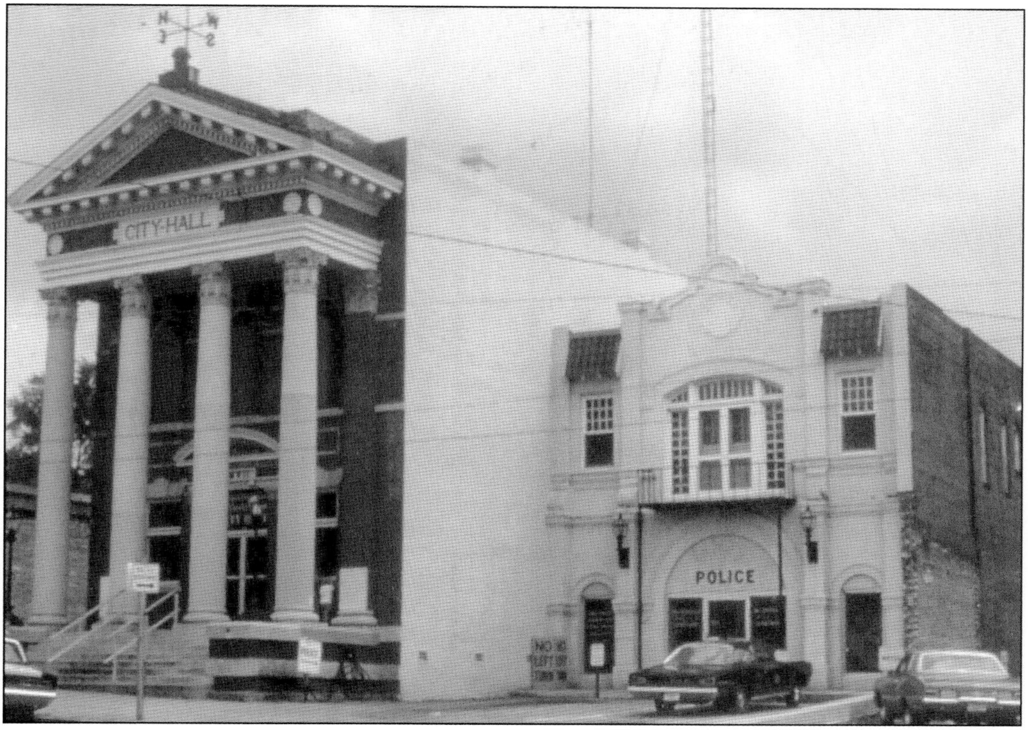

Taken in the early 1970s, this photograph shows the police station, formerly the location of Jeanes and Robinson's livery stables, next to city hall, . A fire originating in the stables caused them, as well as the Elks Club, to be left in ruins. The building was reconstructed in 1917. A firewall between the stables and city hall existed on the side opposite the Elks Club at the time and may have protected city hall from the blaze. (Courtesy of the Milledgeville Police Department.)

An effective system for the delivery of water was a crucial element for Milledgeville's growth as a city. In this early-1900s image, a field in Milledgeville is watered by a surface-irrigation system. This type of irrigation causes water to flow over the soil, allowing the entire area to be flooded. Digging small trenches into which the water could flow would channel irrigation. Water and pipe systems were also crucial to the city for improved health and sanitation.

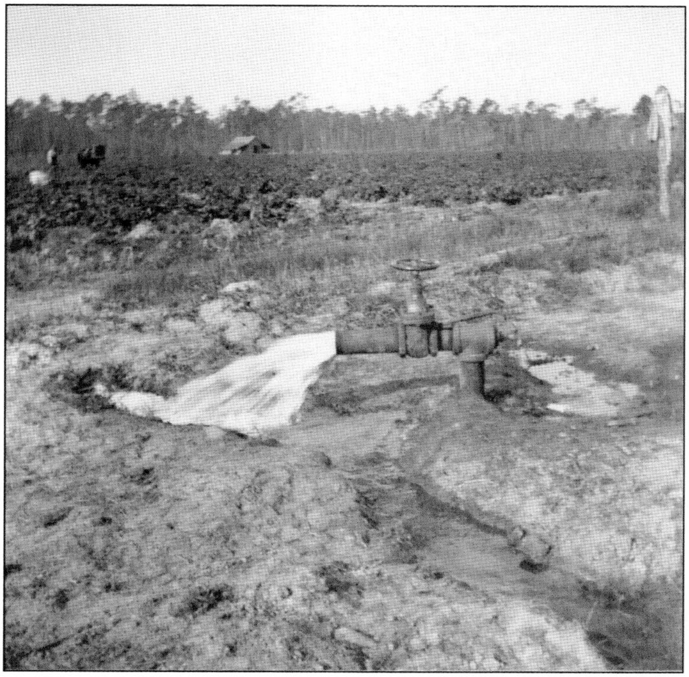

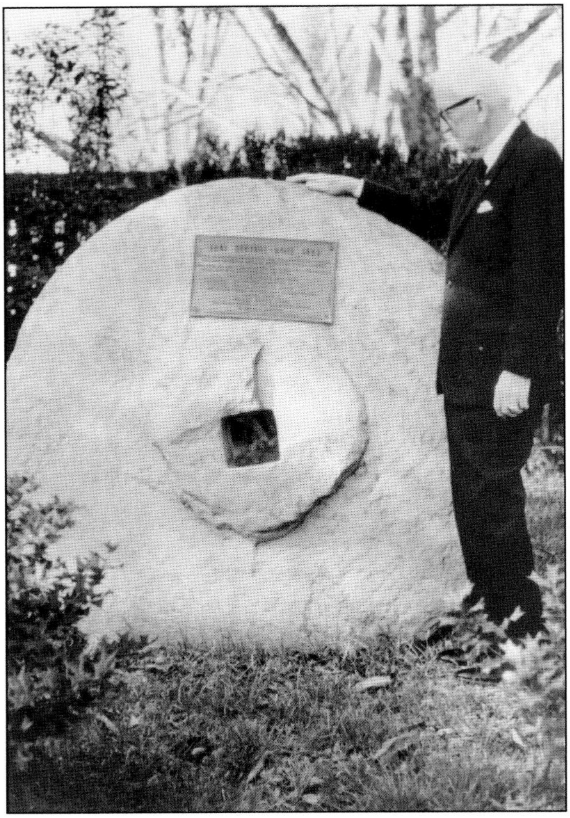

The development of industry was another important factor in the continued growth of Milledgeville. Frank Bone is seen here in 1952, standing beside a millstone from Stevens Pottery, which was used to grind the white clay used in making firebricks. The plaque on the stone reads, "1861 Stevens-Bone 1952." Stevens Brothers and Company Clay Works, also known as Stevens Pottery, was sold in 1891 and became Oconee Brick and Tile Company. (Courtesy of Barbara and Buddy Martin.)

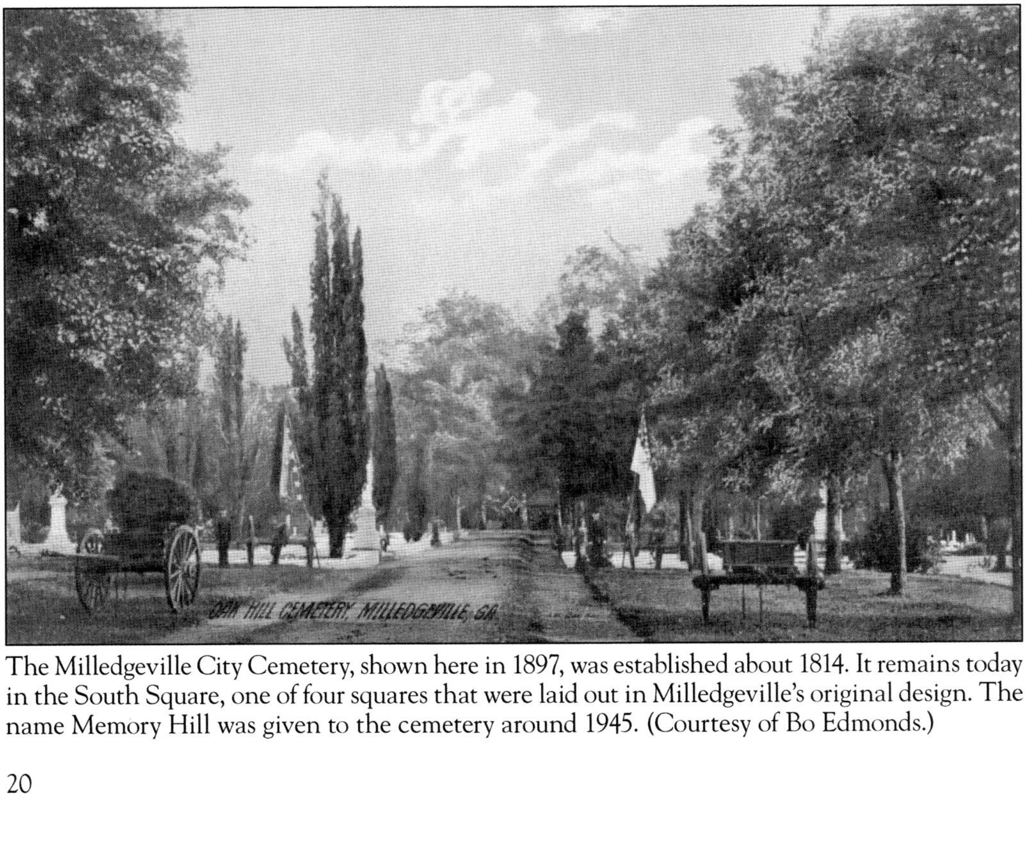

The Milledgeville City Cemetery, shown here in 1897, was established about 1814. It remains today in the South Square, one of four squares that were laid out in Milledgeville's original design. The name Memory Hill was given to the cemetery around 1945. (Courtesy of Bo Edmonds.)

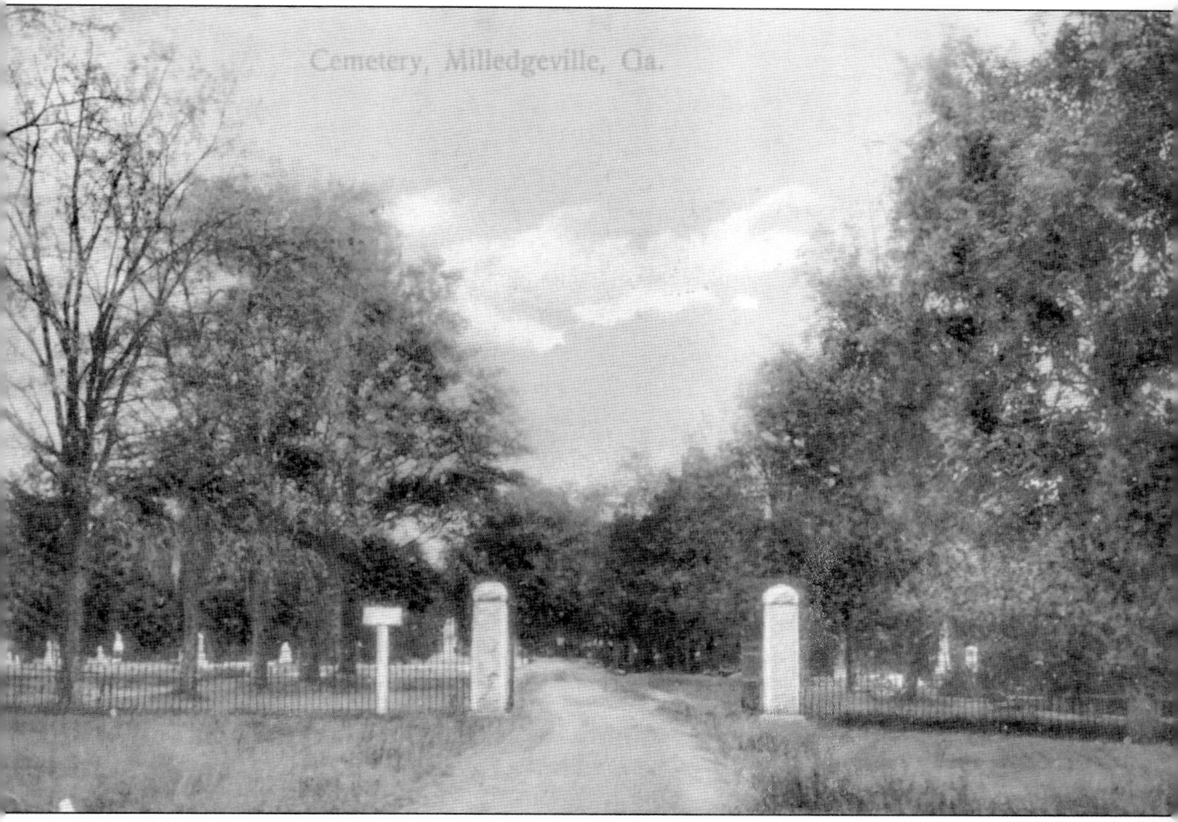

Some of the many notable persons interred at Memory Hill include writer Flannery O'Connor; businessman Marion Wesley Stembridge, who became the basis for a character in the award-winning novel *Paris Trout* by former Milledgeville resident Pete Dexter; unknown Confederate soldiers honored with the *Soldier's Monument*; Bill Miner, who was a notorious stagecoach and train robber who escaped from the state prison several times before dying there; and Dr. Benjamin Judson Simmons, the first black physician in Milledgeville. The cause of his death was reported in *The Milledgeville News* on January 14, 1910, as an illness that lingered for several months. (Courtesy of Bo Edmonds.)

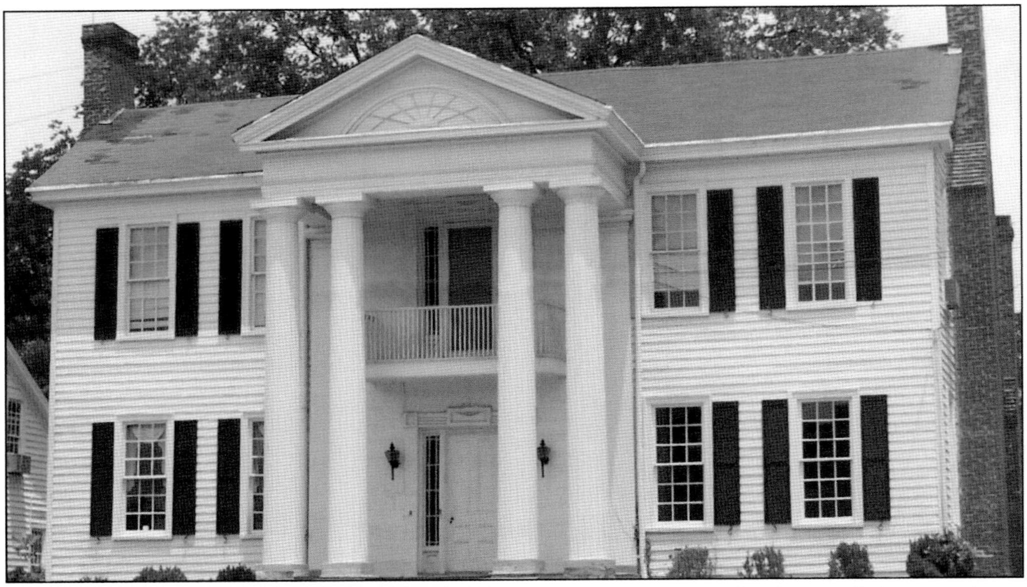

The John Marlor house, located on North Wayne Street, was once the home of the prominent transplanted English architect. It is said that he built the house as a gift to his second wife. In addition to his having designed the Masonic Hall, Marlor's architectural influence can be seen throughout Milledgeville. Now known as the John Marlor Arts Center, it houses the operations of Allied Arts, a multidisciplinary community-arts organization. (Courtesy of Allied Arts.)

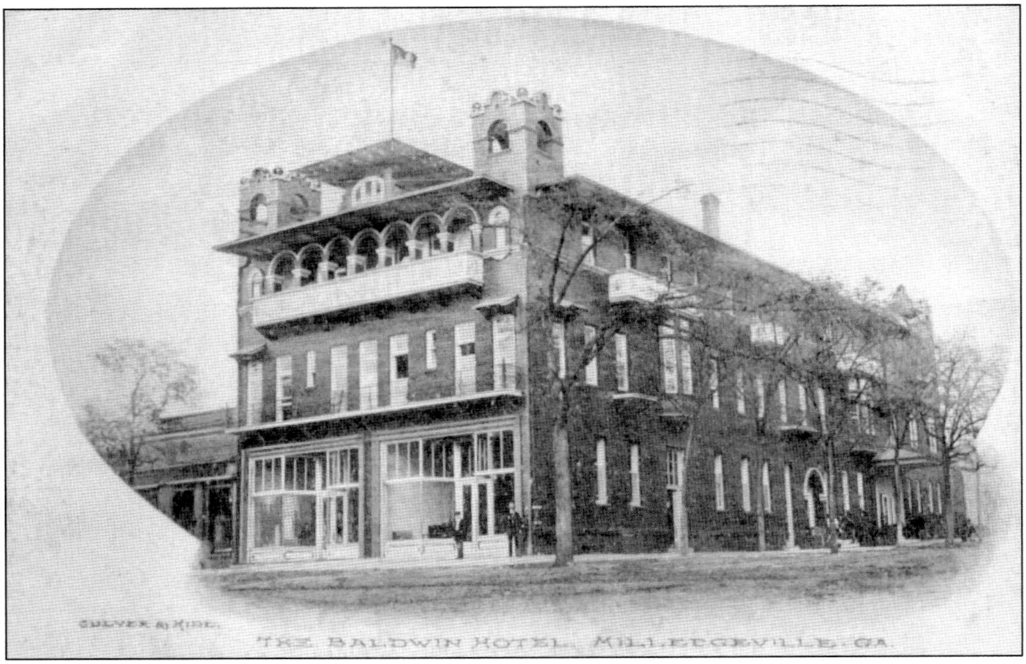

Built in 1855, the Baldwin Hotel, also called the Hotel Baldwin, is shown on this c. 1909 postcard. It was originally called the Milledgeville Hotel and was built on the corner of Wayne and Greene Streets, where the Magnolia Bank is currently located. Comedian Oliver Hardy's mother ran the hotel operations. While living at the Milledgeville Hotel, Oliver managed operations at the Palace Theatre, located across the street from the hotel. (Courtesy of Bo Edmonds.)

Two

AGRICULTURE AND INDUSTRY

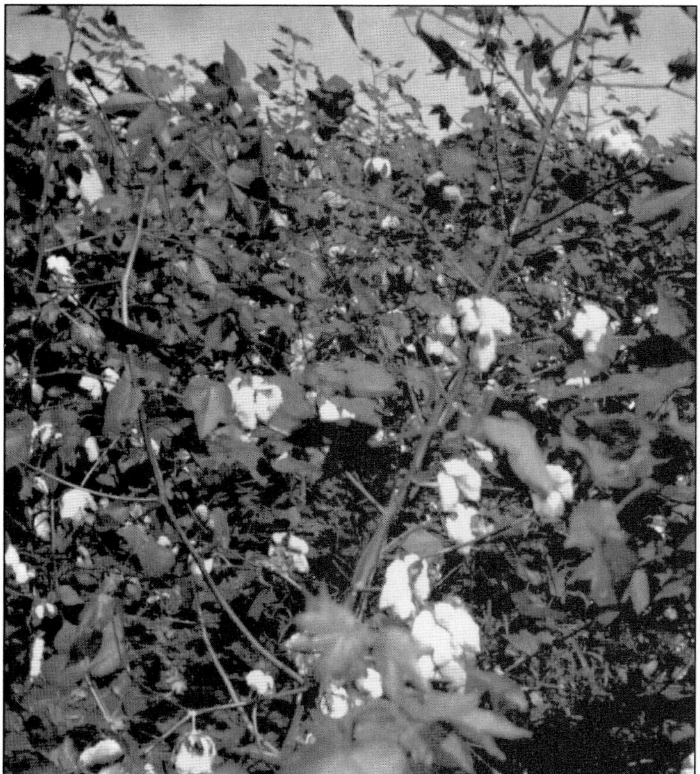

The growing economy of Milledgeville was centered around cotton and the plantation system. In the United States, demand for increased cotton production prompted the invention of the cotton gin by Eli Whitney. The introduction of the sewing machine revolutionized the making of clothing, and interchangeable parts made assembly of products faster and more efficient. In addition, advancements in machines and cultivators in agriculture allowed farmers to continue increasing product output while decreasing the cost of production.

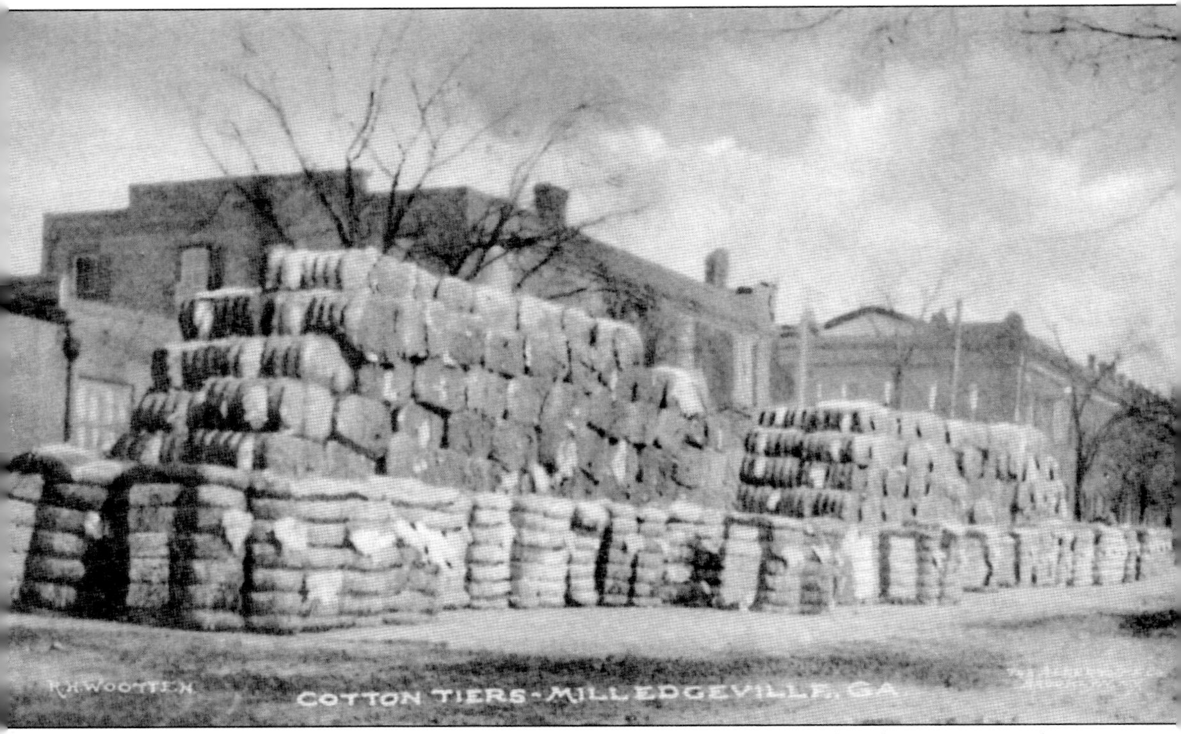

Shown on this card postmarked 1906, cotton bales stacked in tiers for either shipping or warehousing are shown near the southwest corner of Greene and South Wayne Streets in Milledgeville. The staples of Georgia's antebellum economy were tobacco, cotton, and rice. Grain, potatoes, and corn were grown primarily for sustenance. Cotton was the most important commercial row crop in Georgia from 1733 until the beginning of the Civil War, and Georgia produced the most cotton out of any state in the Union. Cotton output increased after Eli Whitney developed his cotton gin. It was also an important export to English textile mills. Milledgeville's cotton industry included farming, ginning, textile-mill processing, storing, and selling cotton. (Courtesy of Bo Edmonds.)

Loss of cotton crops in early-1900s Milledgeville, as well as in many Southern states, was a direct result of the devastation caused by the boll weevil. *The Union-Recorder* encouraged farmers to diversify their crops to prevent substantial losses to their livelihoods. One report stated that about two months away from harvest, a farmer estimated the yield of his crops to be about 5,000 bales of cotton. After the ravaging of his crops by boll weevils, he had three bales suitable for sale. Seen here is an early-1900s farmer displaying a sample of his potato crop. To preserve potatoes after harvesting, it was important to store them in a cool, dark place with good ventilation. In many Milledgeville homes, they were kept in root cellars or in potato mounds.

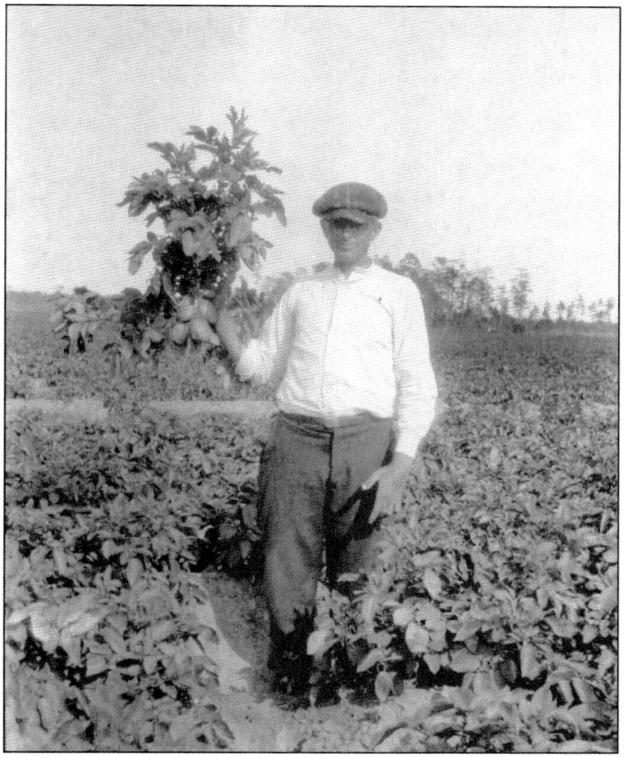

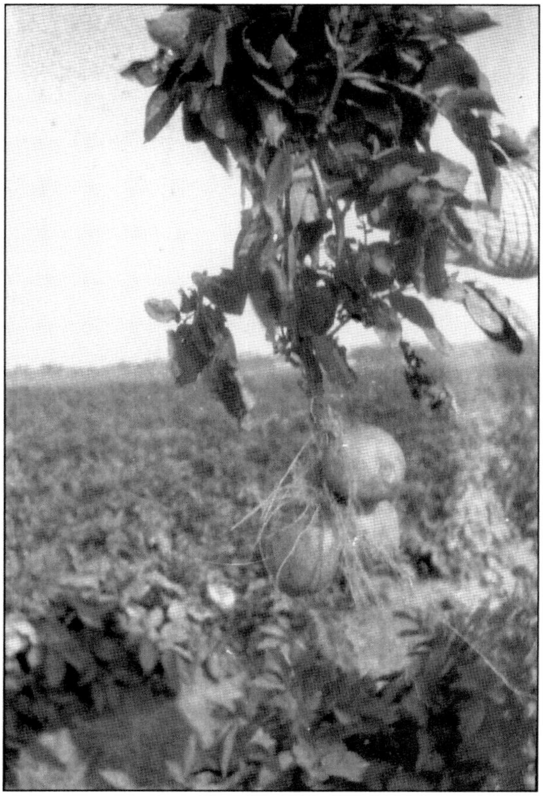

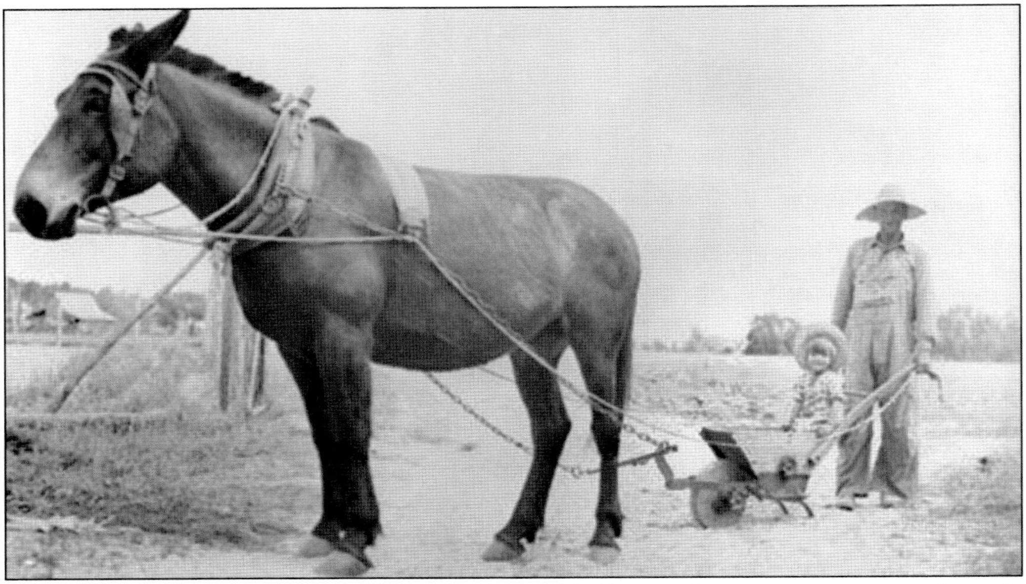

This unidentified farmer and child are plowing the field to seed cotton sometime in the early 1900s. There was substantial profit from successfully growing and selling cotton, and Milledgeville was a center for marketing the crop. Drawn by the allure of growing cotton, a tide of immigrants came from other states and from their tobacco fields. Farmers brought their slaves with them to Milledgeville. This influx of slaves, according to census reports, made the population of African Americans and whites about equal.

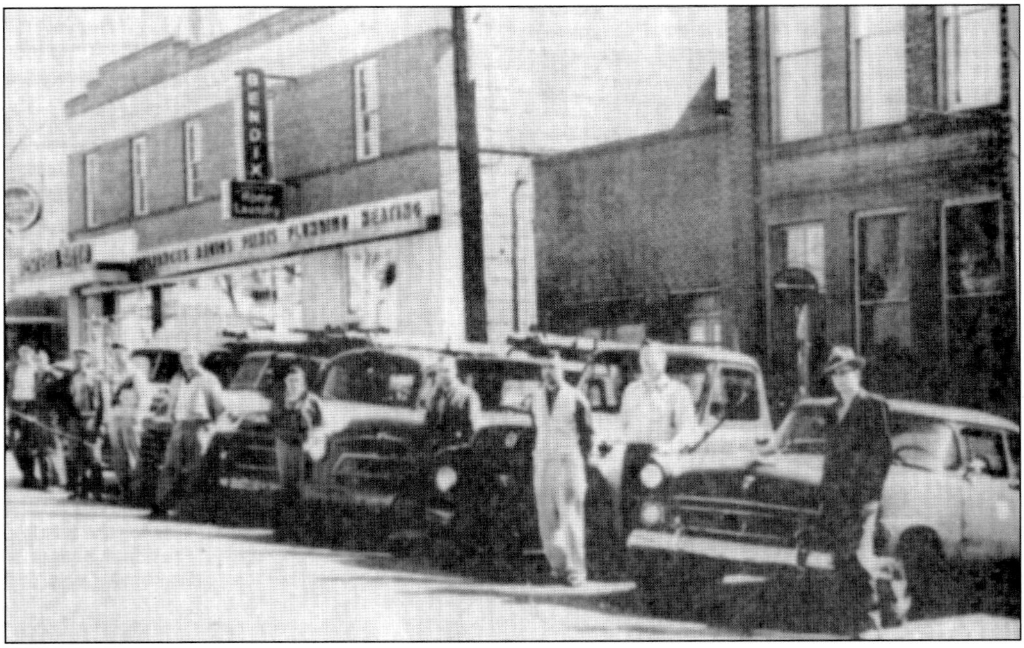

Milledgeville Telephone and Telegraph Company was purchased by General Telephone (GTE) in 1957 and served 3,000 telephone lines at that time. Here, employees of GTE are in front of the former Milledgeville Telephone building. GTE later relocated to North Jefferson Street, and Alltel acquired Milledgeville's phone services in 1993. Windstream spun off from Alltel in 2006, and that business remains at the same location. (Courtesy of *The Union-Recorder*.)

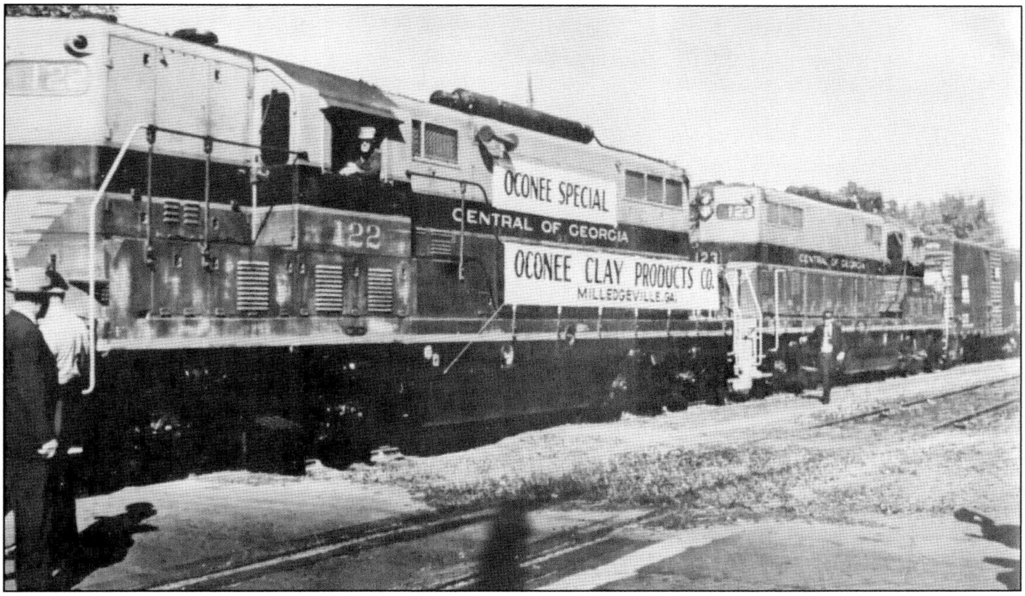

Vital to Milledgeville's businesses shipping and receiving of goods, a Central of Georgia train is shown here in the early 1950s. Although the increased use of trucking in the mid-1900s saw a decline in transport by rail, railroads were still the primary mode used by Oconee Clay Products because of the volume and weight of its shipments, including brick and clay pipe. (Courtesy of Barbara and Buddy Martin.)

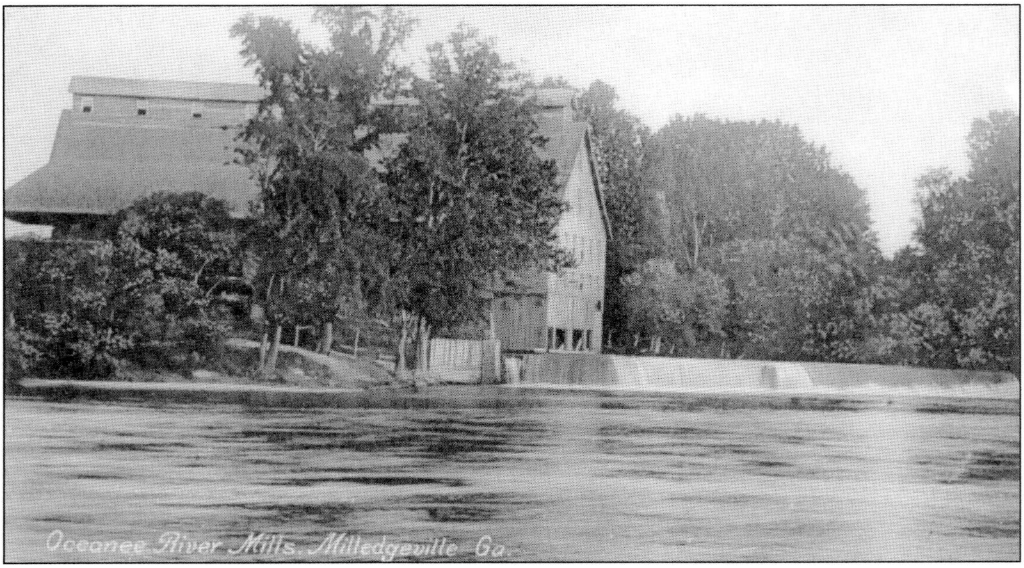

The Oconee River Mills, also known as Treanor Mills, was established around 1821 and was owned by Peter Williams and Hugh Treanor. Farmers would take their corn to the mill for processing and exchange it for meal and grits. Being ground between a fixed lower stone and a rotating upper stone moved by waterpower is how grain was processed. At least a couple dozen mills are documented to have existed in Milledgeville. During the Industrial Revolution, grain mills became more commercial and financially viable. (Courtesy of Bo Edmonds.)

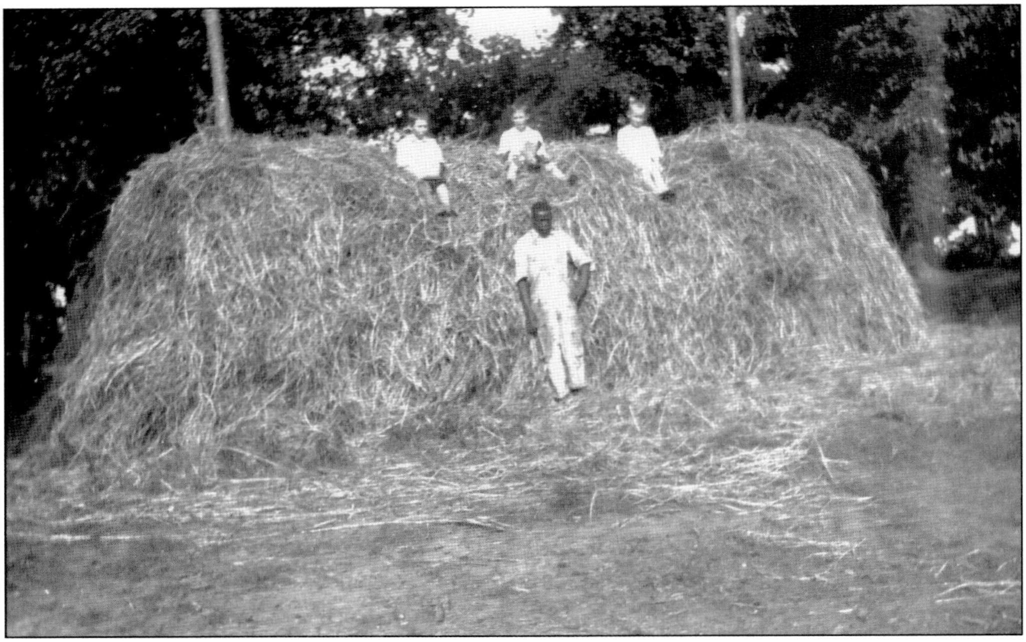

This photograph was taken in the early 1900s, when the practice of sharecropping was common. Sharecropping agreements would specify whether the sharecropper or the landlord was responsible for which expenses to grow a crop and whether the yield would be picked up by or delivered to the landlord. The sharecropper might cut and bale the hay to deliver or leave the landlord's share in his field to be retrieved when needed.

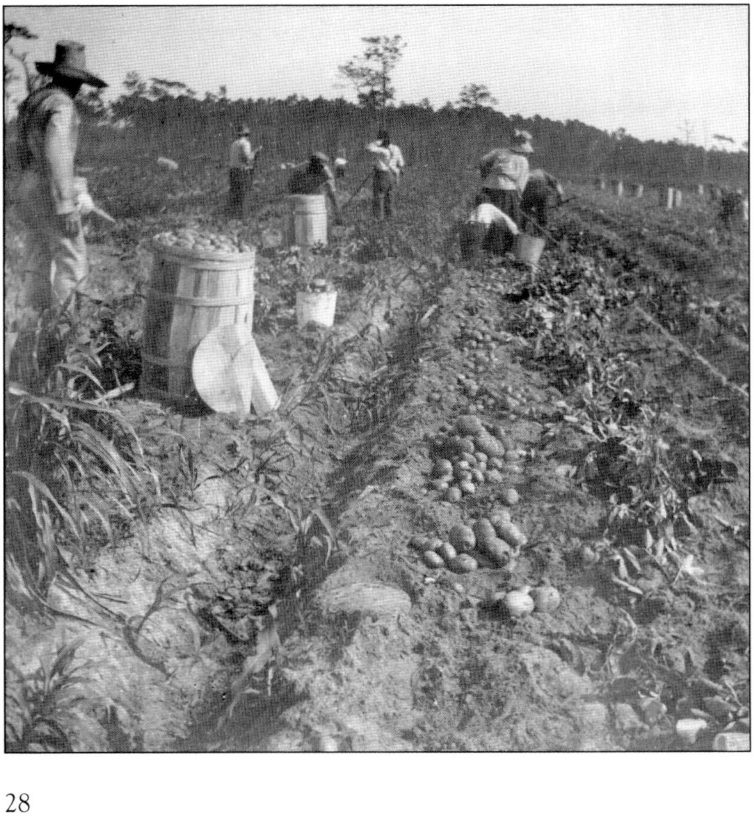

As technology brought new machinery to Milledgeville for faster crop production, the number of people needed in the fields decreased. The practice of sharecropping declined, and sharecroppers, forced from their farms, began moving to work in factories in the North or migrant labor in the West.

Barrels like these would have been used to hold vegetables and fruits. Largely, they stored potatoes directly from harvest to minimize sun exposure and deterioration. The sides of the barrel have holes to allow ventilation, preventing the produce from rotting. The barrels would still have been stored in a root cellar or an equally cool, dark place. This image is from a collection of photographs of Milledgeville taken in the early 1900s.

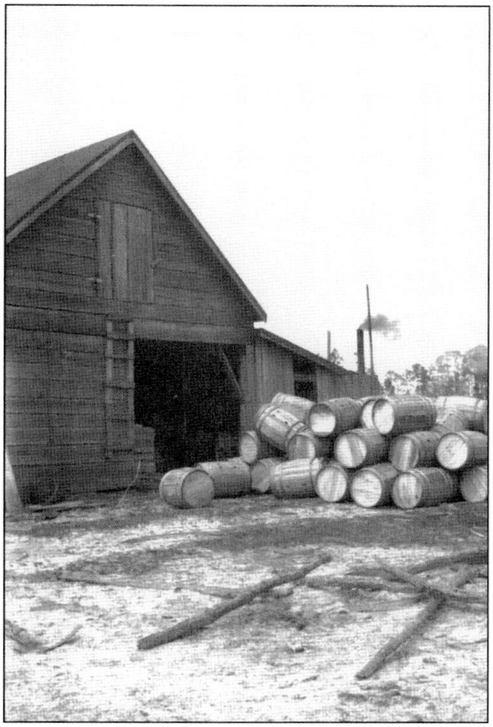

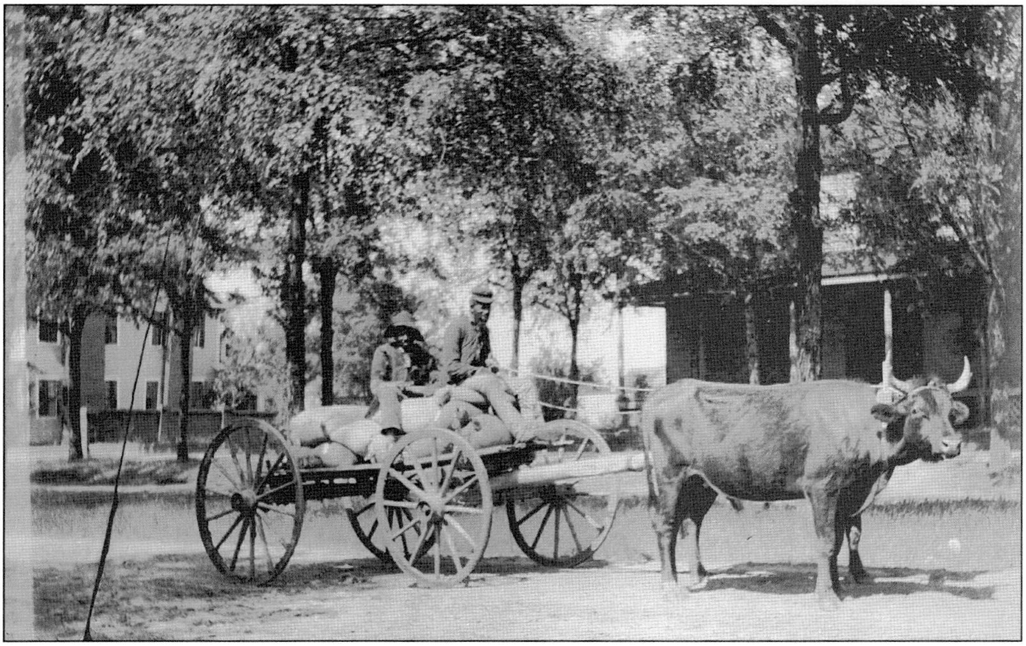

Another sharecropping arrangement could have the sharecropper delivering the landlord's share of the product to market. The landlord would get his share in the form of sale proceeds. The timing of the delivery to market could be crucial for the price of some crops. It would be decided whether the crop would earn more money immediately after harvest, or whether it should be stored until the price rose. These sharecroppers pass the Governor's Mansion on their way to market sometime in the early 1900s.

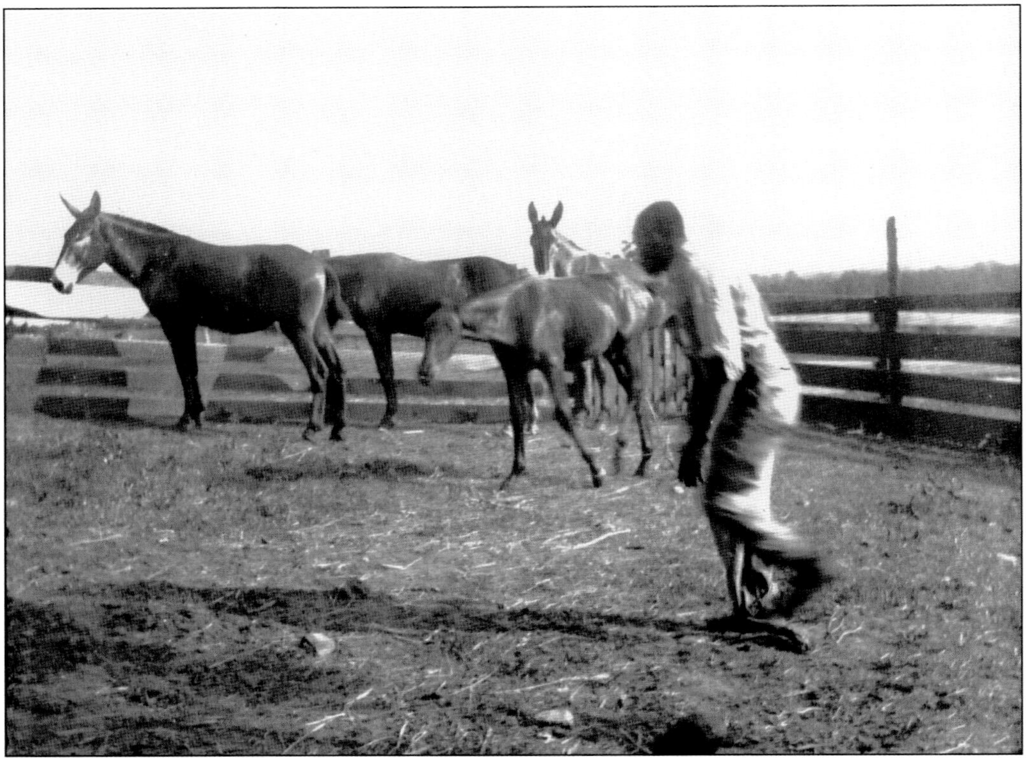

In 1920, farmers in Milledgeville were encouraged to diversify their crops to minimize losses from the boll weevil. This allowed peanuts and other crops to gain a foothold in Georgia's agricultural economy. Diversification of crops also allowed farmers to pursue economic independence. Also, former cotton farmers were turning back to production of livestock for subsistence farming and sale for profit. This unidentified man in Milledgeville is shown engaged in the daily operation of caring for livestock.

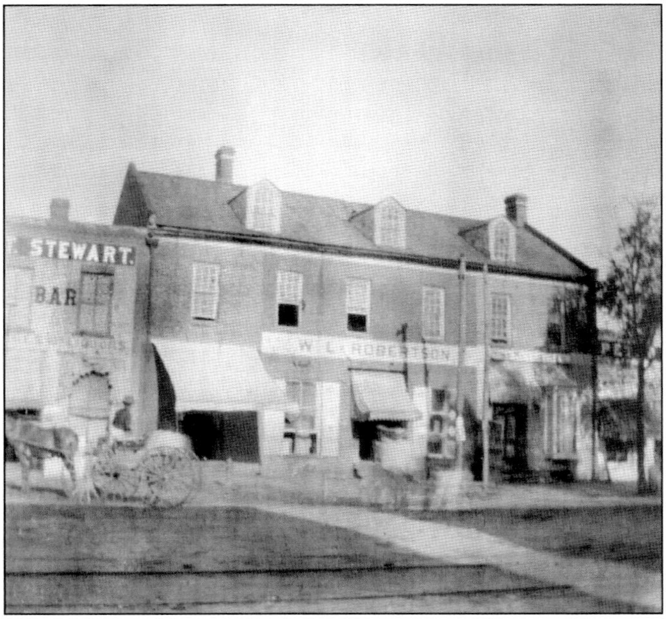

This photograph was taken in the 1890s on the west side of South Wayne Street. Railroad tracks ran down Main Street about a mile south, for four or five blocks, before turning eastward. The train went through town, stopping for an occasional traffic light on Wayne Street. The businesses from left to right are Stewart's bar, W.L. Robertson's, an unidentified business, and Cline's General Goods Store. Access to rail transportation for shipping and receiving of goods was instrumental in the economic growth of Milledgeville.

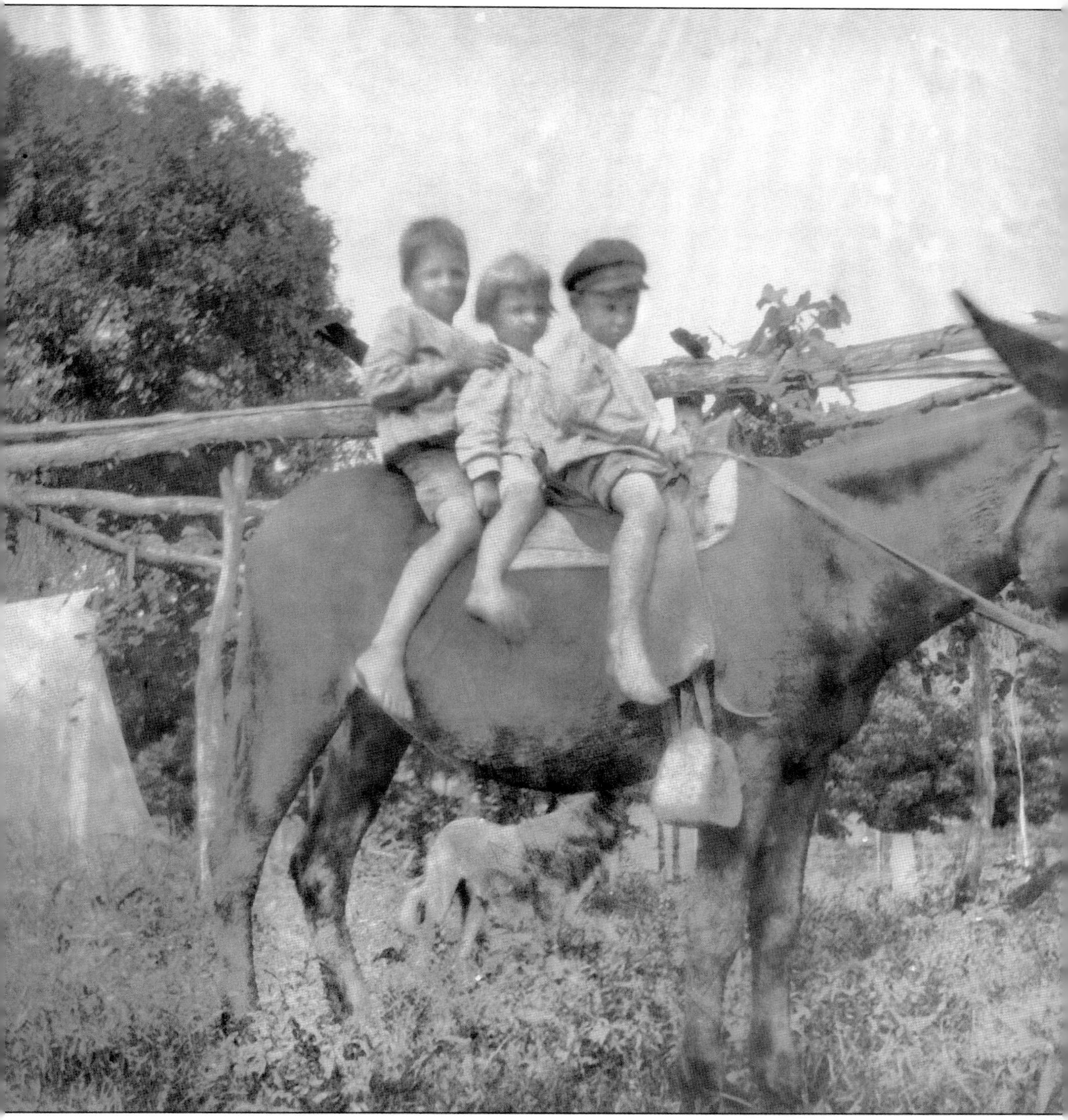

These children living on a farm in Milledgeville would have contributed to the family by working in the fields and helping with household duties. There was limited access to education until in the early 1900s, when compulsory education was introduced. School calendars were scheduled to allow children to help during planting and harvesting. At one time, about 90 percent of Georgians lived and worked on farms. Only two percent of today's population works on farms, but the school breaks related to spring harvest, summer work, and weekend work remain.

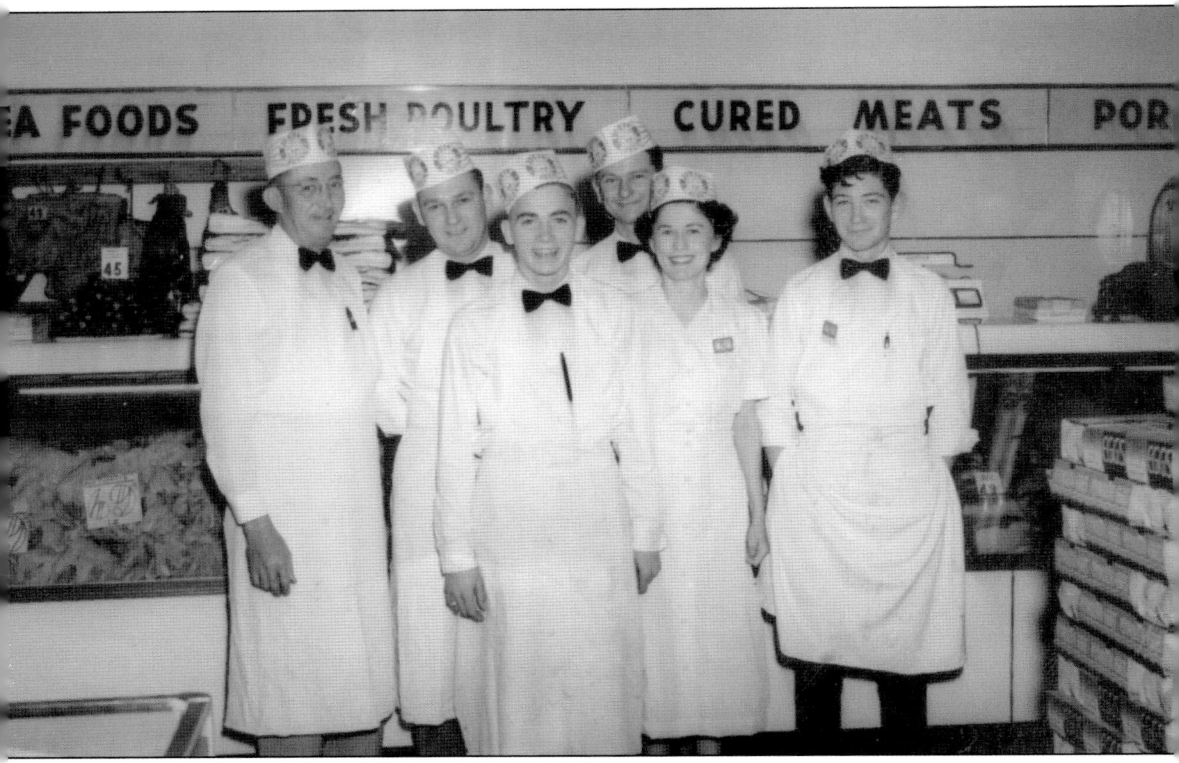

These employees of Piggly Wiggly grocery store are shown on the day of the store's opening around 1951. They are, from left to right, Fred Mercer, Floyd Lord, Buddy Martin, Ed Brannen, Eloise Lord (Floyd's wife), and Ray Corbin. Prior to the 1930s, small independent stores were common in many communities. Orders by telephone, home delivery of goods, and monthly credit accounts were services included for customers. Piggly Wiggly was an example of the new chain store, a retail innovation that affected every aspect of economic and social life. Numerous technological advances were also adopted as a result of use in larger chain stores. The variety of goods and services, media marketing, and price awareness are a sampling of the advances that changed the shopping experience. Larger stores made jobs available to women and gave them the freedom to shop and travel alone. Such retailers were forerunners of the current-day shopping center housing many different stores, and goods, under one roof. (Courtesy of Barbara and Buddy Martin.)

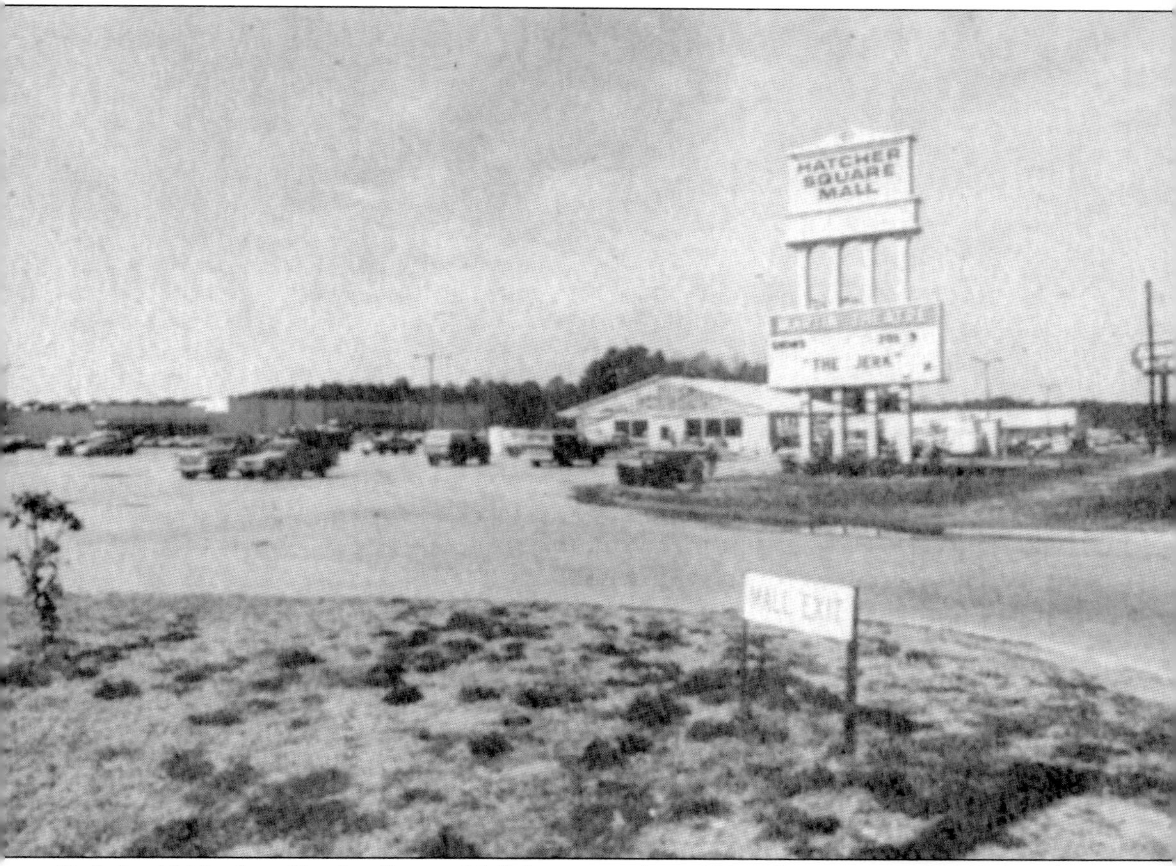

Built by Al Hatcher, Hatcher Square Mall first opened in 1972 and was renamed Milledgeville Mall in the 1990s. Al was known as the man who moved Milledgeville, since no retail centers existed on Highway 441, and the crossroads became one of the highest traffic-volume intersections after the mall was constructed. In the late 19th century, the general store, providing convenience and easy accessibility to a large variety of goods, gained prominence. Car-friendly strip malls were developed in the United States in the 1920s, and shopping malls corresponded to the growth of suburban living after World War II. (Courtesy of *The Union-Recorder*.)

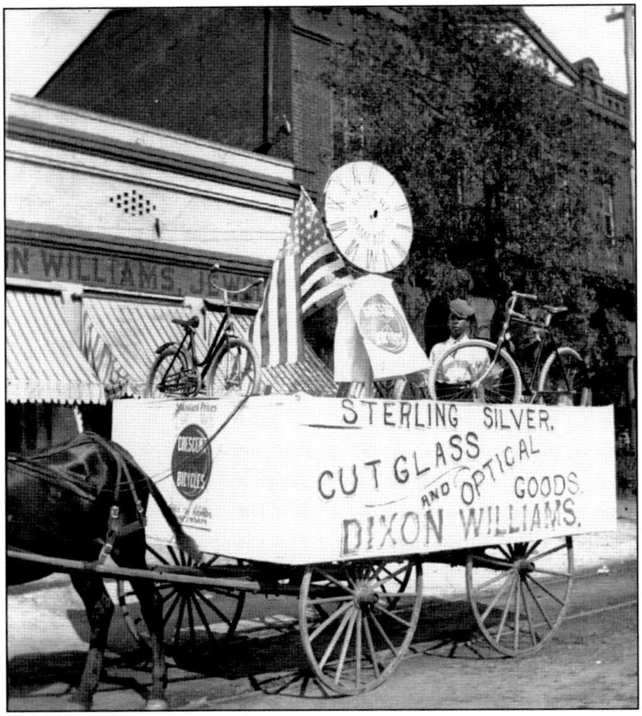

Businesses in this early-1900s photograph are Dixon Williams's jewelry store and the Baldwin Hotel on South Wayne Street. The unidentified young man in the photograph would ride the cart of goods through town, promoting and selling for Williams's store. The jeweler is advertising bicycles, watches, sterling silver, diamonds, cut glass, and optical goods.

In the early 1900s, an elderly man rides a donkey on Wayne Street in downtown Milledgeville, while others look on. Behind him is the Dixon Williams jewelry store. Williams would run advertisements in the newspaper about once a month to notify customers of the optician who would come from Macon for a day and give eye exams and fit glasses.

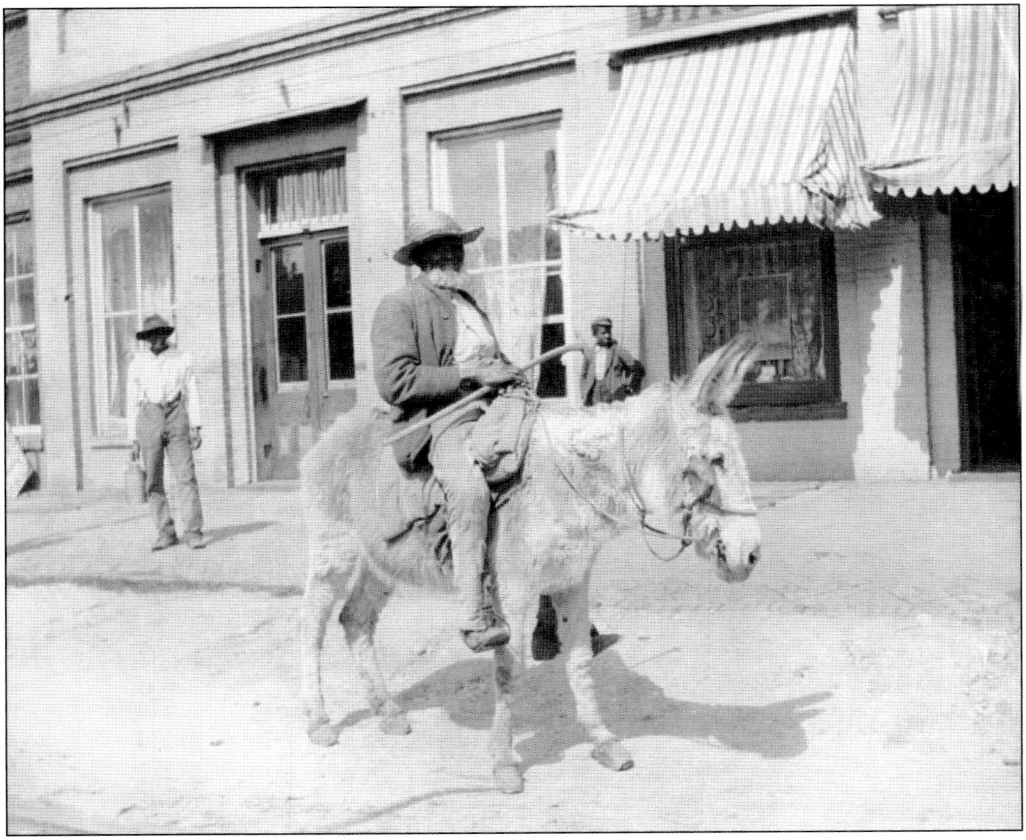

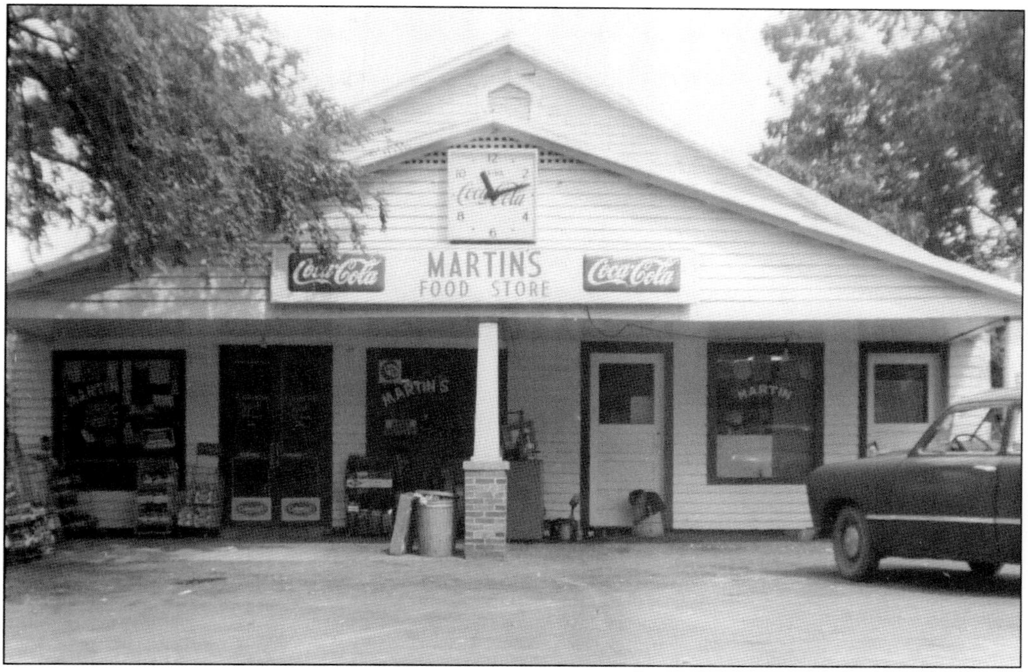

Pictured above in the 1970s is Martin's IGA Grocery Store on Allen Memorial Drive in Milledgeville. Martin attributes his long-term business success to his remaining constant in employment practices and customer service through years that saw social and economic transformation. Although the supermarket was introduced to many areas in the 1930s, it was not until after the World War II era that it flourished. Changes in urban transportation, development, and rapid expansion of suburbs, food production developments, and newfound household affluence were factors that led to the continued progression of the supermarket. The sale of refrigerators in the US rose dramatically, and households increased their storage of perishable food, thereby lowering the frequency of shopping trips a household had to make. As the amount of disposable income available for food and nonfood items grew, the supermarket inevitably expanded to meet suburban demands. Below, retail stores in the early 1900s are shown in this eastward view down Hancock Street. These older retailers would have been smaller businesses with less selection, in contrast to the chain stores that would open in later years. (Above, courtesy of Barbara and Buddy Martin; below, courtesy of Bo Edmonds.)

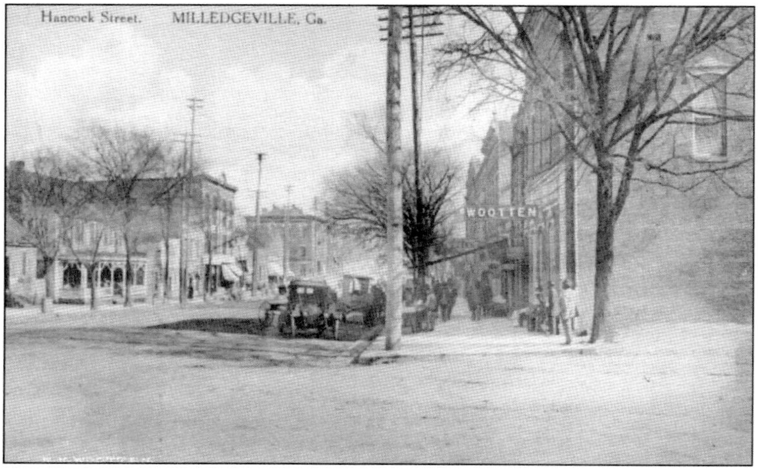

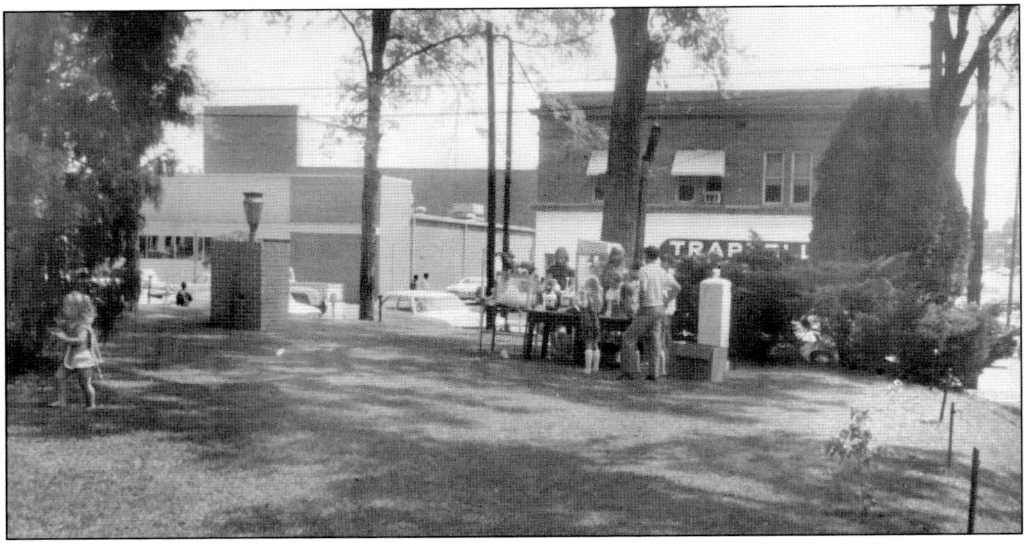

Seen from the front lawn of the old courthouse on Hancock Street, downtown businesses are shown where the new and present-day courthouse was constructed in the early 1970s. In the background on the right is the Sanford Building. (Courtesy of John Milledge Academy.)

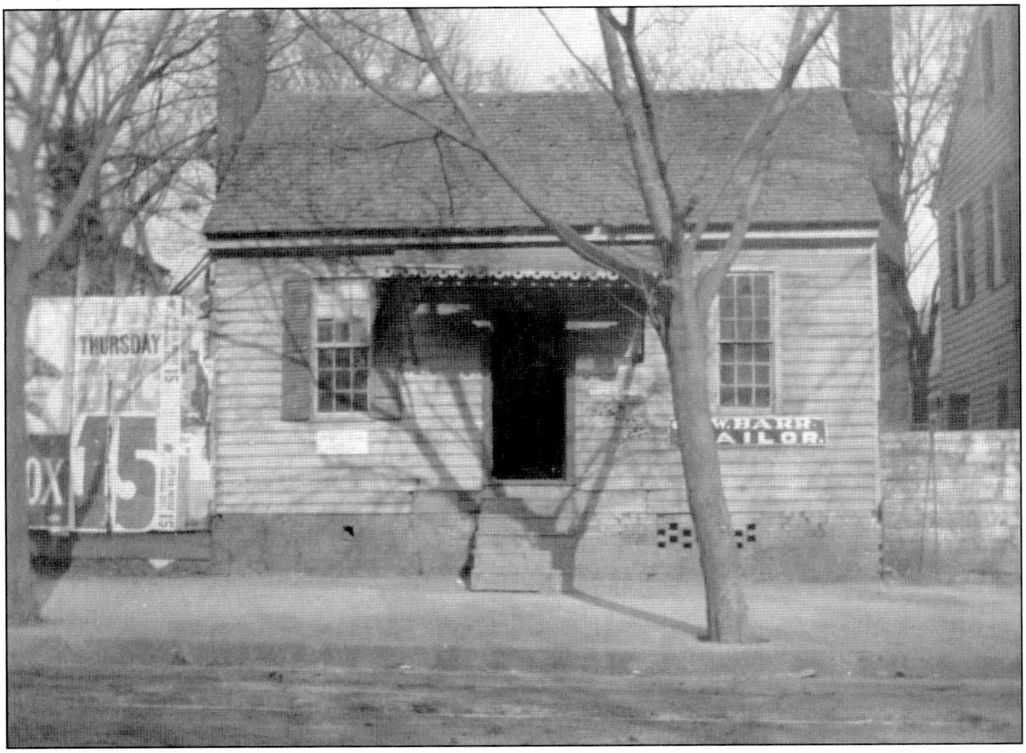

George Barr's Tailor Shop is seen here at the Root house in Milledgeville in December 1910. Laundry and pressing services were done by William Gautier and were accepted on Mondays and Tuesdays for delivery to the customer on Thursdays and Fridays. An advertisement is posted to the left of the house for a production of *The Man On the Box* presented by Bert Leigh at the Opera House Theatre on December 15. (Courtesy of the University of Georgia Special Collections, Joseph and Elizabeth Grisham Brown Papers.)

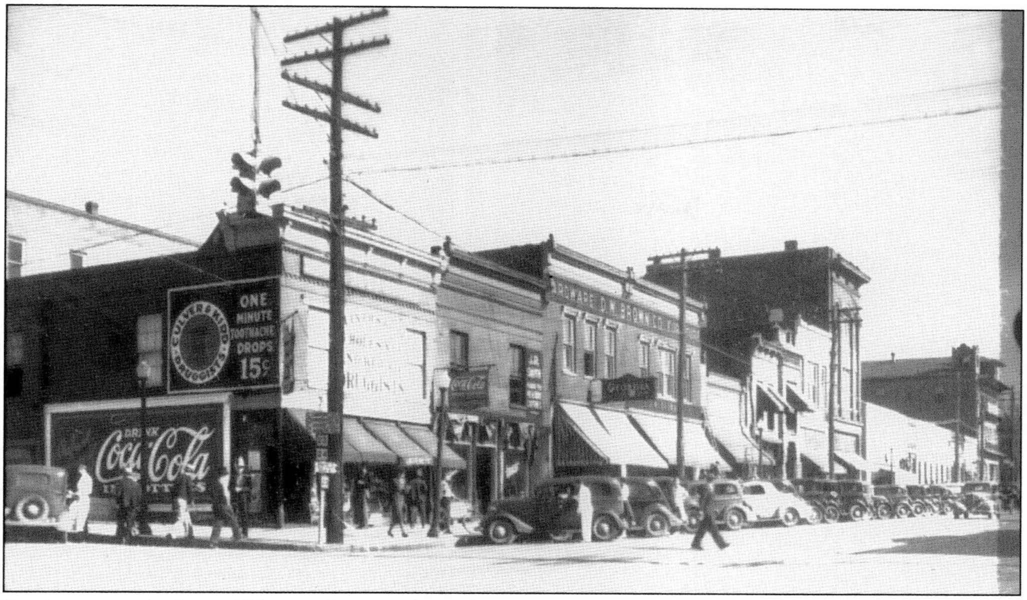

Looking south down Wayne Street, these businesses are, from left to right, Culver and Kidd Druggists; Star Theatre, serving Coca-Cola with fountain service; J.R. Smith Taylor, above the Star Theatre; Georgia Power; and D.W. Brown Furniture. Currently, the Culver and Kidd building is still owned by the Kidd family.

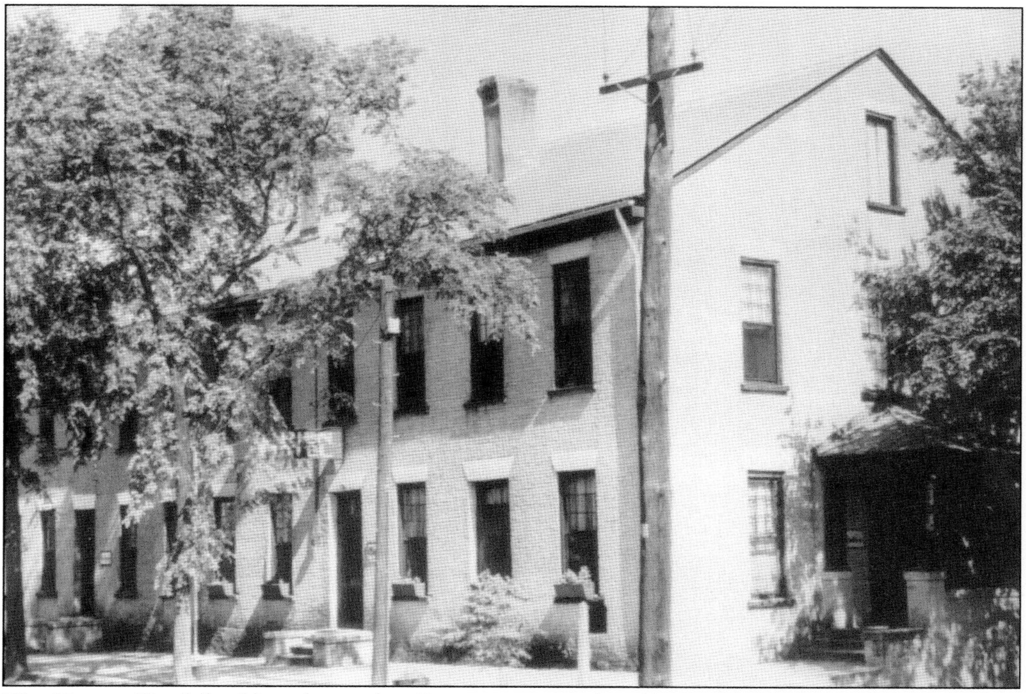

The Darien Bank building located at East Greene and Wilkinson Streets was constructed in 1818. The bank was the meeting place for the Masons until construction of their lodge. Since housing Darien Bank, the building has also been home to a newspaper, a private school, students from the Georgia Military College, apartments, and the Darien Hotel. This photograph shows the Darien Hotel around 1940 to 1941.

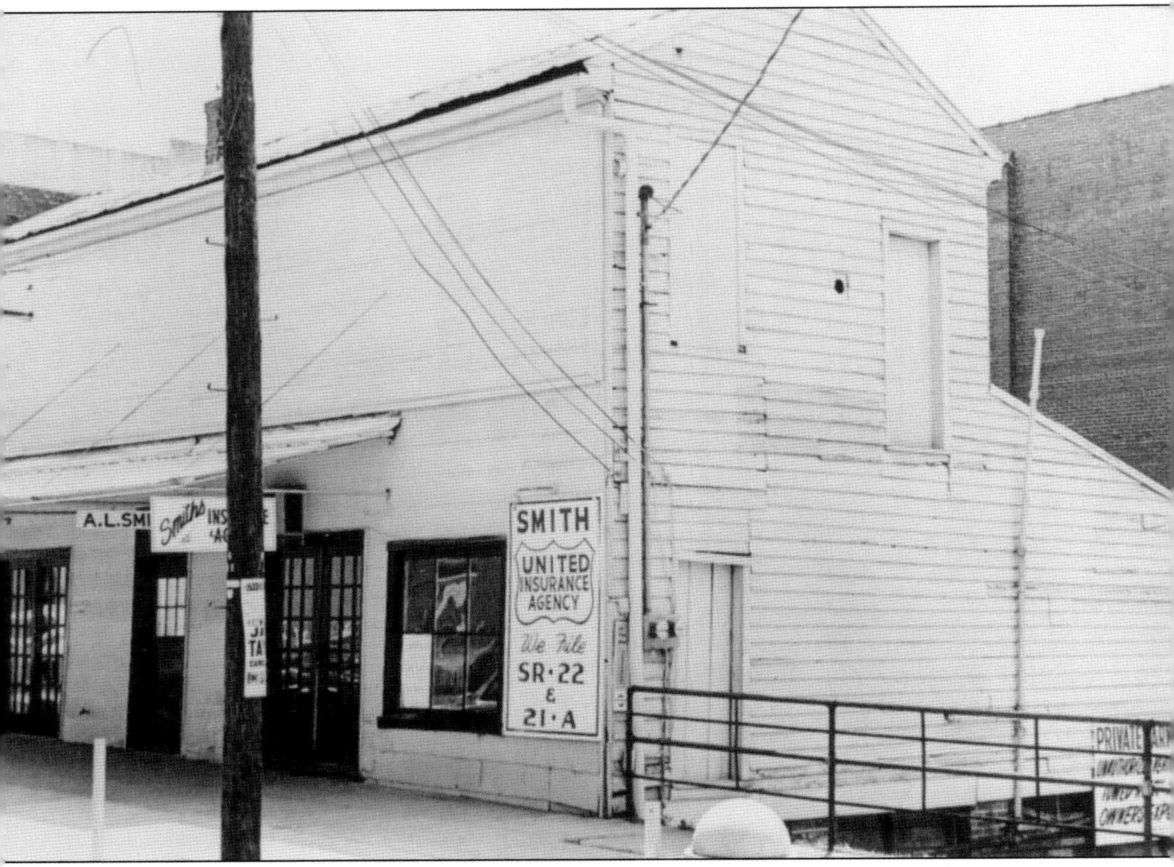

Shown here around 1970, Smith's United Insurance Agency was located on North Wayne Street. This was one of the oldest commercial structures in Milledgeville from the time period when wood was the predominant building material. To the left of the agency is a redbrick firewall. In later years, the building burned when vagrants built a fire on the lower level to keep warm on a cold night. (Courtesy of the Georgia Archives, Vanishing Georgia, bal-124.)

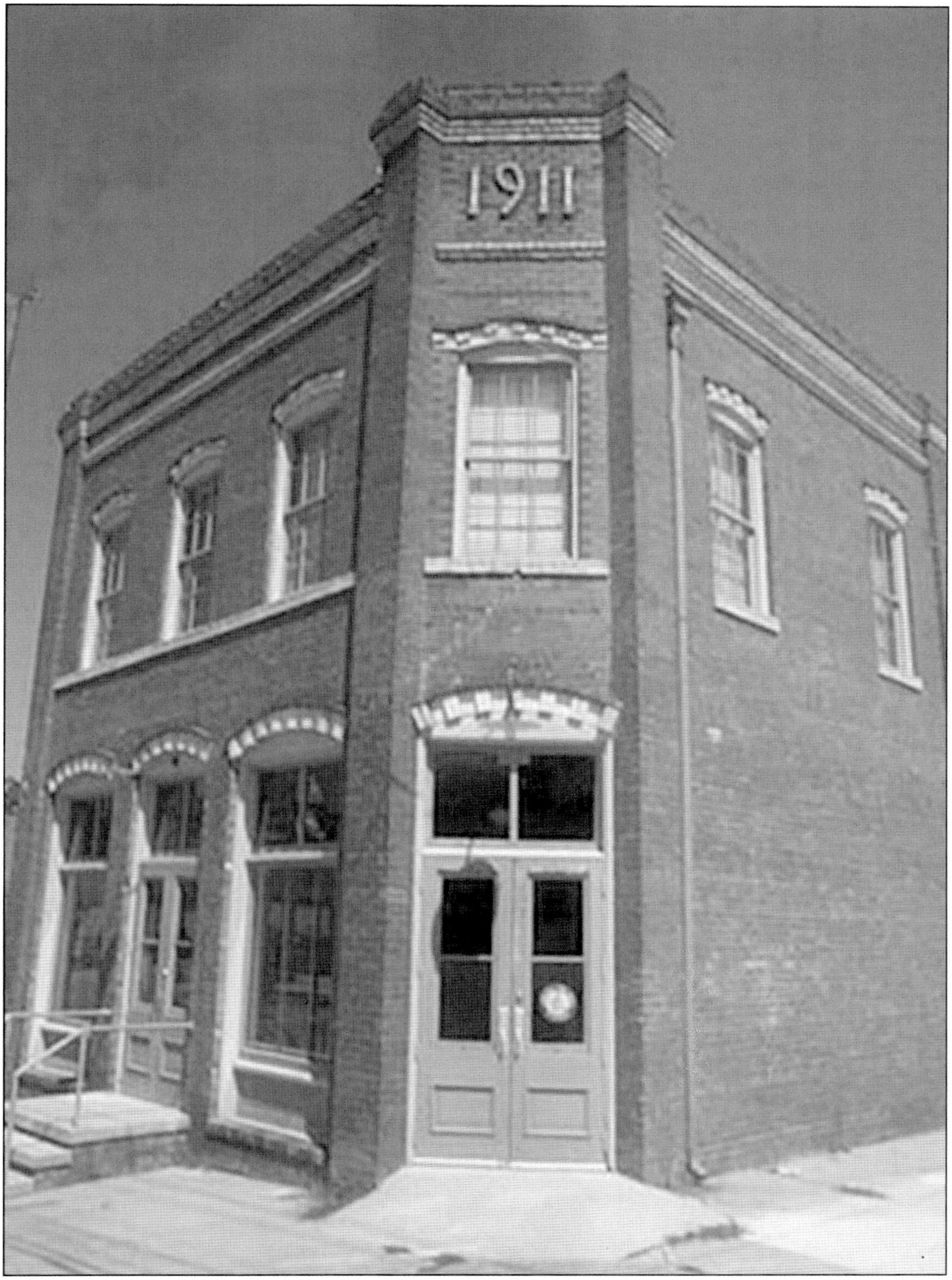

Shown here is the Allen's Market building, located on the corner of North Wayne Street and East McIntosh Streets. Allen's Market was constructed in 1911, and has housed several businesses, including grocery retail and a funeral home. Since the 1980s, the building has been part of the facilities of Milledgeville–Baldwin County Allied Arts and is used to stage theatrical, musical, and dance productions and to conduct art classes for youths and adults. The market building is also available as rental space for individual and group events. (Courtesy of Allied Arts.)

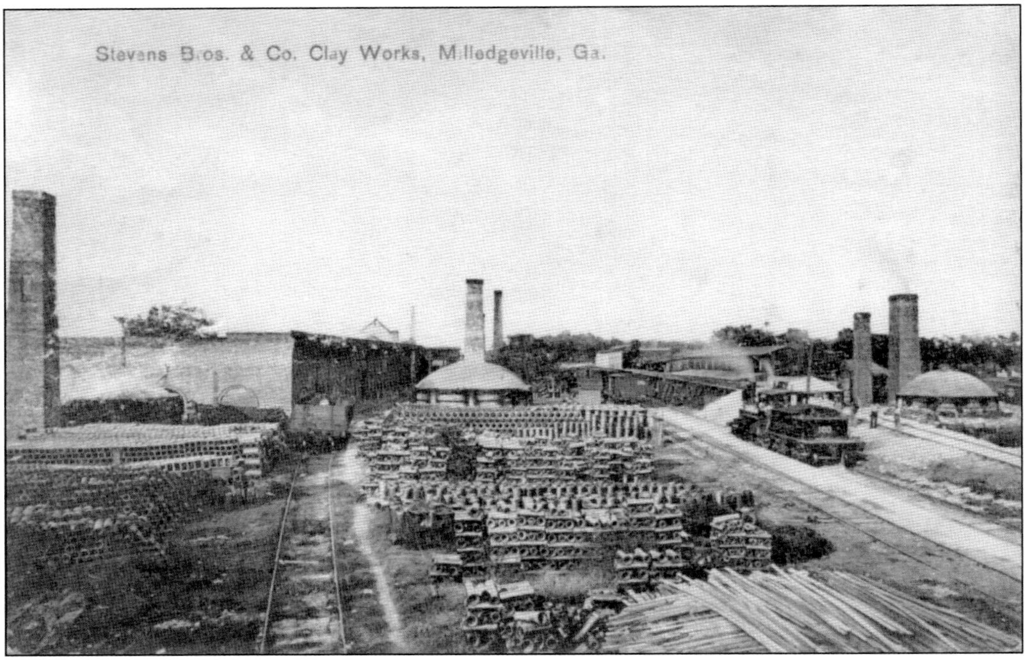

Stevens Brothers and Company Clay Products promoted itself as "the old reliable clay workers" in a 1902 advertisement in *The Union-Recorder*. The company was a producer of sewer piping for streets, public roads, and households, as well as flue pipe and chimney tops, firebrick for boilers and chimney backs, brick for grating, churns, jars, jugs, flowerpots, vases, and urns. In both of these postcard photographs, completed pipes and kilns can be seen, as well as a railway car above and a horse and buggy below. Both forms of transport were used to take goods to and from the company. (Both, courtesy of Bo Edmonds.)

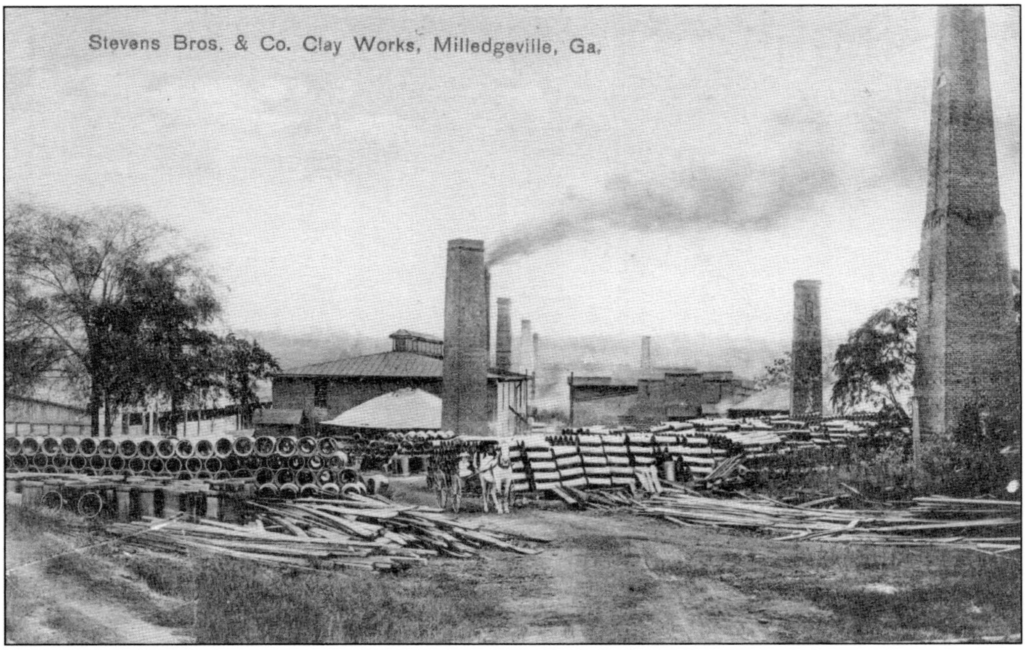

Three

Religious and Service Organizations

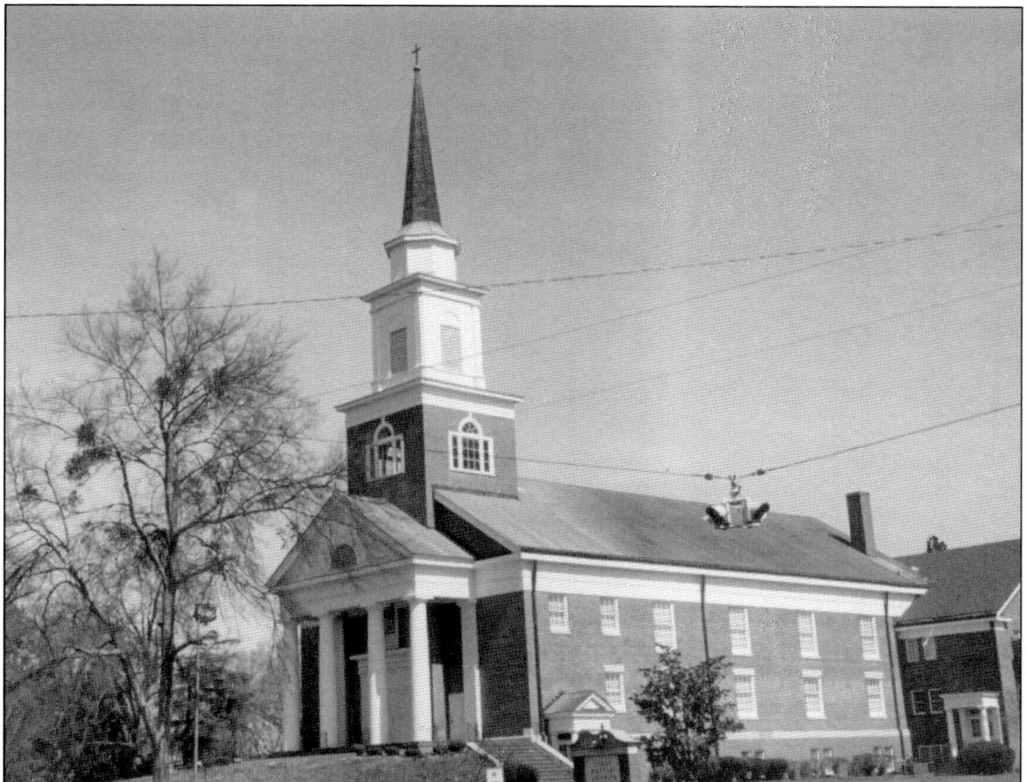

At its formation in 1806, Milledgeville Baptist Church was originally Mount Zion Baptist Church. The church adopted its new name in 1834 when, along with Baptist churches at Antioch and Indian Creek, it withdrew from the Ocmulgee Association and joined with Eatonton to form the Central Baptist Association. Differing doctoral opinions regarding atonement as well as the ability of individuals to dismiss themselves from church membership led to the division of the Ocmulgee Association. (Courtesy of Bo Edmonds.)

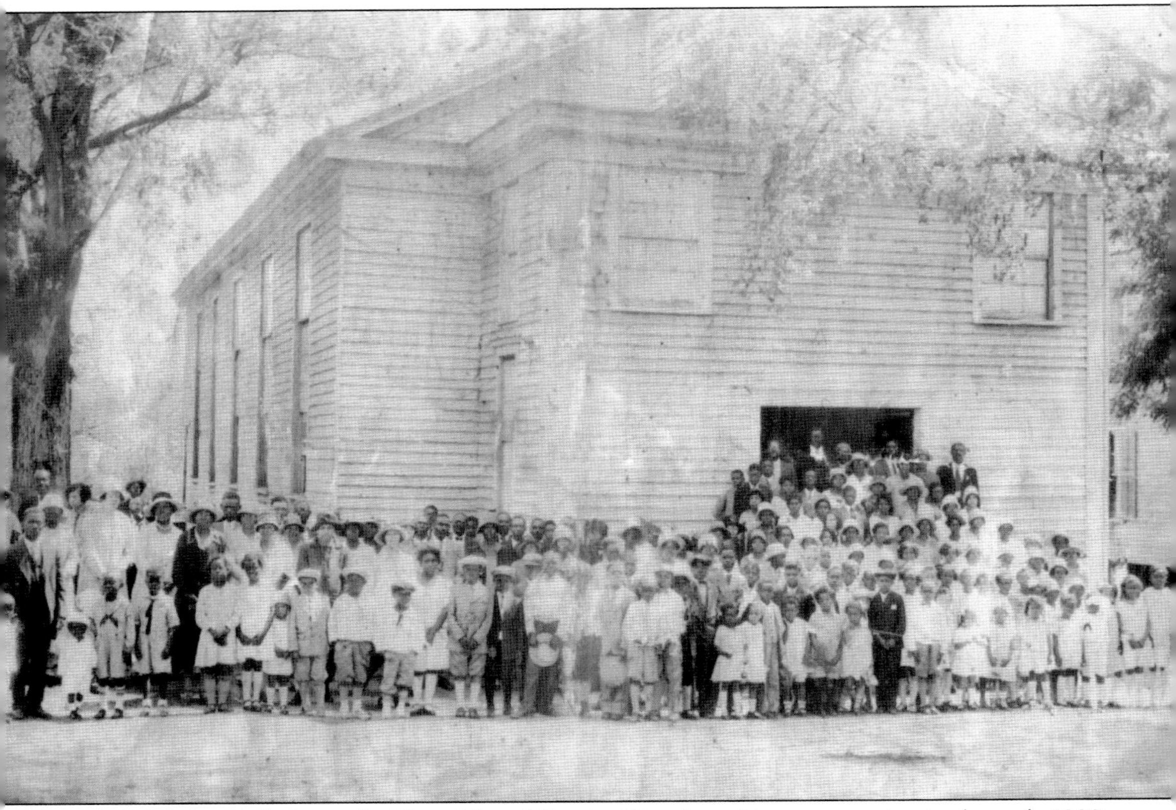

This photograph shows the Flagg Chapel Baptist Church and its congregation in the early 1900s. Located on Franklin Street, the church was founded in the early 1860s. It was destroyed by fire in 1973, but the church was rebuilt at the same location. Wilkes Flagg is credited with being instrumental in establishing the church. Flagg was a slave in the household of Dr. Tomlinson Fort. His trade was a blacksmith, as reported by the 1830 census report, and he became a master blacksmith over the shop, located on North Wayne Street, with two or three other smiths and their strikers. By saving money that was earned while working as a blacksmith, Flagg later purchased the freedom of his wife, his son, and himself. He formed a school for African Americans at Flagg Chapel Baptist Church. Recognition was made of his accomplishments in education by the American Missionary Society and, along with the Freedmen's Bureau, Milledgeville was selected as the site for the new Eddy School, which would be the only educational institute in Milledgeville for African American students. The Eddy School was founded in 1882 and operated with all grades until 1947. It was located behind Flagg Chapel on West Franklin Street. (Courtesy of Flagg Chapel Baptist Church.)

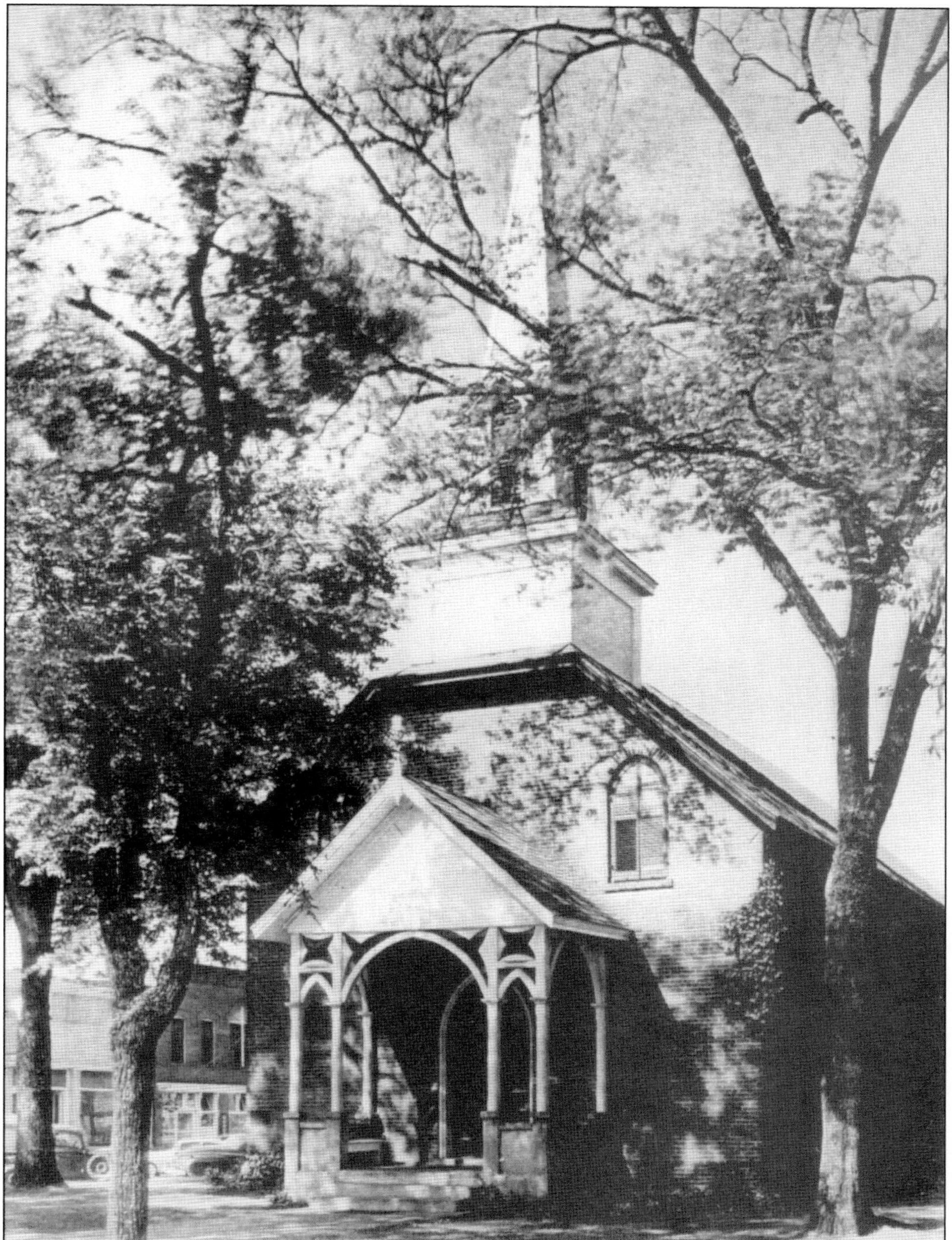

In the mid-19th century, a rapid influx of Irish and German immigrants made Catholicism the largest religion in America. Sacred Heart Catholic Church was established in Milledgeville when, in April 1845, the first documented mass was officiated by the Rev. J.J. McConnell in the Newell Hotel room of Hugh Donnelly Treanor, the great-grandfather of Flannery O'Connor. One year after a meeting to discuss building a new Catholic church—and after approval was received, the location determined by a generous endowment of land by O'Connor's great-grandmother, and a campaign conducted to raise building funds—construction of the church was completed in April 1874. (Courtesy of the Library of Congress, Carnegie Survey, LC-J7-GA-1445.)

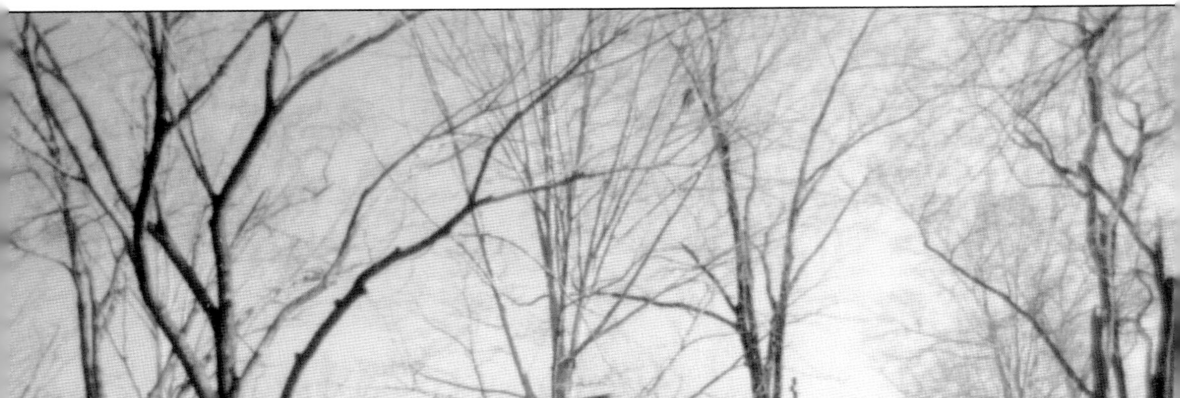

Bishop Stephen Elliot organized St. Stephens Episcopal Church in 1841, and construction of the church was completed in 1843. The building was damaged in 1864, when Federal troops used dynamite to blow up the nearby arsenal. In 1864, when Gen. Tecumseh Sherman led his 30,000 troops into Milledgeville on his March to the Sea, some of his soldiers burned the church pews, stabled their horses in the sanctuary, and poured molasses down the organ pipes. The organ was replaced in 1909 by George Walbridge Perkins Sr., former vice president of New York Life Insurance Company and partner at J.P. Morgan and Company, after he heard it was damaged by Union troops during their passage through Milledgeville. John Pierpont Morgan, with whom Perkins was partner, was a prominent member of and major benefactor to the Episcopal Church who also played a central role in the preservation of arts and history. (Courtesy of St. Stephen's Episcopal Church.)

Although it is not known whether the sign was temporarily removed or if it fell down, the photographer captured the humor in this sign having been propped in this particular orientation until it could be rehung outside the offices of St. Stephen's Episcopal Church and. (Courtesy of Saint Stephen's Episcopal Church.)

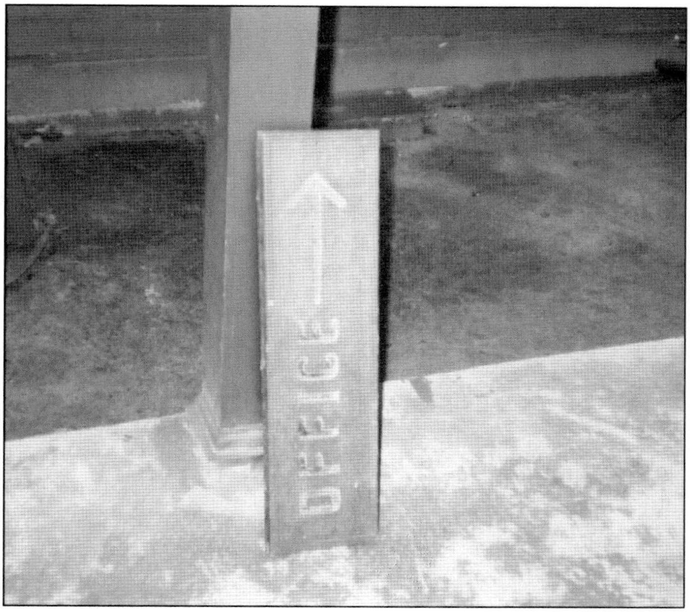

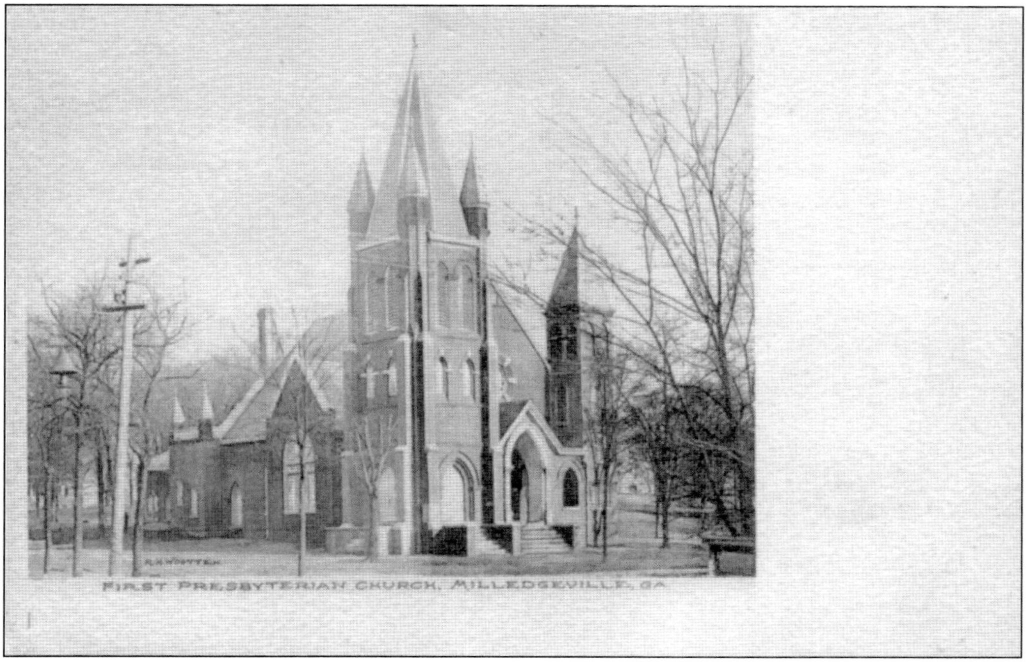

Six charter members organized the Presbyterian church on June 11, 1826. Rev. Joseph Stiles and Dr. John Brown were primarily instrumental in the organization of the church. The sanctuary was constructed in Statehouse Square where the Methodist, Baptist, and Episcopal churches were also located. The cornerstone of the structure was brought over from Scotland and was laid by the Masons in a ceremony on October 20, 1904, and the name of the church changed to First Presbyterian Church of Milledgeville. (Courtesy of Bo Edmonds.)

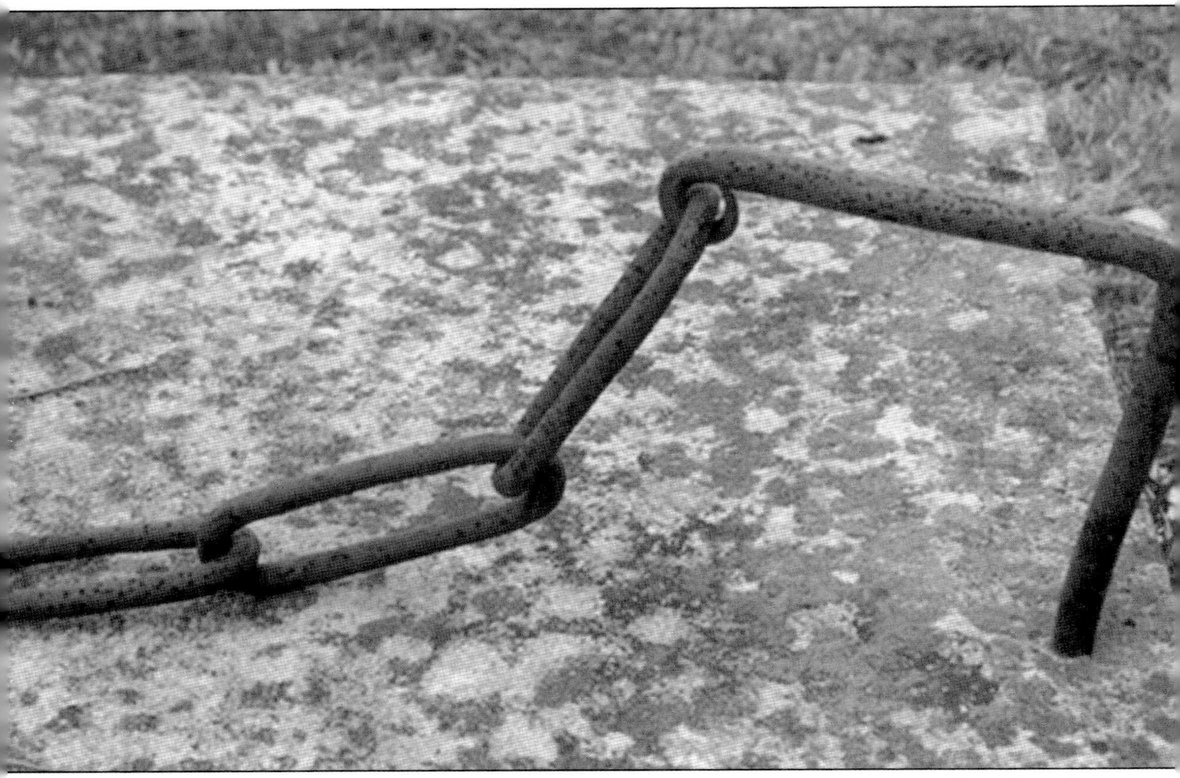

These chain links mark some graves in Memory Hill Cemetery. Although they have long been associated with slavery, the links actually memorialize the interred as having been a member of the Odd Fellows fraternal order. As stated in the *Official History and Manual of the Grand United Order of Odd Fellows*, "Odd Fellowship is an institution formed by good men for the advancement of the principles of benevolence and charity." The Grand United Order of Odd Fellows (GUOOF) was chartered directly from the international headquarters in England to serve African Americans at time when the Independent Order of Odd Fellows in the United States was segregated. Lodges were founded in both 1885 and 1889 in Milledgeville. In 1897, a three-story brick structure was financed and built by the GUOOF on Wayne Street, north of the Masonic Hall near the Baptist church. The first floor was a grocery store owned and managed by African Americans, and the Odd Fellows Hall was located on the building's third floor. The lodge was located on the site currently occupied by Chandler Brothers Ace Hardware store. (Courtesy of author.)

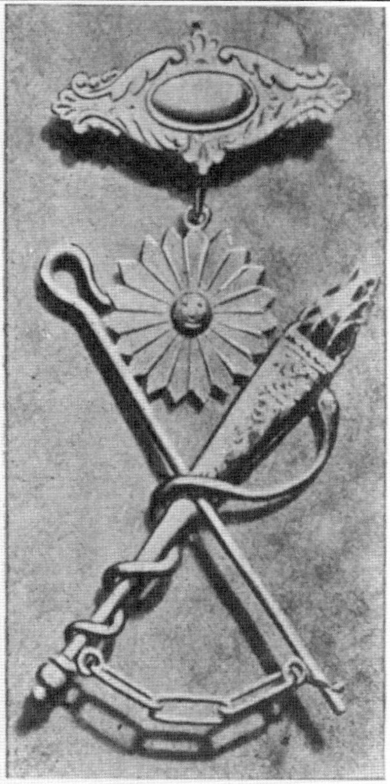

PATRIARCH'S JEWEL,
of the Patriarchie, G. U. O. of O. F.,
America.

In the early 19th century, it was considered an oddity in society for a group to be organized for the purpose of charity and giving without need of recognition. Shown is a Patriarch's Jewel pin worn by members of the Grand United Order of Odd Fellows, America. As published in the *Federal Union*, Odd Fellows emblems are detailed as follows: "the shining sun, which points to the Son of Righteousness; the crook reminds us that patriarchal shepherds were Odd Fellows and that God is our shepherd; the bundle of rods shows the importance of union in our benevolent endeavors; the serpent is to represent the brazen serpent erected by Moses, according to God's direction; the three links is to remind us that the only chain by which we are bound together is that of friendship, love, and truth." (Courtesy of author.)

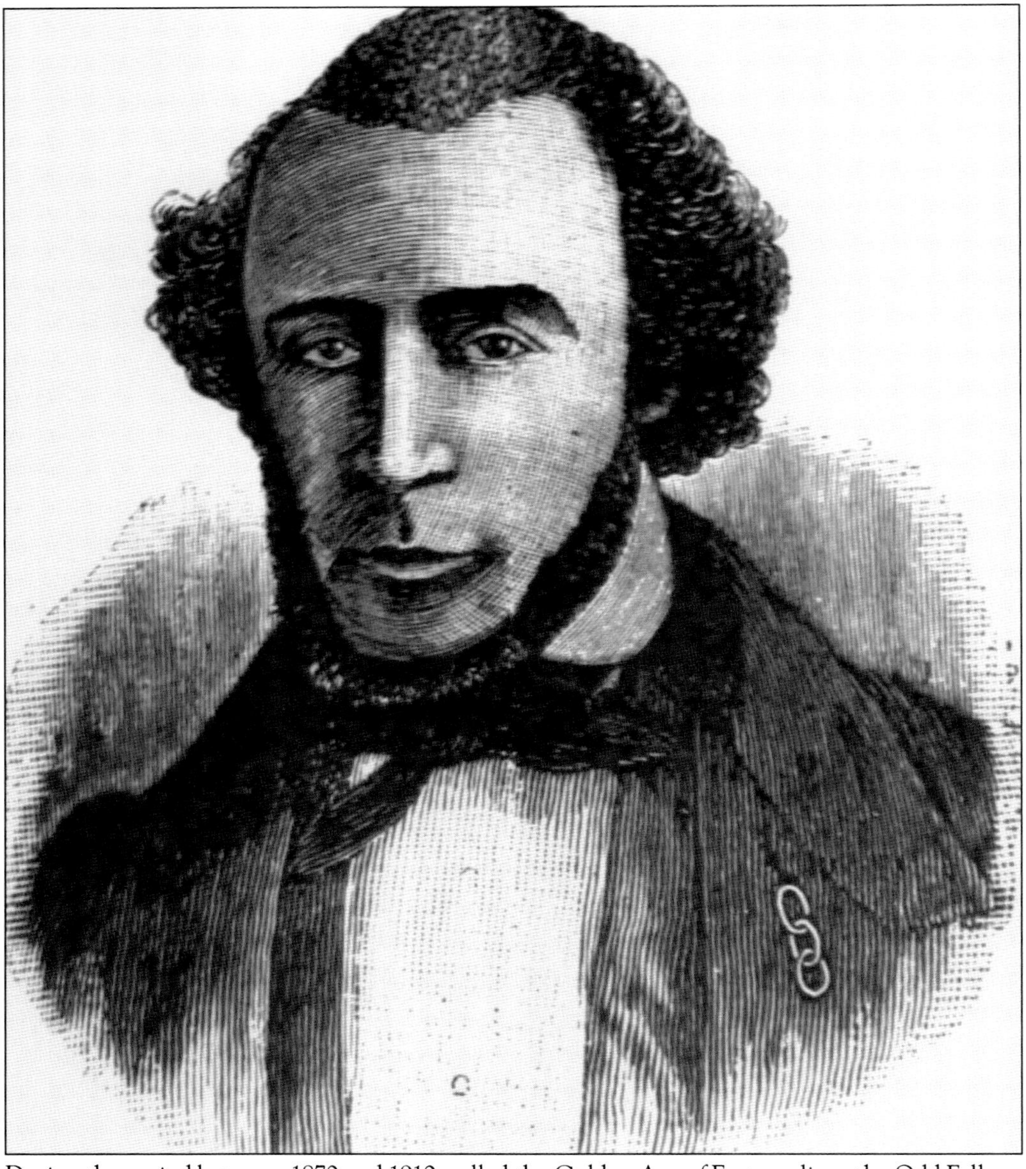

During the period between 1870 and 1910, called the Golden Age of Fraternalism, the Odd Fellows had more members than the Freemasons. Peter Ogden was the founder of the Grand United Order of Odd Fellows in America. Note the pin of three chain links he wears on his lapel. In the manual of the Odd Fellows, the belief and motto of the order is stated, "The Fatherhood of God and the Brotherhood of man, then, are the great principles of our Order, embodied in the motto, 'Friendship, Love, and Truth.' " The three joined links of chain form the organization's symbol for that motto. (Courtesy of author.)

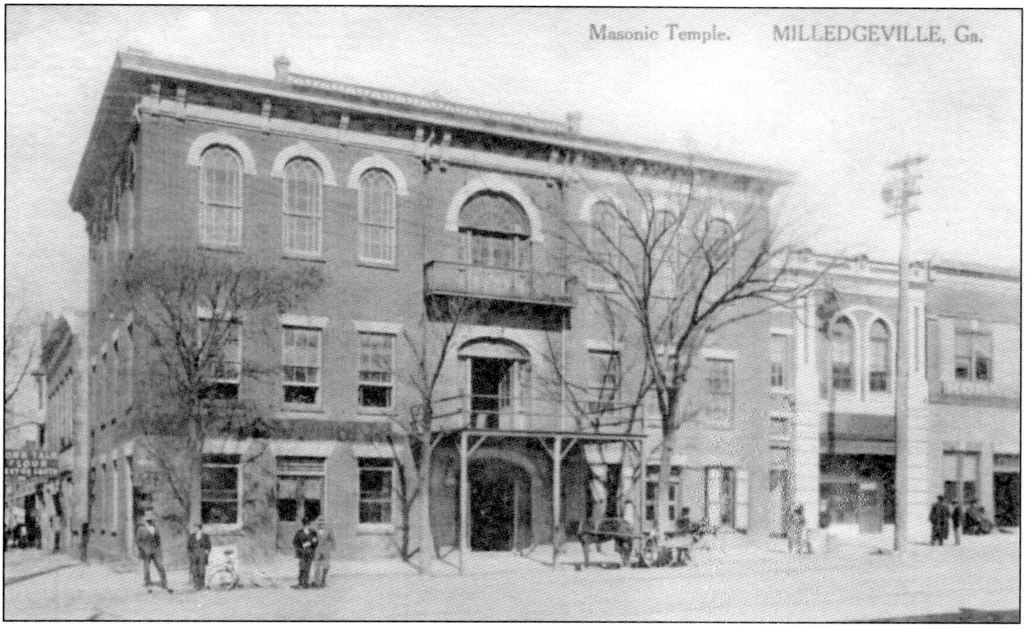

The Freemason Lodge, home to the Benevolent Lodge No. 3, was designed by prominent Milledgeville architect John Marlor between 1832 and 1834. Before construction of the lodge, Masonic meetings were held at the Darien Bank on South Wayne Street. The Freemasons are sometimes referred to as a secret society, so called because methods of recognition such as grips, words, signs as well as induction ceremonies are kept private. The photograph below was taken between 1880 and 1890, and the lodge currently remains at the intersection of Wayne and Hancock Streets.

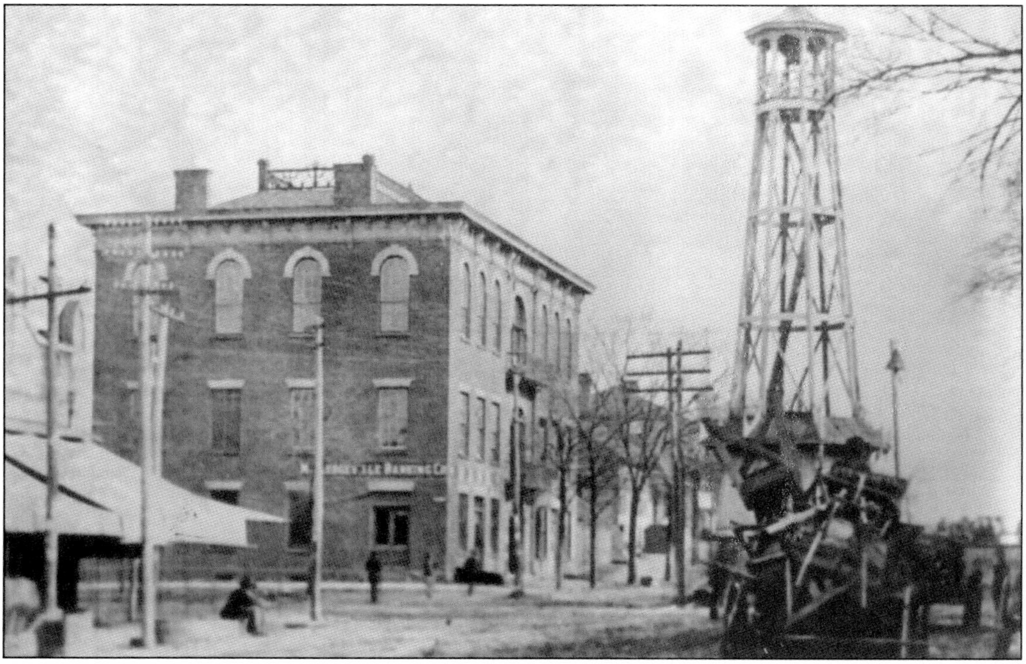

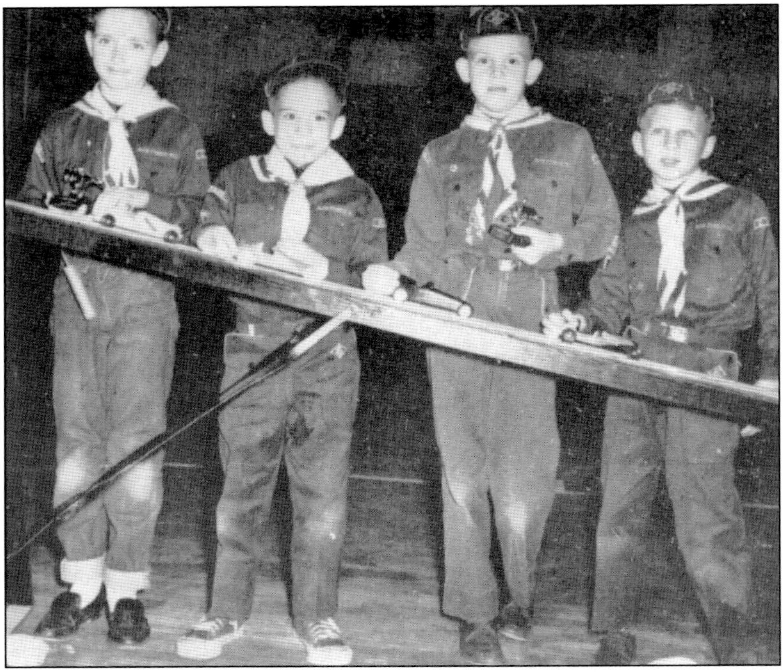

In this image taken April 3, 1962, Boy Scout Cub Pack 70 competes in the annual Pine Wood Derby. Pictured are, from left to right, Raymond Raley, trophy winner for car design; Jim Davis, first-place winner in the race; Jimmy Durden, third-place winner in the race; and Lindsey McCoy, trophy winner for car design. (Courtesy of *The Union-Recorder.*)

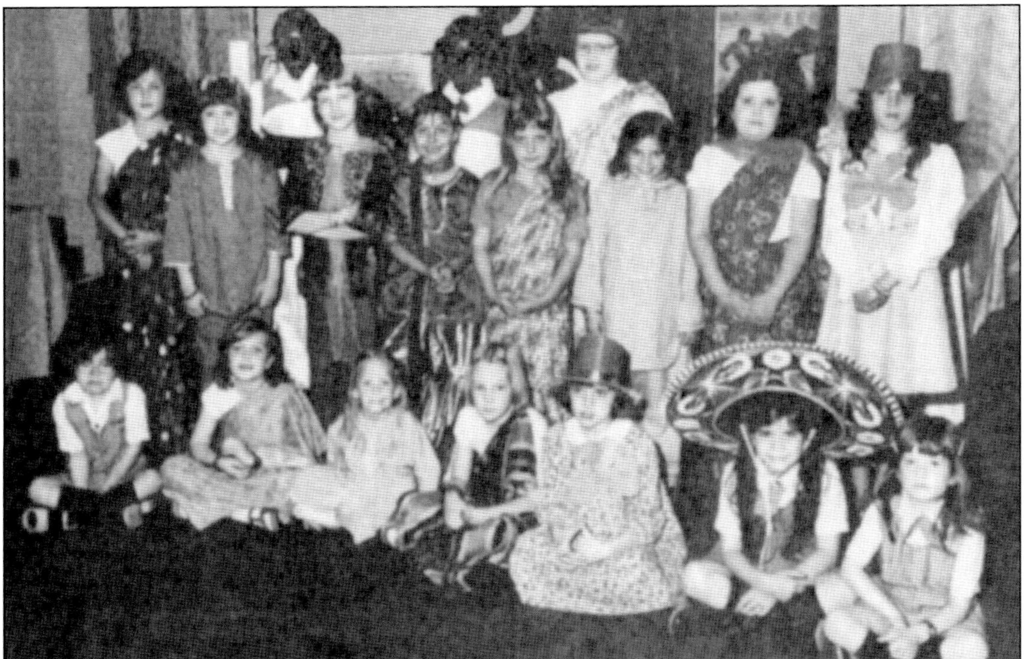

The Girl Scouts of Milledgeville celebrate Girl Scout Week by hosting an International Taster's Tea. In this late-1970s photograph, they wear costumes honoring such countries as Korea, Ireland, India, and Nigeria. Pictured are, from left to right, (first row) Tara Smith, Denise Jones, Brenda Benson, Marty Bird, Donna Shell, Heather Diaz, and Monica Moxley; (second row) Leslie Todd, Erin Smart, Dawn Schwartz, Robia Karatella, Christine Foreman, Patricia Lavendar, Wendy Grimes, and Wendy Register; (third row) Jerri Dean Vasser, Sonya Horne, and Heather Schwartz. (Courtesy of *The Union-Recorder.*)

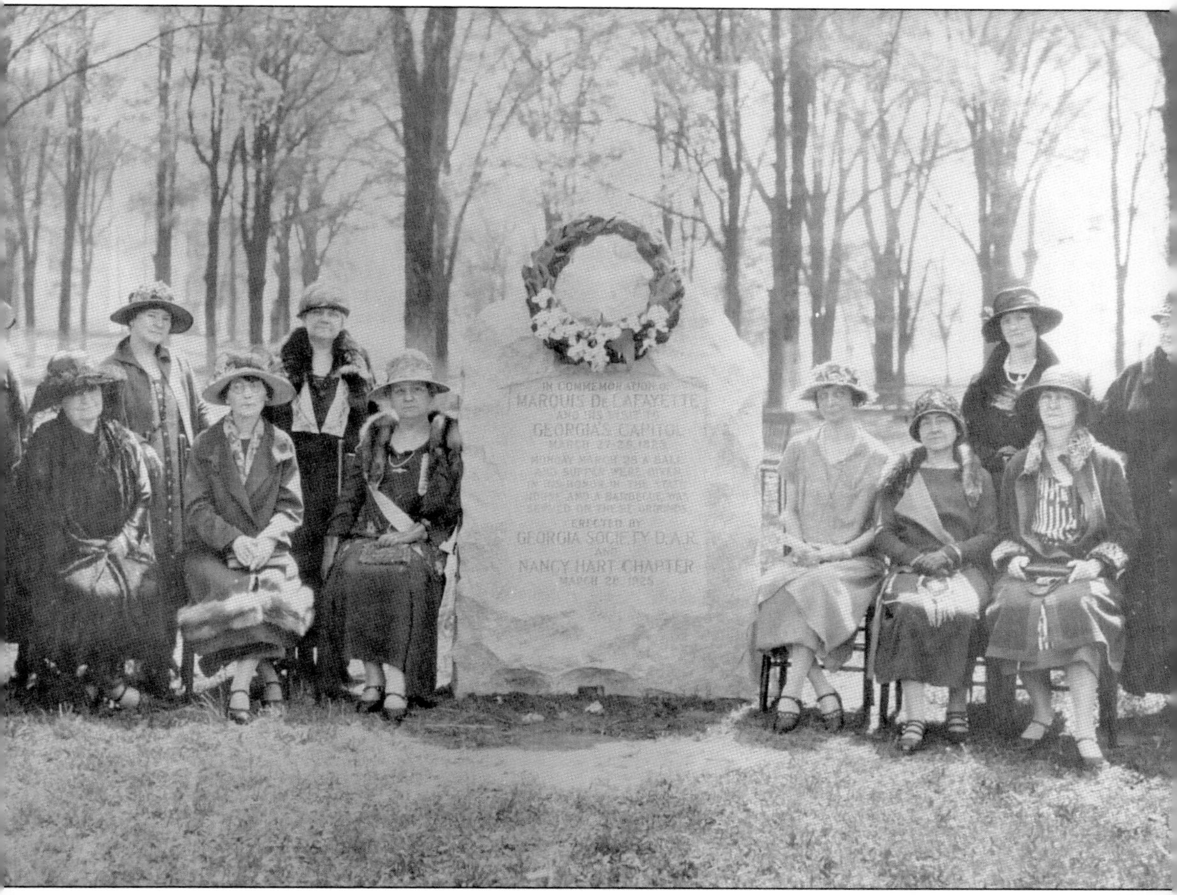

The Nancy Hart Chapter of the Georgia Society Daughters of the American Revolution is shown at the March 28, 1925, dedication of the monument to commemorate 100 years since the visit of the Marquis de Lafayette to Milledgeville. Lafayette visited the town as part of his tour, at the invitation of Pres. James Monroe, to visit all 24 states. The monument is located on the grounds of the former capitol. Pictured are, from left to right, (first row) Laura Singleton Walker, Eli Thomas, state regent Mrs. Howard McCall, Sarah Hearn Garrard, Leola Selman Beeson, and Clara Williams Pottle; (second row) Gertrude Horne Hutchinson, unidentified, Sarah Cantey Whitaker Allen, Leila Lamar, and A.B. Scott. (Courtesy of Allied Arts.)

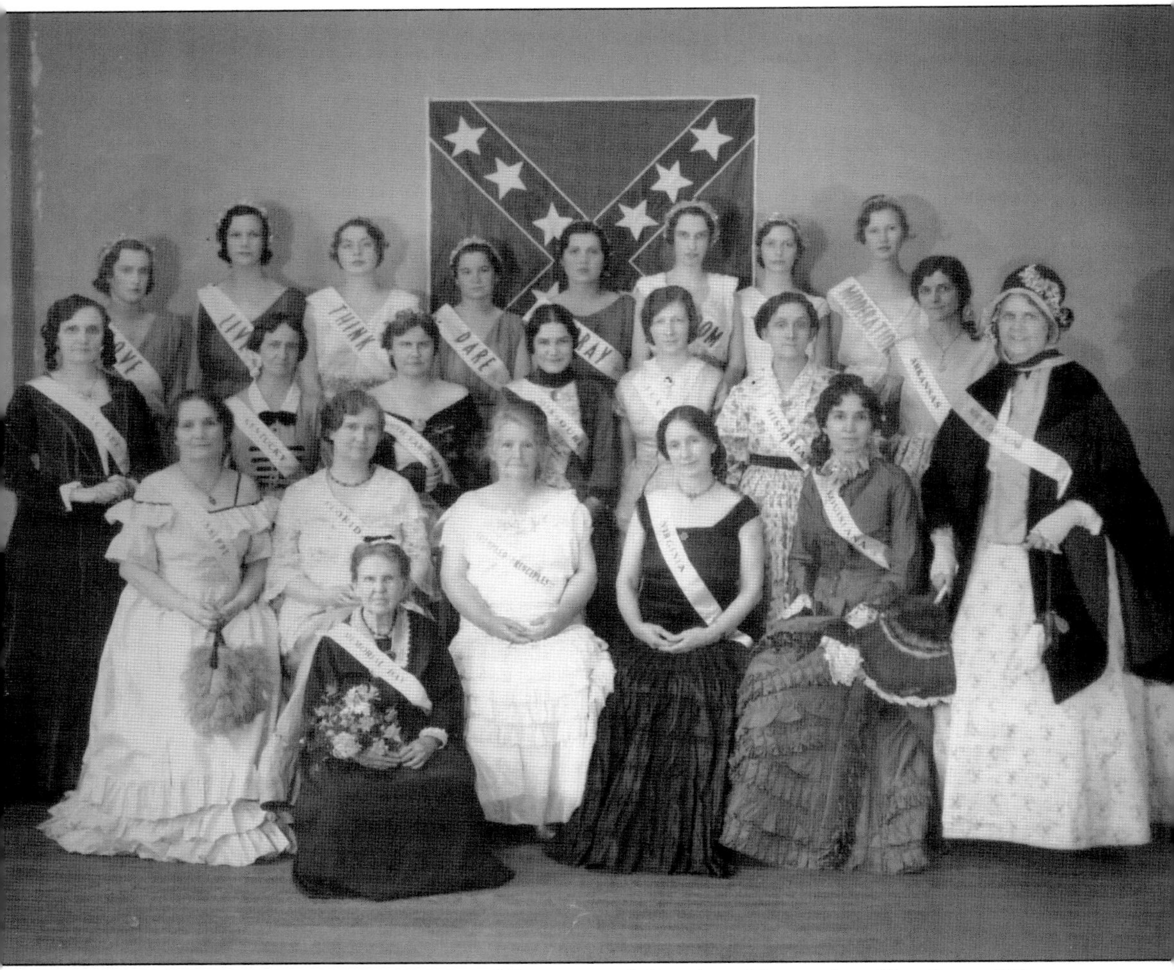

Founders Anna Davenport Raines of Georgia and Caroline Meriwether Goodlett of Tennessee organized the National Association of the Daughters of the Confederacy in 1894. The organization changed its name to the United Daughters of the Confederacy (UDC) in 1895 and was formally incorporated in 1919. The c. 1910 UDC in Milledgeville is shown here. The motto of the UDC is "love, live, pray, think, dare." The objectives of the organization are historical, educational, benevolent, memorial, and patriotic. Among some of the UDC's undertakings have been petitioning the Georgia legislature to endorse compulsory education, defining the age of consent, and supporting a bill allowing women to practice law in the state of Georgia. (Courtesy of Allied Arts.)

Four

Reform, Health Care, Education, and Recreation

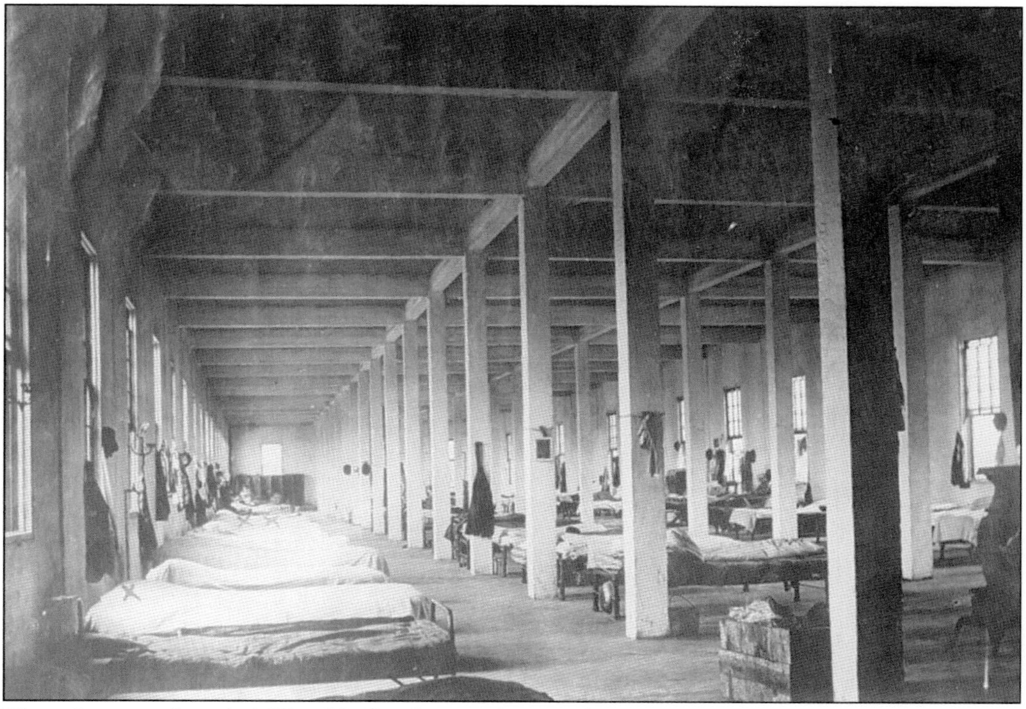

This photograph, titled "Frank's Cot," was taken at the state prison in Milledgeville in 1915. One of the most controversial trials of the 20th century, the Leo Frank case was representative of many complex issues of the day, including child labor, North versus South, white versus black, Jews versus Christians, and industrialist versus agrarian. (Courtesy of the Library of Congress, Bain Collection, LC-B2 3571-8.)

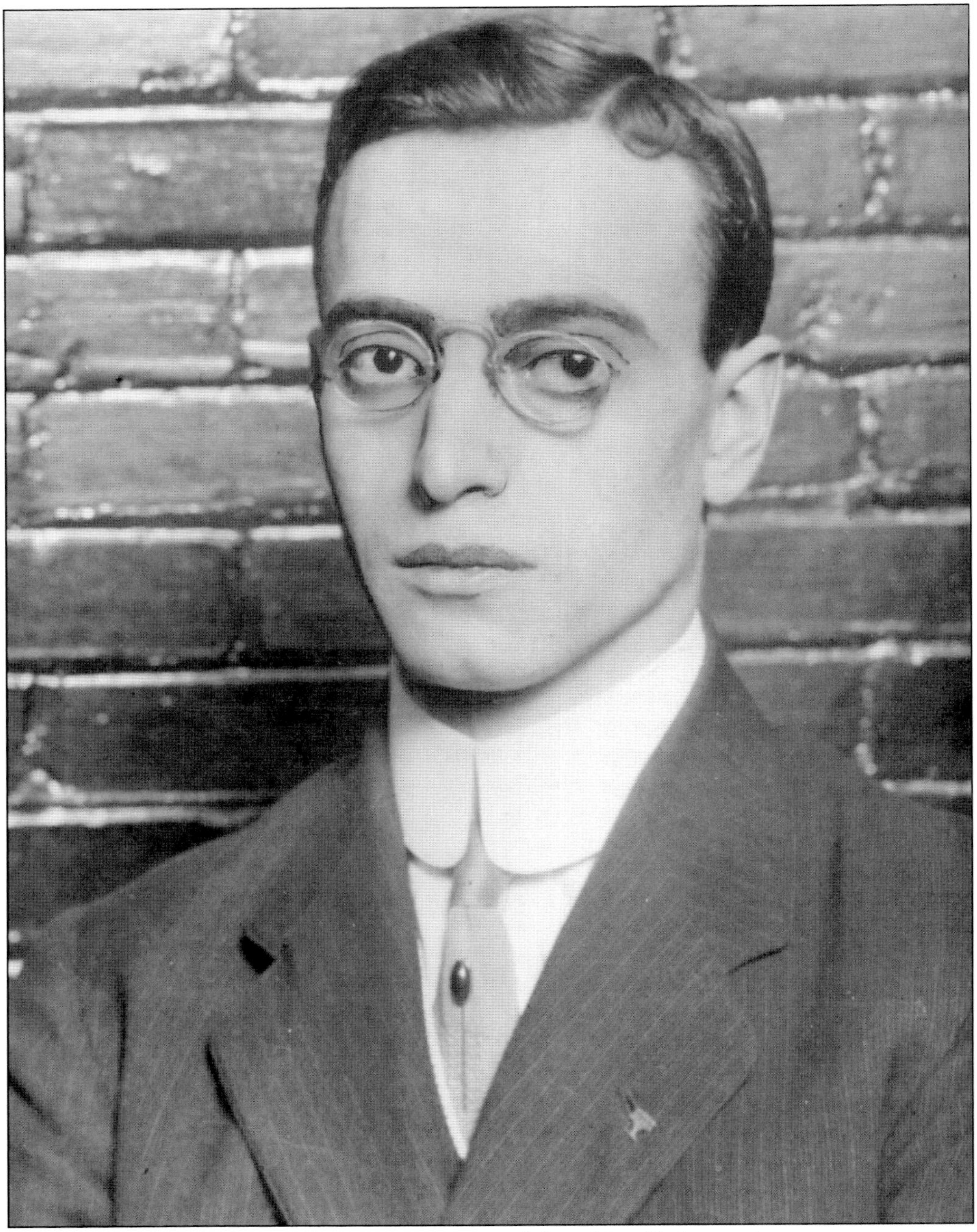

Leo Frank was a Jewish American man who moved from New York to Atlanta to supervise the National Pencil Company factory. Frank was later tried and convicted for the murder of Mary Phagan, a 13-year-old child laborer, who was found dead in the basement after having gone to collect her paycheck at the factory. Frank appealed his case all the way to the country's highest court, and the governor of Georgia commuted his sentence in 1915. After surviving an attempt on his life by another inmate at the Milledgeville prison, Frank was abducted by a mob of about 25 men, who drove him to Marietta, Georgia, where they hanged him from a tree. Almost 100 years later, the case remains debated and unresolved, although the Georgia Bureau of Pardons and Paroles granted Frank a posthumous pardon in 1986. (Courtesy of author.)

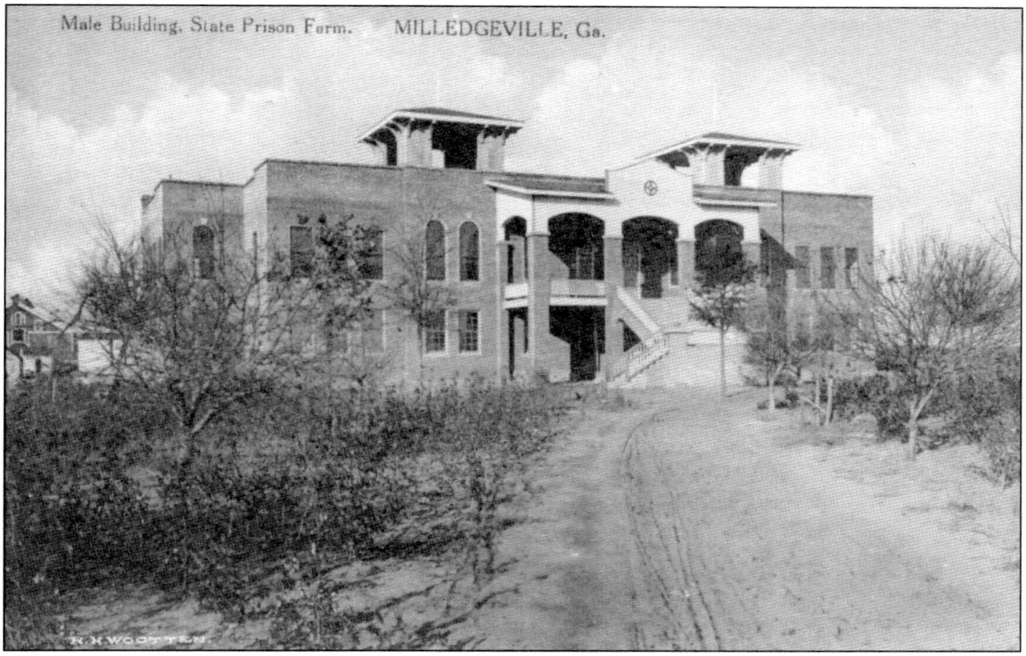

The men's building at the State Prison Farm in Milledgeville, shown here in 1911, replaced the structure lost to fire in 1910. The prison farm was developed in 1899 to house infirm, aged, and juvenile convicts. The youngest prisoner, age nine, was confined to the facility in 1901. (Courtesy of Bo Edmonds.)

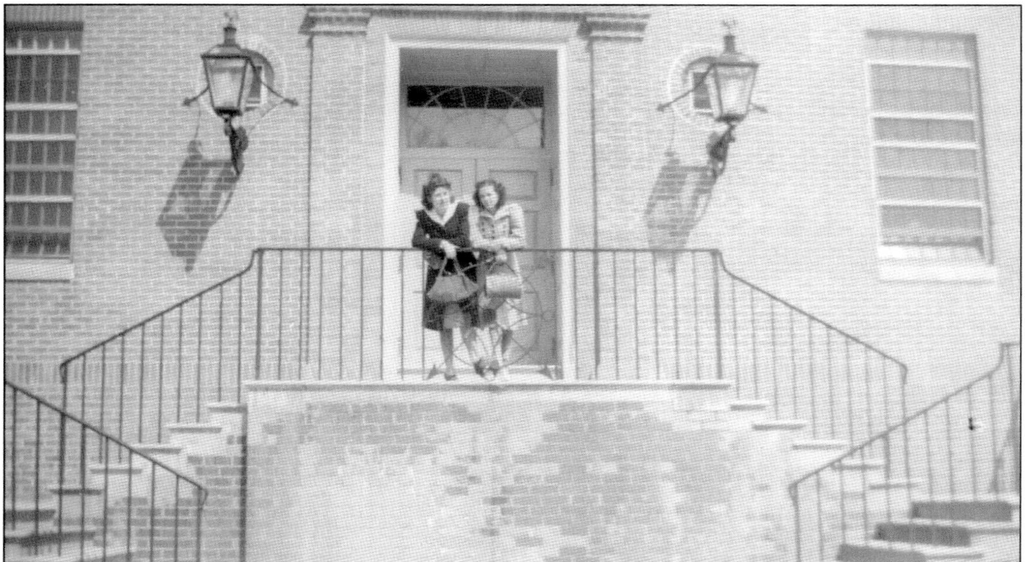

Marion Kinney Garland (left) and an unidentified woman pose at the top of the staircase of the L.M. Jones Building at Central State Hospital in the 1940s. The building was constructed between 1928 and 1929. (Courtesy of Ken Garland.)

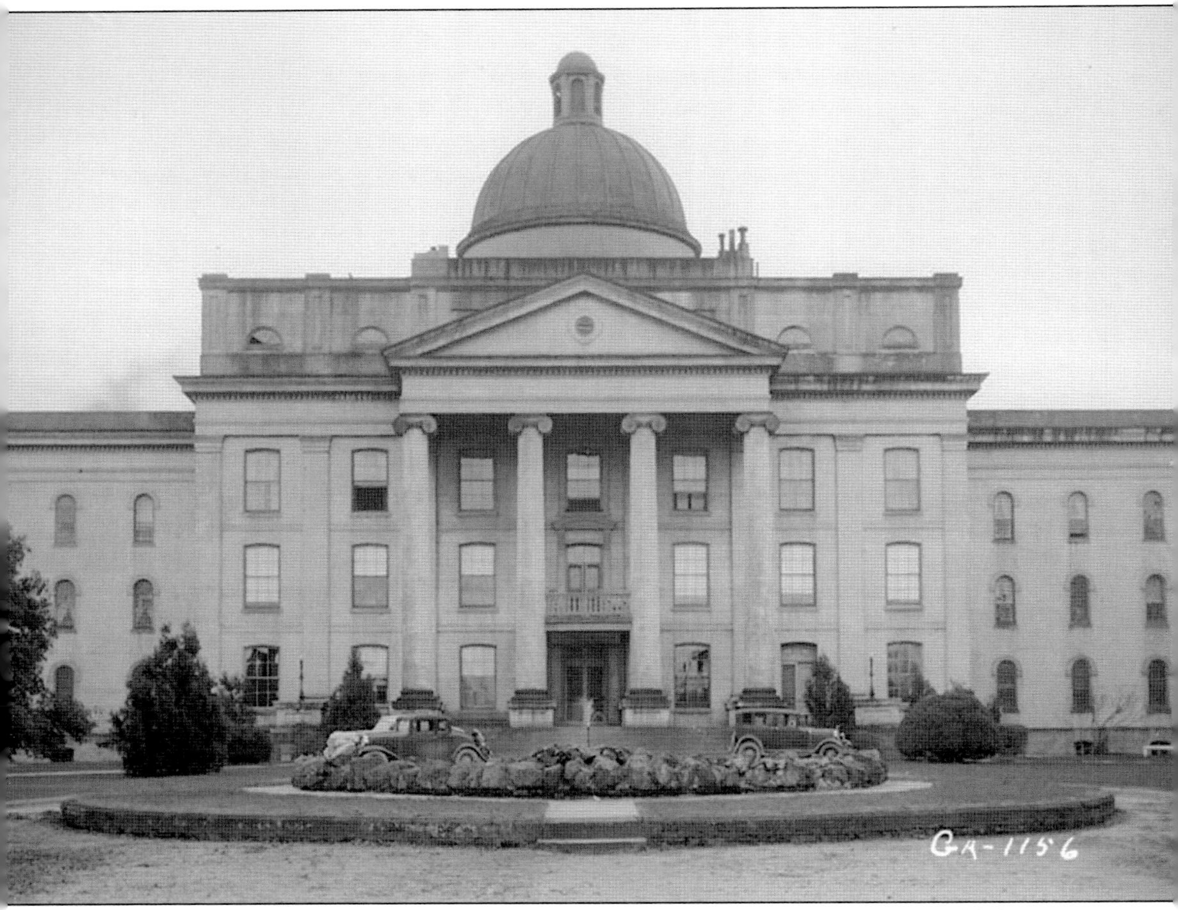

In 1837, Georgia legislators responded to movements across the nation to establish state-run hospitals for the mentally ill by passing a bill to create a "State Lunatic, Idiot, and Epileptic Asylum." Construction of the facility was completed in 1842, and the first patient was admitted the same year. The name of the asylum was later changed to the Georgia State Sanitarium in 1898, to Milledgeville State Hospital in 1929, and the current Central State Hospital in 1967. The Powell Building is shown in this early-to-mid-1900s photograph. (Courtesy of the Library of Congress, Historic American Building Survey, HABS GA-1156.)

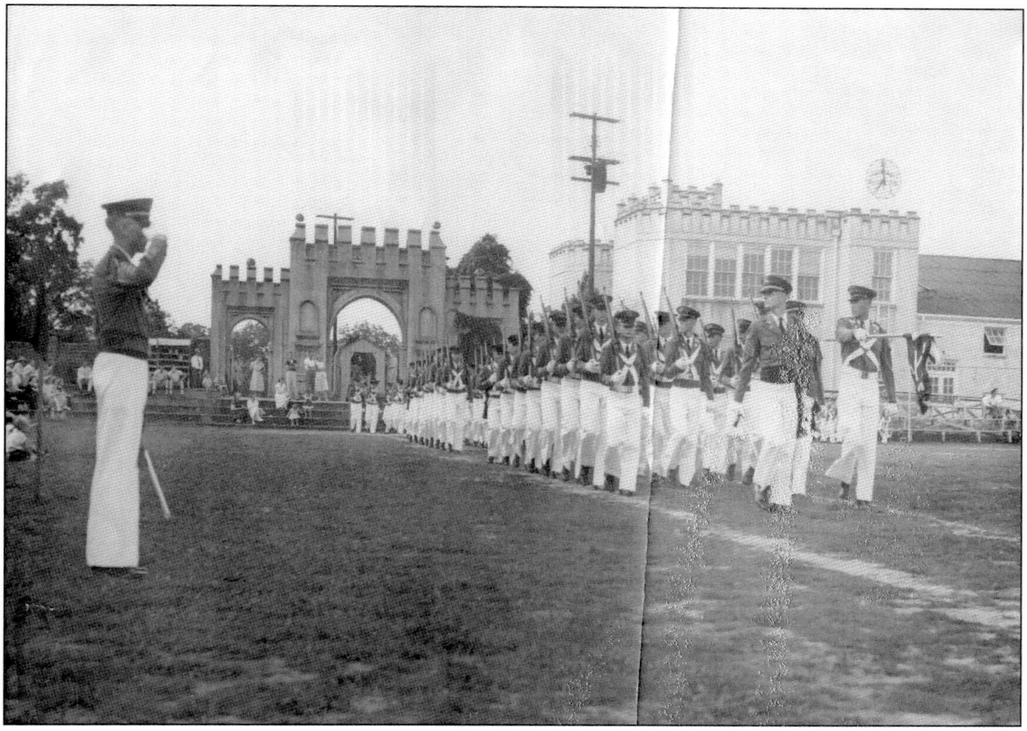

Cadets at Georgia Military College are seen here in 1953. Shown in formation is the prestigious Charlie Company, a saber company at the college. (Courtesy of Barbara and Buddy Martin.)

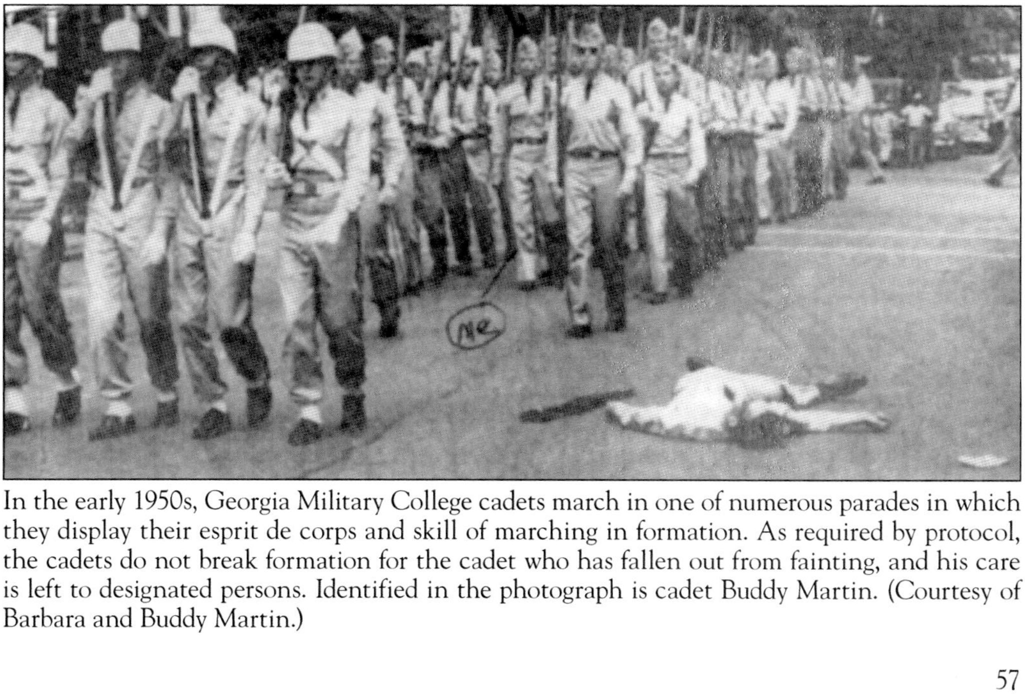

In the early 1950s, Georgia Military College cadets march in one of numerous parades in which they display their esprit de corps and skill of marching in formation. As required by protocol, the cadets do not break formation for the cadet who has fallen out from fainting, and his care is left to designated persons. Identified in the photograph is cadet Buddy Martin. (Courtesy of Barbara and Buddy Martin.)

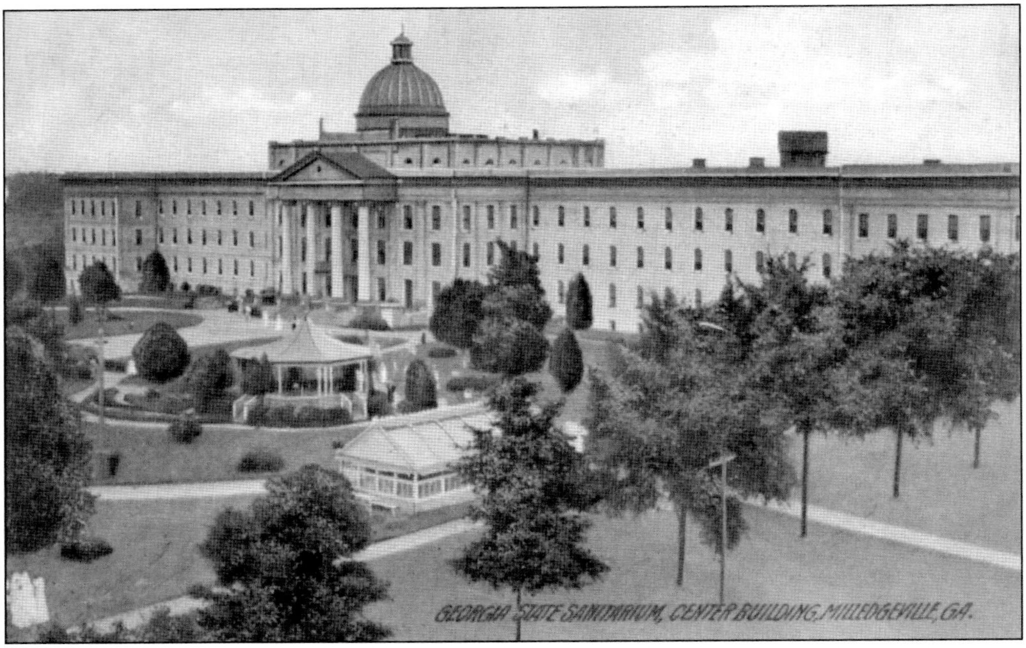

Shown here is the Georgia State Sanitarium central building and grounds. In Milledgeville, as well as in mental hospitals across the nation, patients were classified by the amount of control that they had over their own behavior rather than a diagnosis of the symptoms presented. Despite the efforts of administration to effectively manage patients, by 1872, the ratio of patients to physicians was 112 to 1 and remained so for about the next 100 years. (Courtesy of Bo Edmonds.)

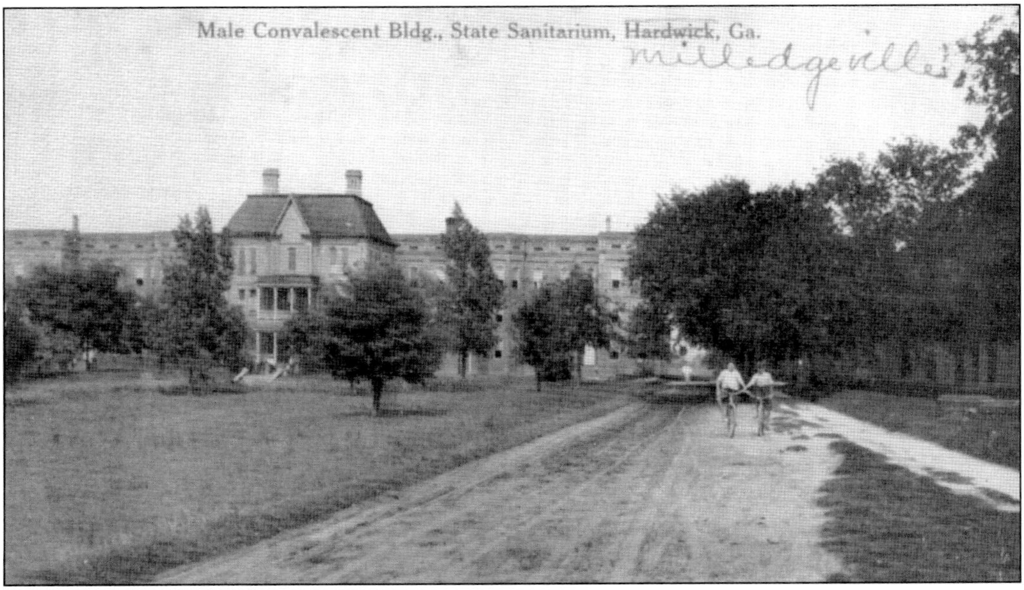

The Male Convalescent Building at the State Sanitarium in Milledgeville, Georgia, is shown here in the early 1900s. Known as the Walker Building, it was constructed in 1887 and served as intake for white, male convalescent patients. The practice of segregating patients by race continued until around the 1940s. The first building for African American patients was constructed in 1889, and its design was much more advanced than most health care facilities in the South at that time. (Courtesy of Bo Edmonds.)

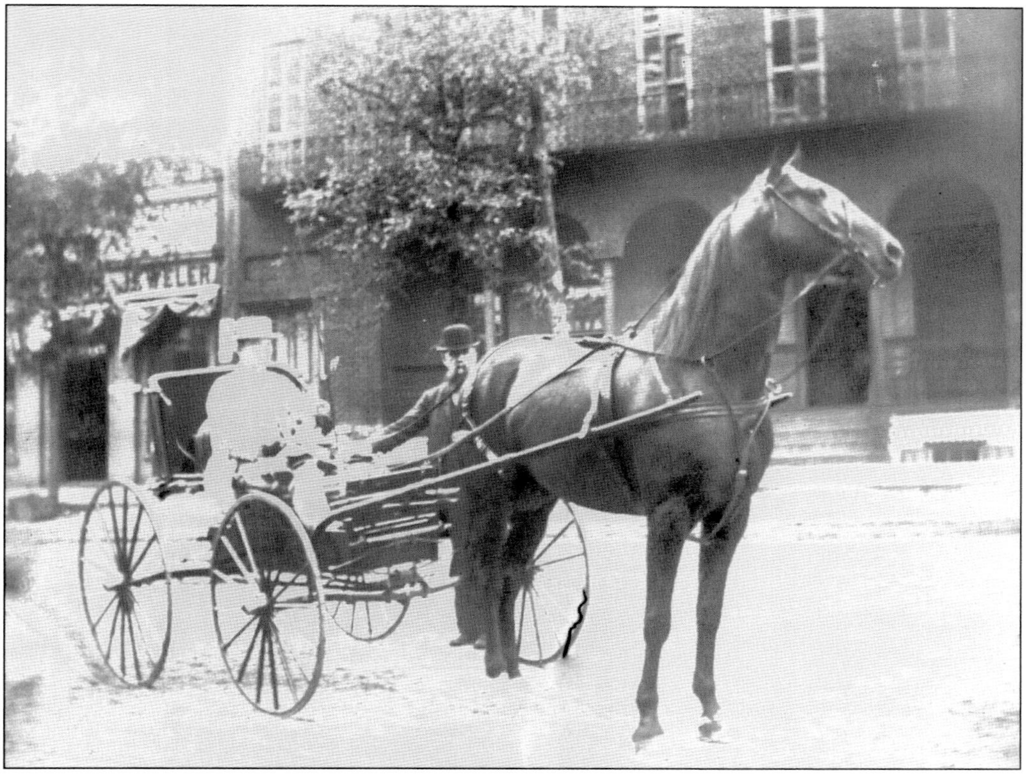

At the corner of Greene and South Wayne Streets, around 1890, Dr. Henry Dawson Allen Jr. is standing beside a buggy. Thalian Hall, shown above, was a dormitory built in the late 1850s at Oglethorpe College; it is no longer standing. Sidney Lanier, an American musician and poet, attended Oglethorpe College and roomed at Thalian Hall. The property was later purchased by Dr. Allen and used for the establishment of Allen's Invalid Home. As reported by the *Milledgeville News*, the invalid home was "a private hospital for the treatment of nervous disease" and among its patients were "numerous ex-soldiers wounded or disabled by [World War I]."

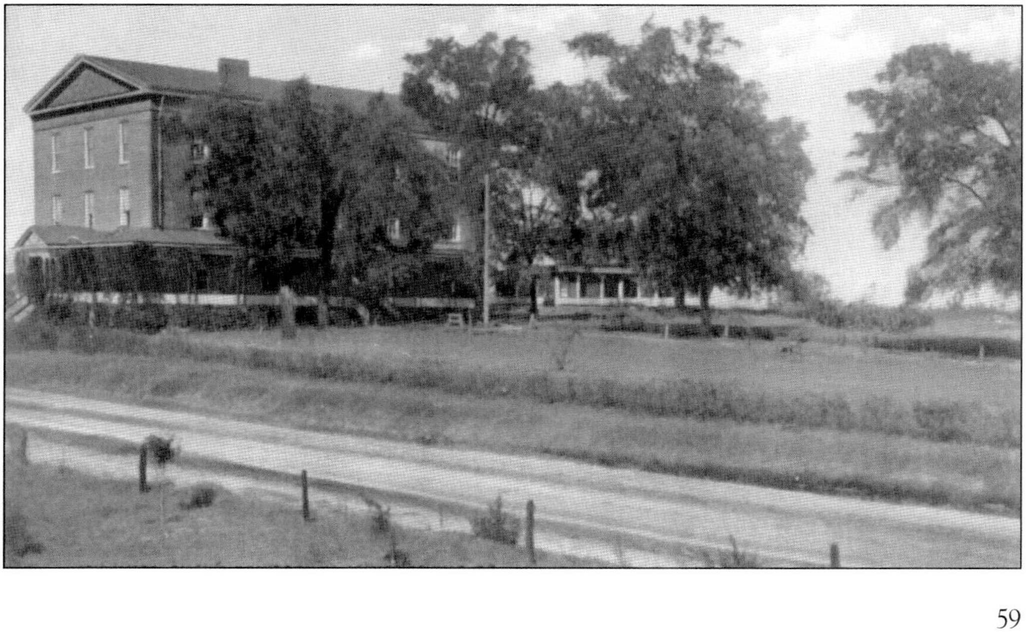

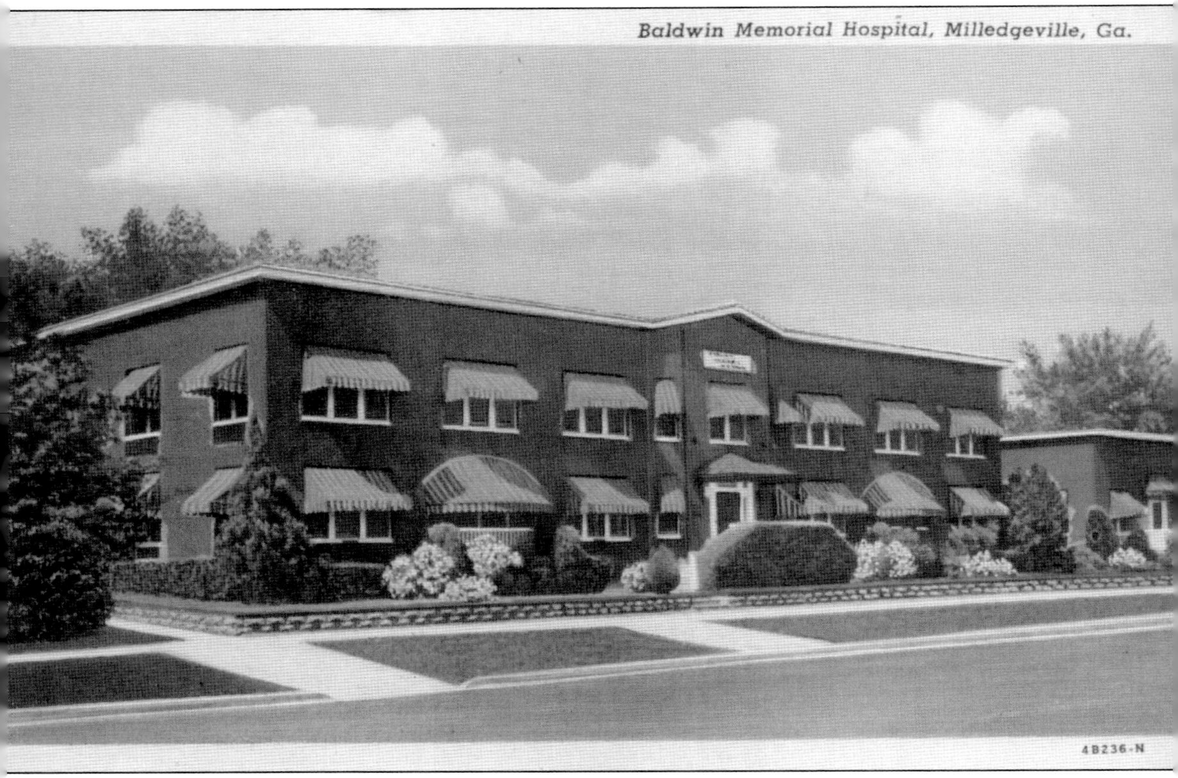

Baldwin County Hospital opened in Milledgeville in March 1957. Located on Greene Street, it took the place of two doctor's clinics that served Baldwin County and also provided hospital services for surrounding areas. At its opening, the hospital employed about 120 staff and had capacity of 160 beds. In the 1950s, the price of health care doubled. By the 1960s, more than 700 companies were selling health insurance, and major medical insurance contributed to the rising cost of medical care. The elderly and those outside of the workforce began to have difficulty affording insurance, pushing Pres. Lyndon Johnson to sign Medicare and Medicaid into law. Concern about a shortage of health care manpower led to federal measures to increase education in the health professions, and the number of doctors reporting themselves as full-time specialists rose from 55 percent to 69 percent. In the 1980s, there was a shift in hospital structure and governance, as health care facilities were primarily operated as individual units and not as part of larger medical body. (Courtesy of *The Union-Recorder.*)

A front view of the high school building, Midway School, is shown in the late 1930s. The first school year with a senior high school at Midway began in 1938. There were five graduates in that class—James Davis, Mattie Lingold, Grace Califf, Lily Kate McCluney, and Joe Davis. (Courtesy of Barbara and Buddy Martin.)

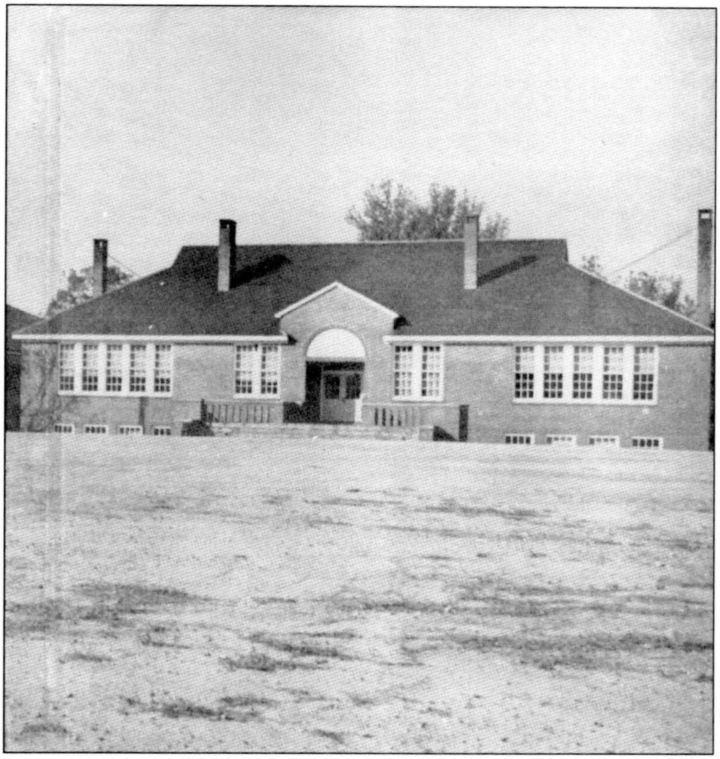

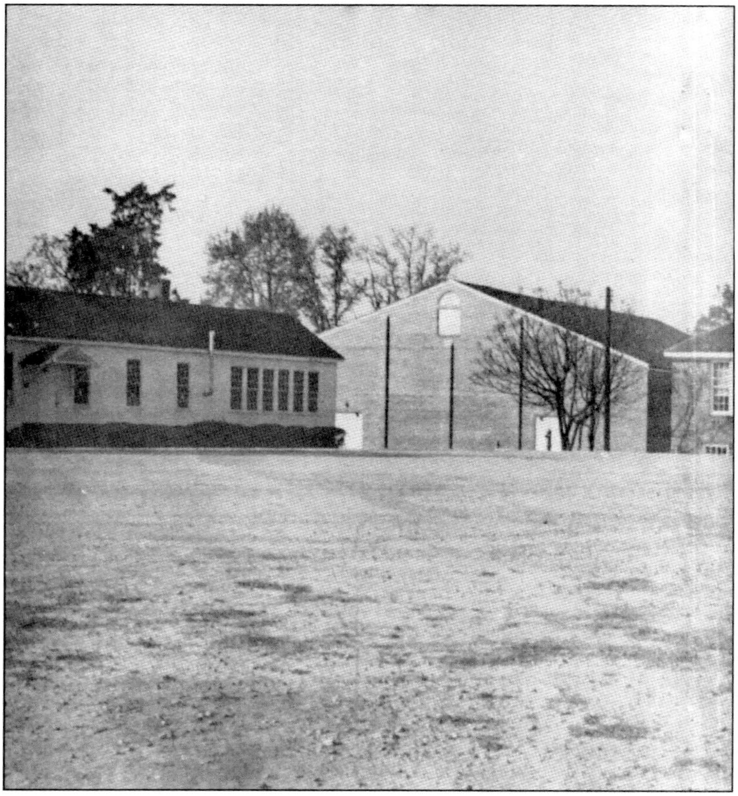

The land on which the Midway School sits was deeded to the school in 1842. Previously, the land and building was home to a Midway Female Seminary for more than 10 years. This late-1930s photograph shows the primary school building to the left and the auditorium in the back. (Courtesy of Barbara and Buddy Martin.)

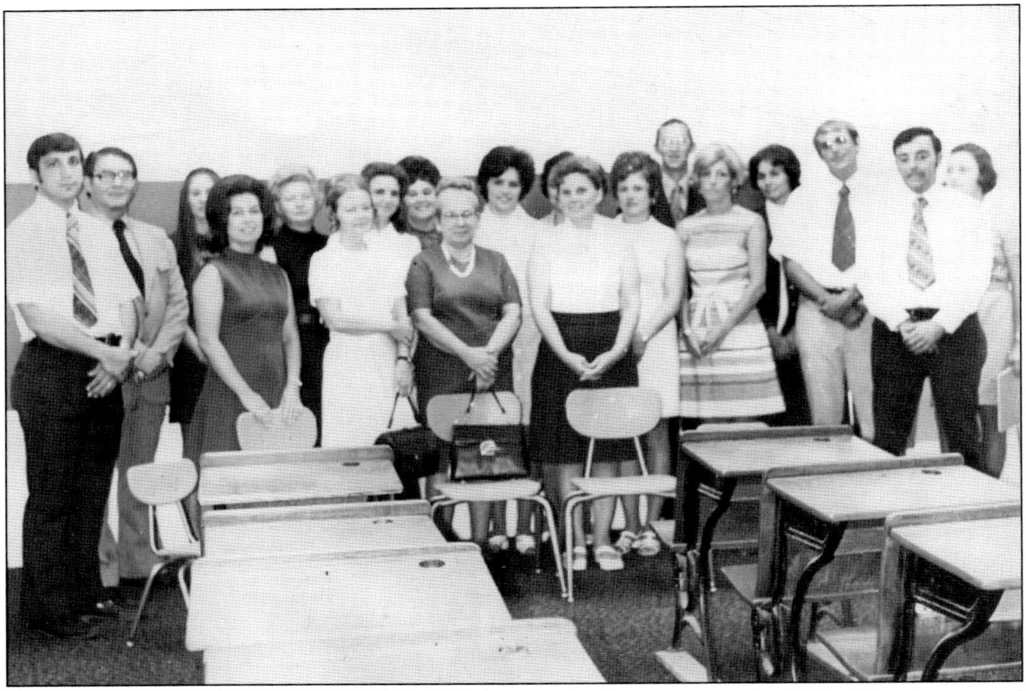

Seen here are John Milledge Academy teachers and administration in 1973. They instructed the first class of students that started at the school in its opening year. In the 1970s, educational instruction shifted from a focus on high-achieving students to measuring success by the treatment of those students not making satisfactory achievement. (Courtesy of John Milledge Academy.)

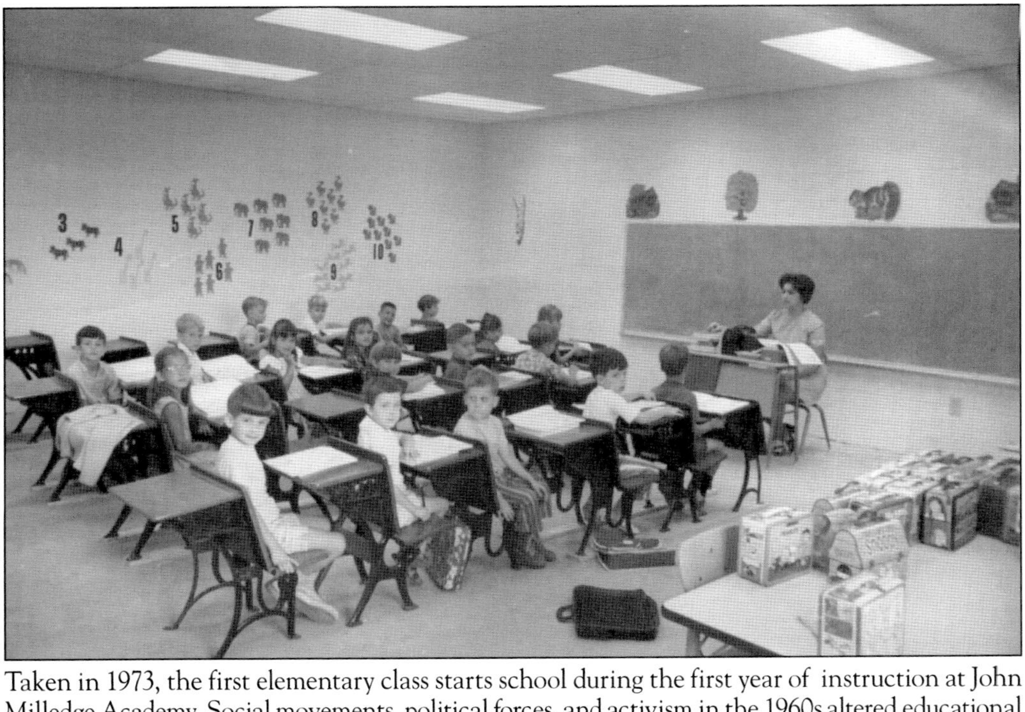

Taken in 1973, the first elementary class starts school during the first year of instruction at John Milledge Academy. Social movements, political forces, and activism in the 1960s altered educational curricula and student interests in the 1970s. (Courtesy of John Milledge Academy.)

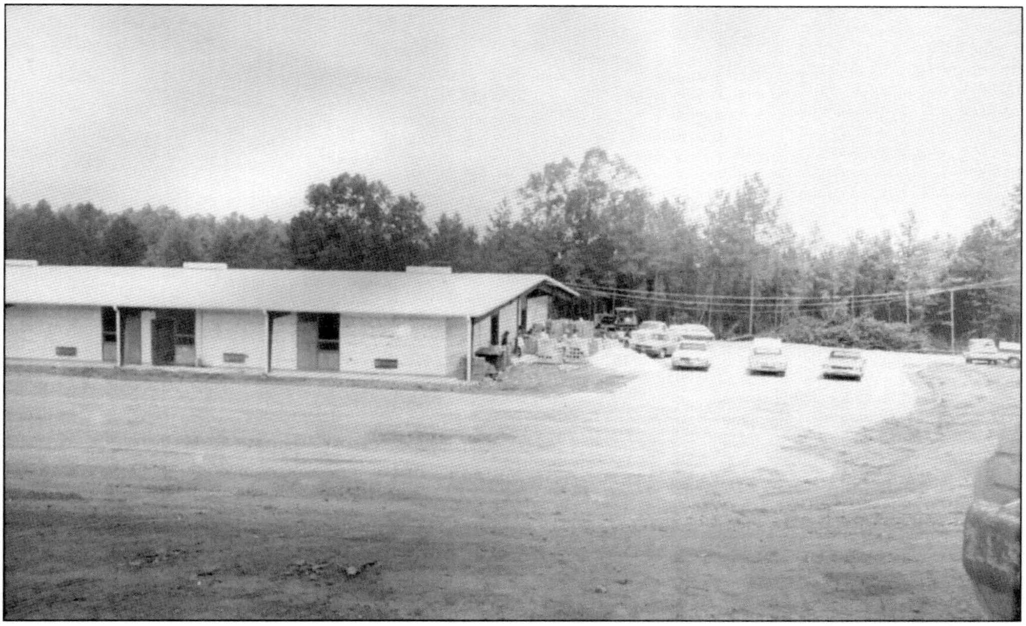

In 1971, construction was underway to complete the new John Milledge Academy (JMA). This building now houses the elementary school students and the school library. JMA currently offers education to students from pre-kindergarten through 12th grade. (Courtesy of John Milledge Academy.)

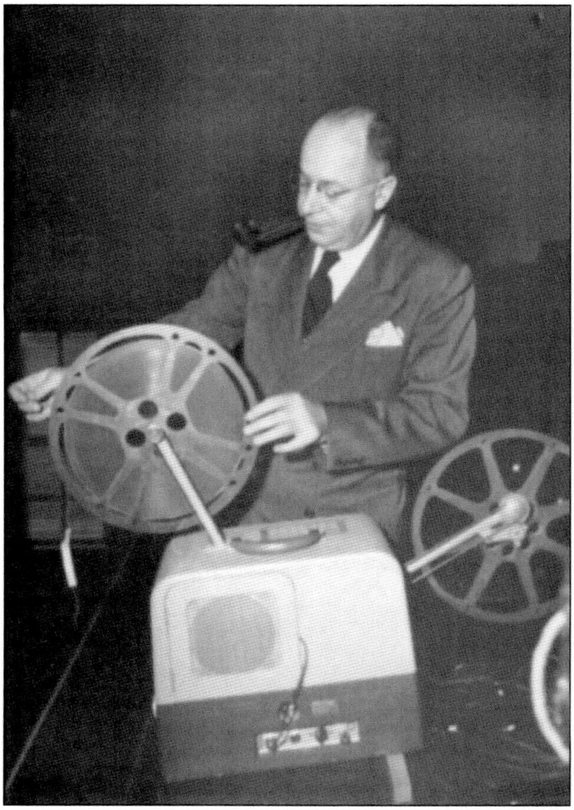

In this image from the early 1950s, Herbert Meyer operates a film projector at Georgia College. Meyer was a comptroller at Georgia College at the time. As advancements have been made in technology, the medium with which to instruct students has continued to expand. (Courtesy of Larry Houston.)

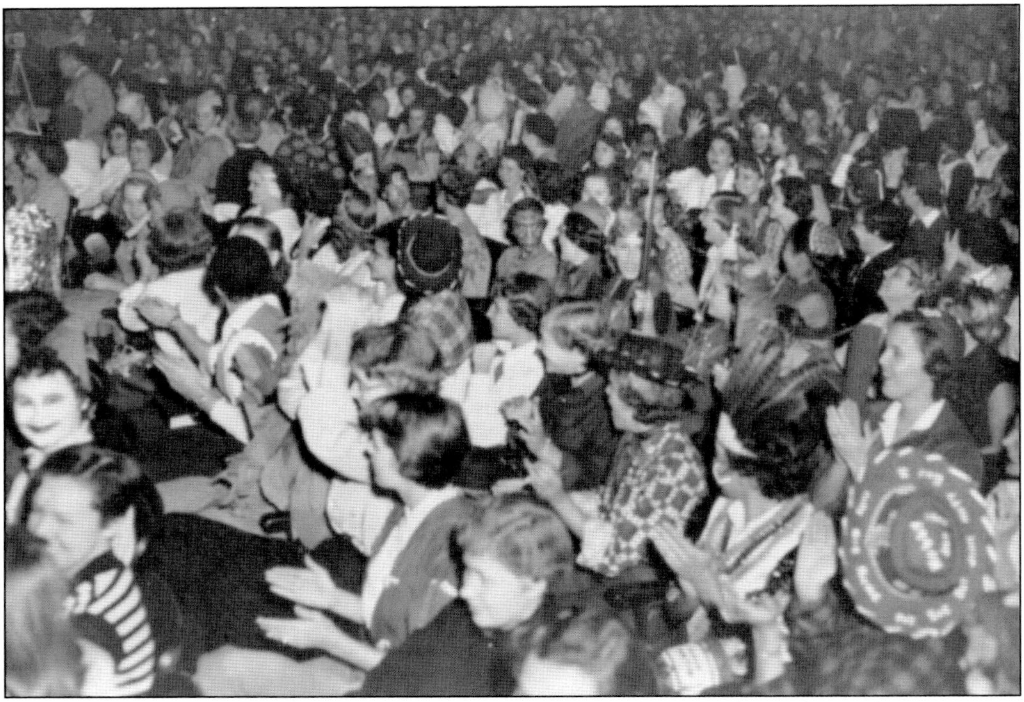

Education and competition are often interrelated and have been used together to better prepare students for the competition that occurs naturally and under varying circumstances in society. In this early-1950s photograph, students in costume for the Golden Slipper theater competition pack Russell Auditorium. (Courtesy of Larry Houston.)

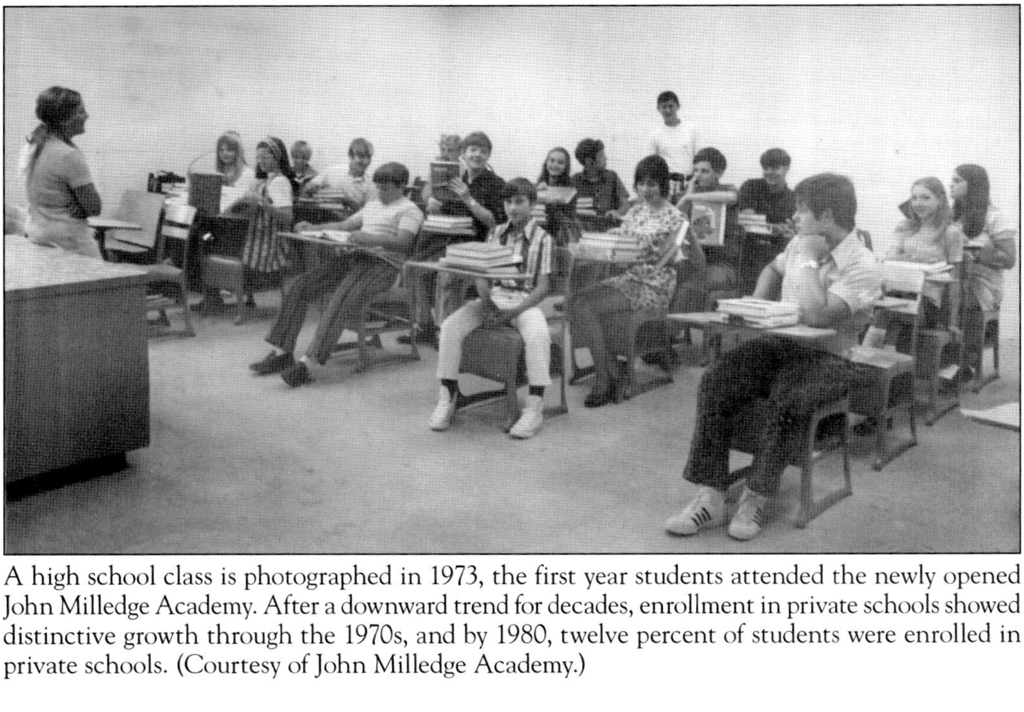

A high school class is photographed in 1973, the first year students attended the newly opened John Milledge Academy. After a downward trend for decades, enrollment in private schools showed distinctive growth through the 1970s, and by 1980, twelve percent of students were enrolled in private schools. (Courtesy of John Milledge Academy.)

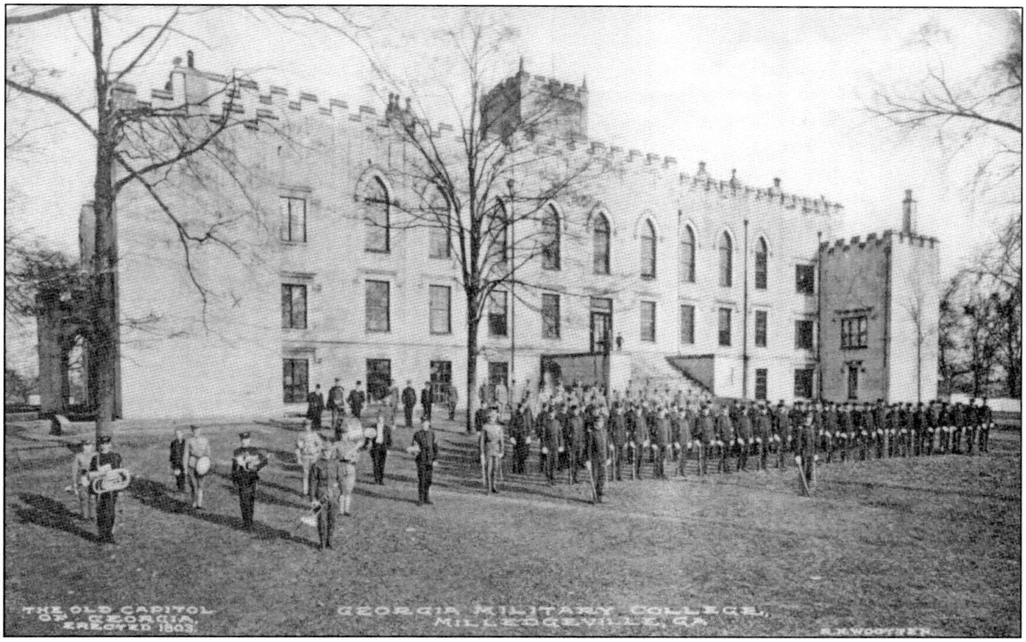

A postcard shows cadets in formation in front of the Old Capitol Building, now part of Georgia Military College (GMC). The school was originally established as part of the University of Georgia. GMC changed its name from Middle Georgia Military and Agricultural College in 1900, since relatively few agricultural classes were being taught. (Courtesy of Bo Edmonds.)

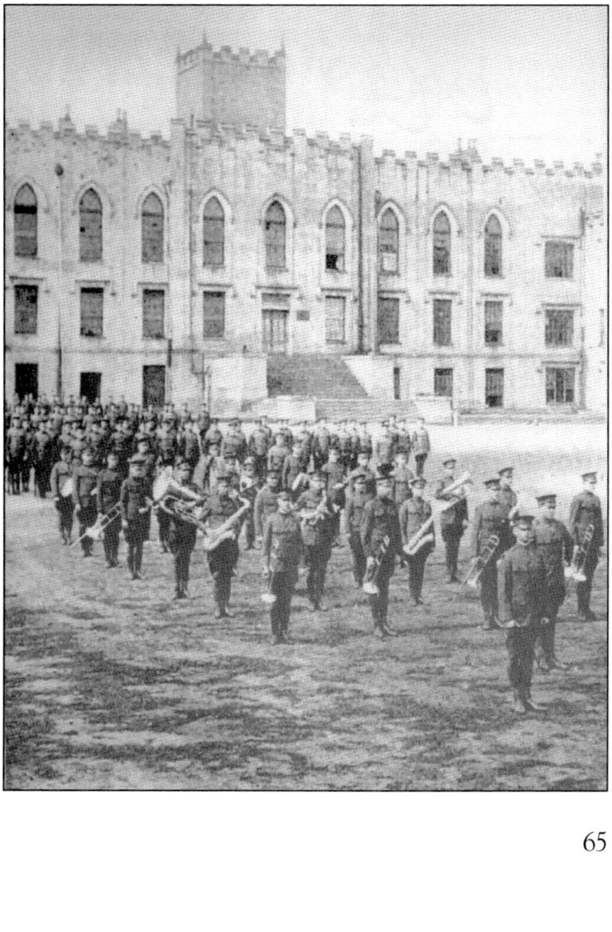

From 1879 until 1952, GMC served as a high school for Milledgeville–Baldwin County. In the 1920s, the association of GMC with the University of Georgia was officially terminated by the legislature. A junior college division was developed in the 1930s, with the support of a state-awarded grant. GMC is currently run as a public and independent educational institution. (Courtesy of Georgia Military College.)

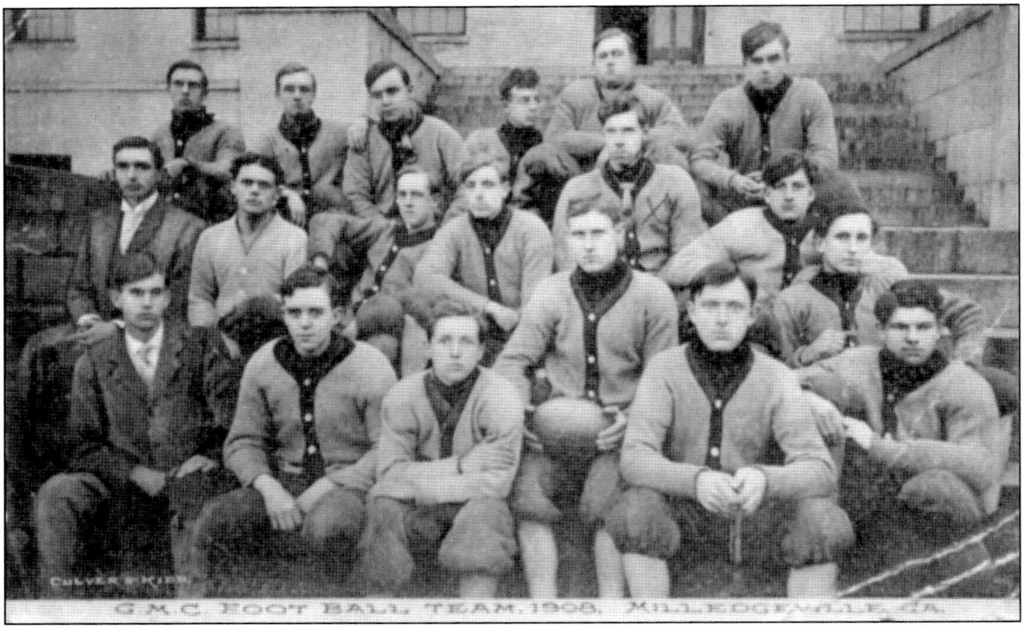

This postcard, sold at Culver and Kidd Drugstore, shows the 1908 GMC football team. In the United States, college football expanded greatly in the last two decades of the 19th century—growing from about eight university fielded teams in 1880 to 43 by 1900. Drastic changes were made to game rules after threats by Pres. Theodore Roosevelt to shut the game down nationwide after 19 player fatalities in 1905. (Courtesy of Bo Edmonds.)

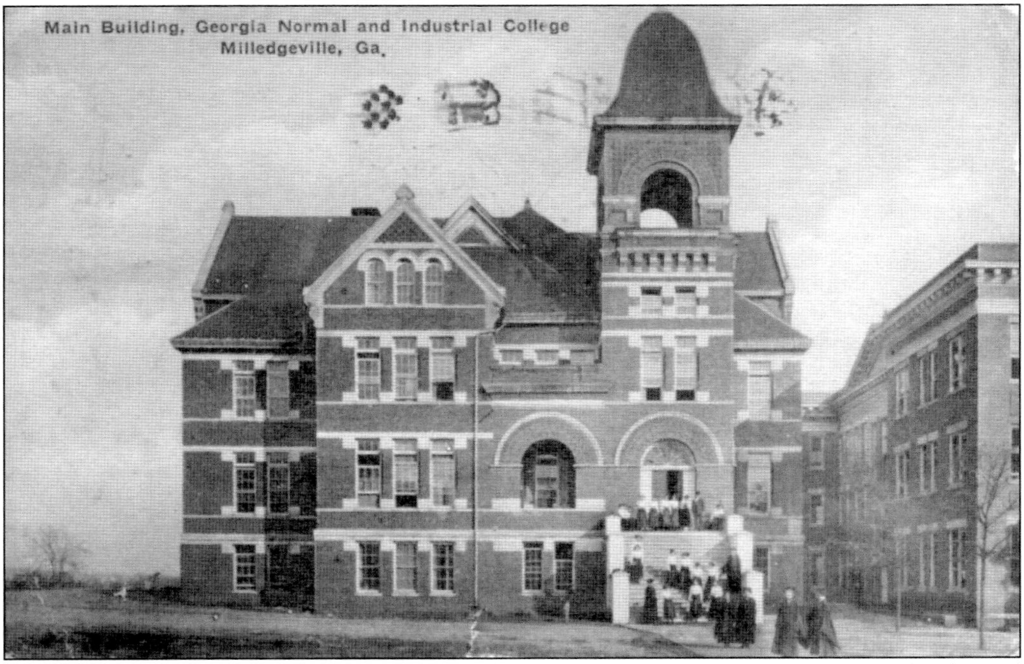

Construction was completed on the main building, or Old Main, of Georgia Normal and Industrial College in 1891. In December 1924, the building burned and, as a result, college records prior to 1924 were lost. Old Main's cornerstone still remains on the site in what is now the president's garden between the Russell Auditorium and Parks Hall buildings. (Courtesy of Bo Edmonds.)

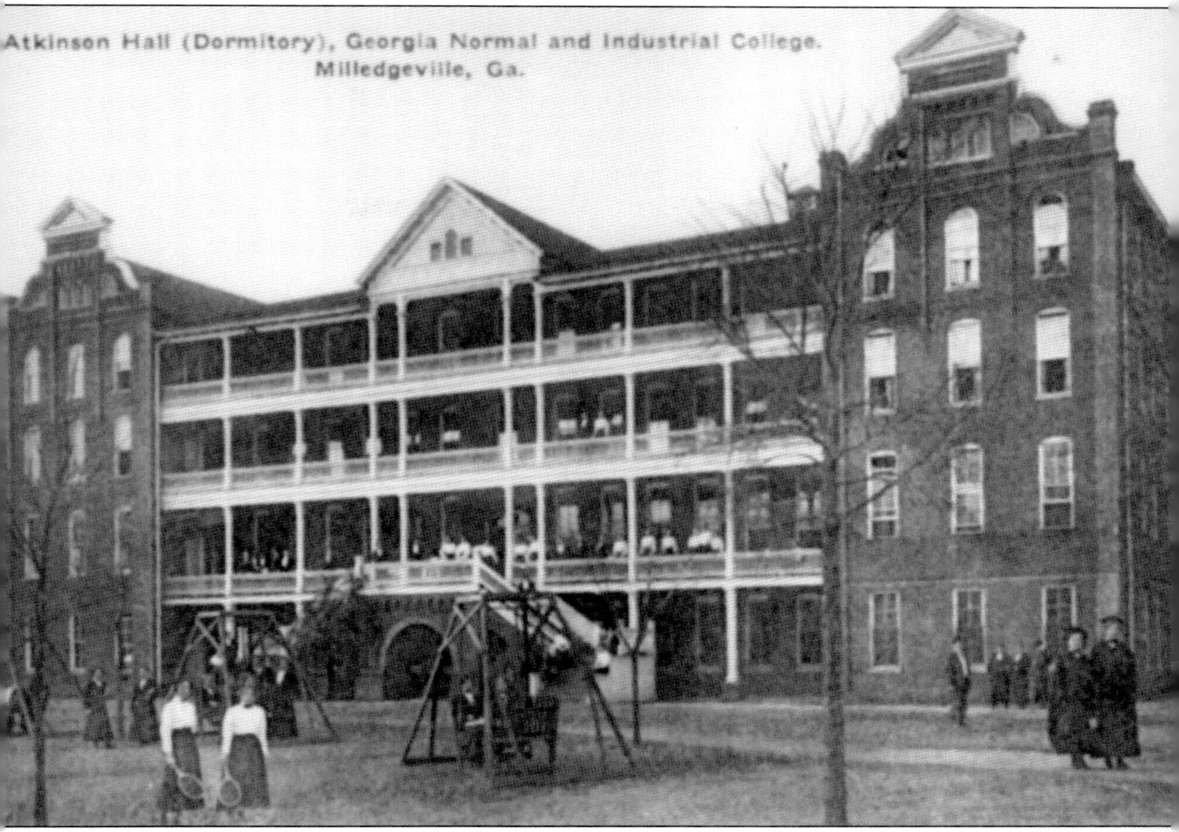

Atkinson Hall was constructed in 1896 and is one of the oldest buildings remaining on campus. The structure is part of the main campus square, on which the Georgia State Penitentiary was located from 1818 until the 1870s. The building is named for William Atkinson, whose wife, Susan Cobb Milton-Atkinson, was friends with Julia Flisch, an advocate for the development of higher education opportunities for women. She lobbied and gained support for a publicly funded college for women with the purpose of equipping them with the knowledge and skills to be prepared for an increasingly industrial society. (Courtesy of Bo Edmonds.)

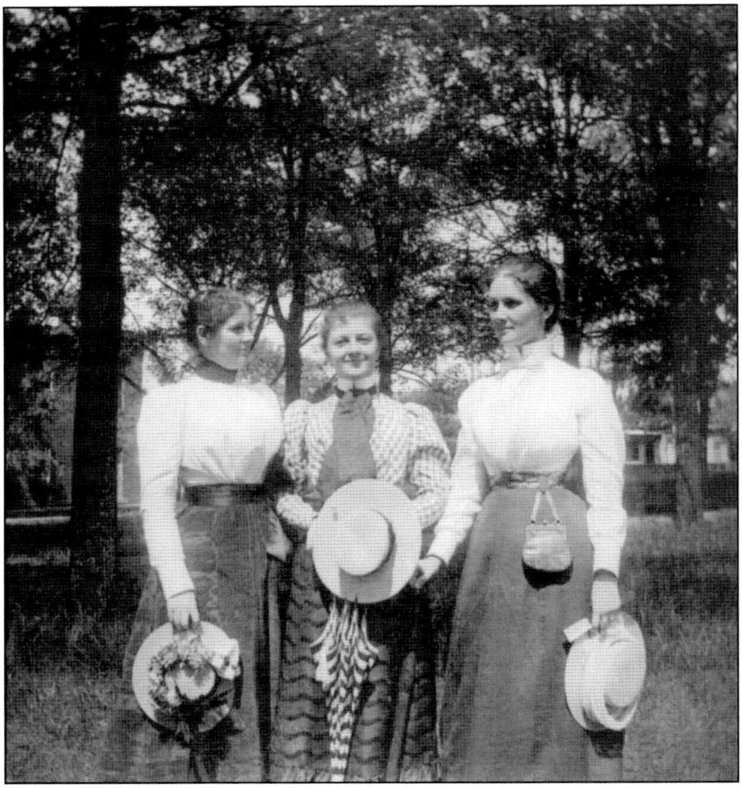

During Julia Flisch's career, she taught at Georgia Normal and Industrial College, Tubman High School for Girls in Augusta, and the Junior College of Augusta that later became Augusta State University. In 1889, she was instrumental chartering a two-year college in Milledgeville named Georgia Normal and Industrial College. Programs of study at the college focused on teacher training and business skills. Shown here are college students at an afternoon outing on the lawn of the Governor's Mansion in the early 1900s.

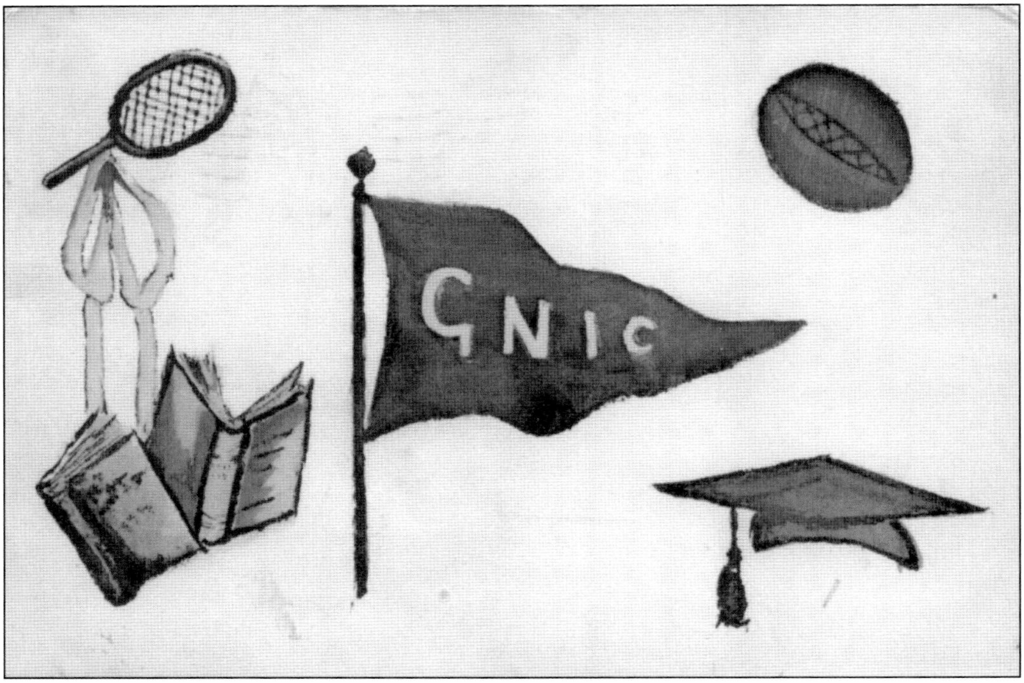

A c. 1910 postcard features hand-drawn art showing academic emphasis and the popular activities of tennis and basketball that were played at Georgia Normal and Industrial College. (Courtesy of Bo Edmonds.)

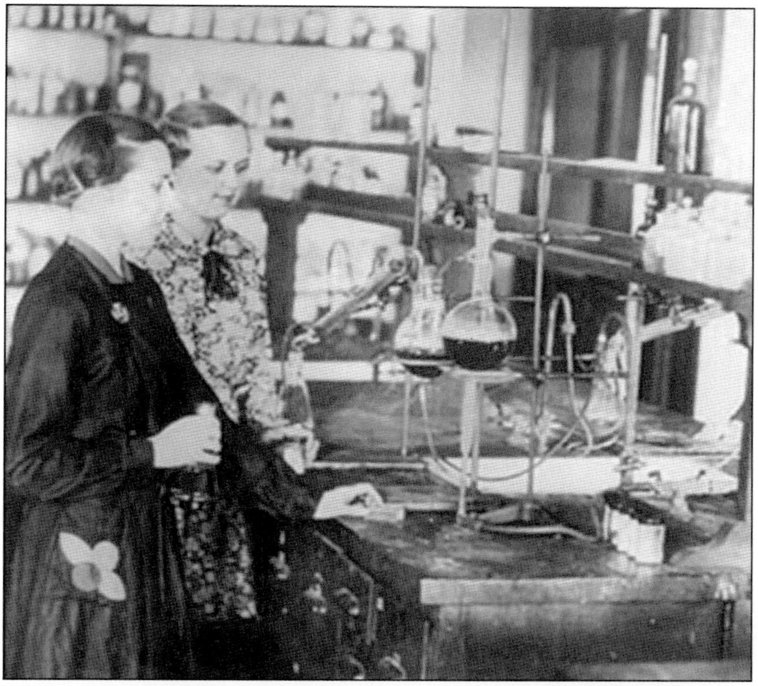

Under the leadership of Pres. Marvin Parks, Georgia Normal and Industrial College became one of the leading schools in the Southeast. Parks put together a faculty that taught contemporary subjects such as educational psychology and secured the authority to grant four-year degrees. These Georgia College students are shown in a chemistry lab in the late 1920s. (Courtesy of the Georgia Archives, Vanishing Georgia, bal-104.)

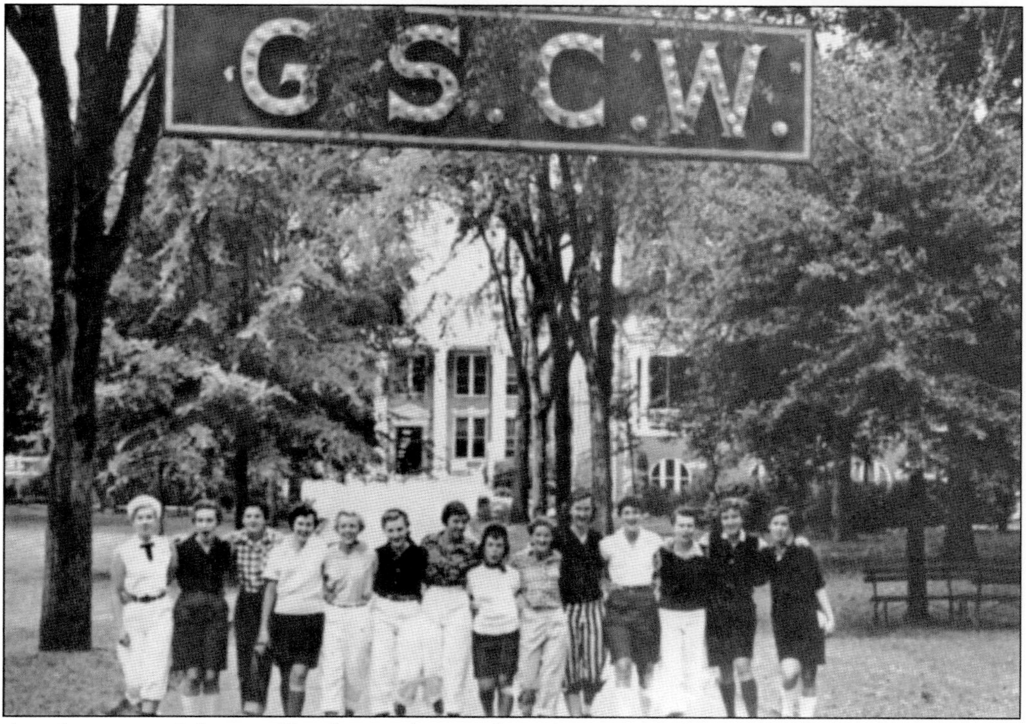

A wider range of classes offered to students reflected corresponding changes in women's roles in society. Courses offered to women expanded beyond subjects related to the traditional women's roles, such as dressmaking, stenography, and cooking. The college changed its name to Georgia State College for Women in 1922. Shown here are freshmen and sophomores on the campus in the early 1950s. (Courtesy of Larry Houston.)

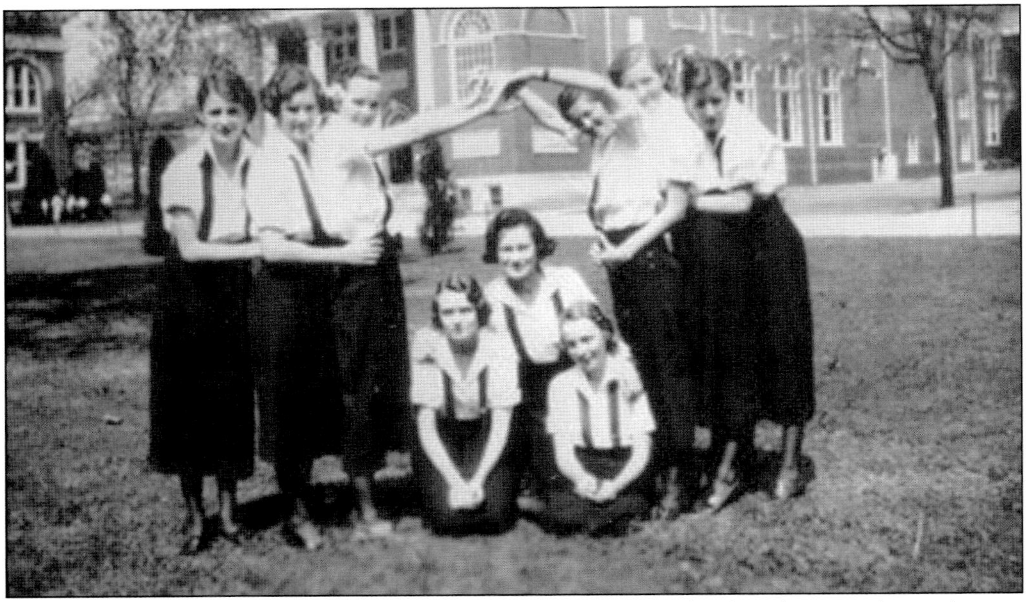

In 1933, a group of students, among the last to wear mandatory school uniforms in the graduating class, pose for this photograph. The first student government association was formed in 1934, and in the same year, uniforms became optional by petition of the students and authorization of college president Guy Wells. (Courtesy of Georgia Archives, Vanishing Georgia Collection, bal-164)

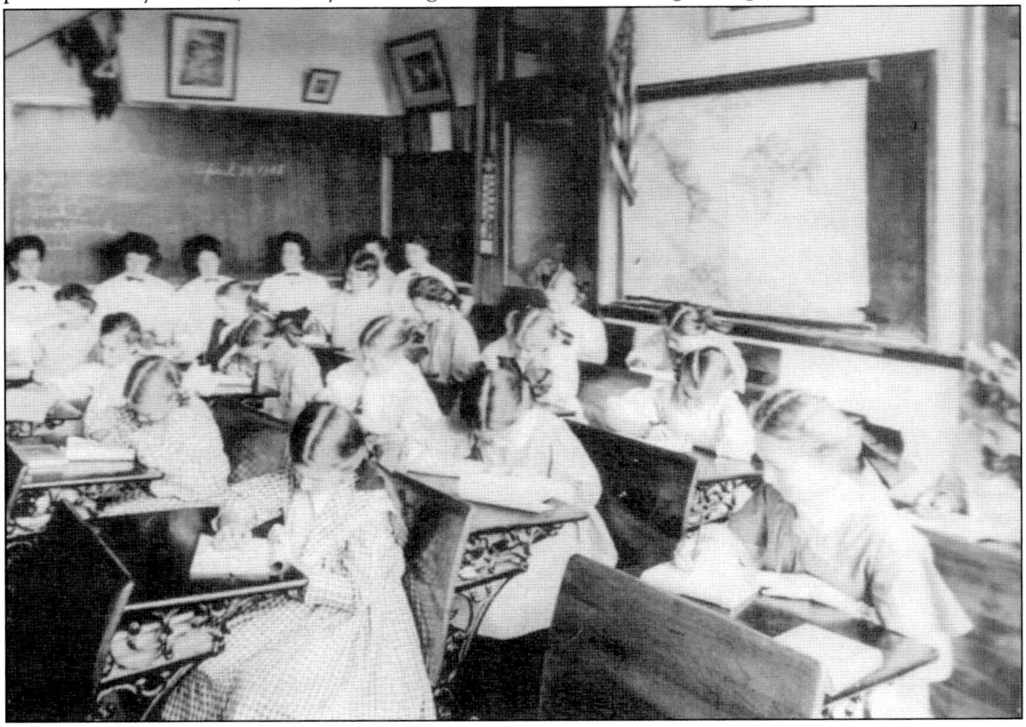

Peabody Model School was opened in 1891 as part of Georgia Normal and Industrial College's supplement to the program of teacher education. The purpose of the model school was to give students in the teaching program approximately 120 to 150 hours of experience before beginning their first teaching job.

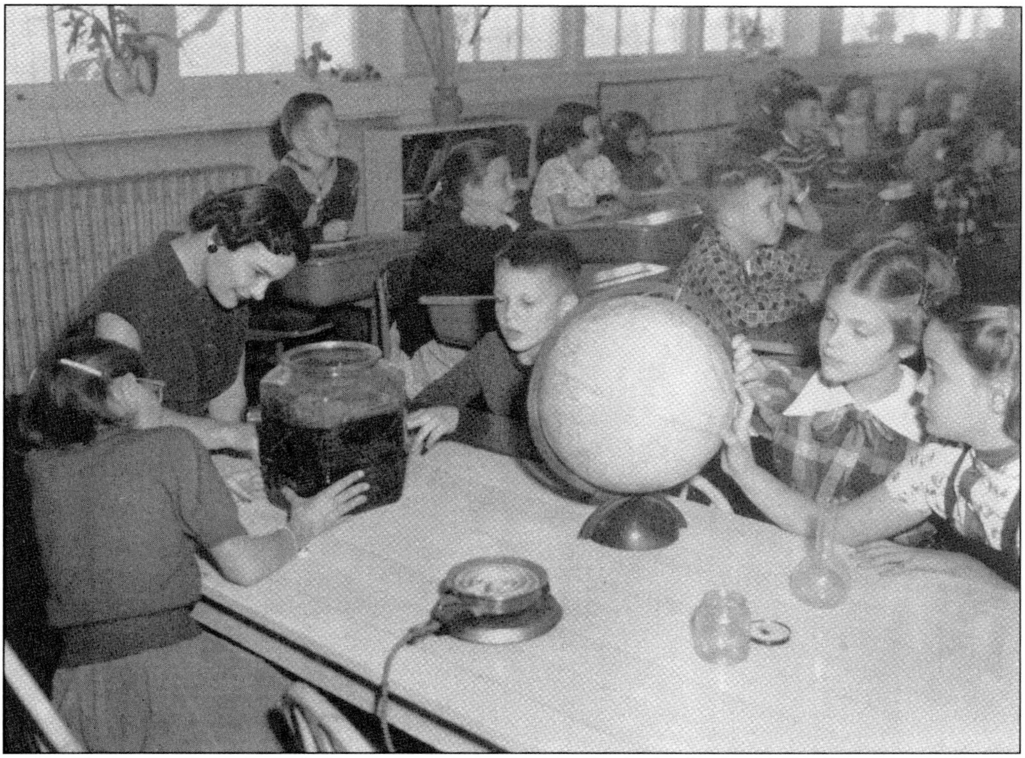

Peabody also served as Baldwin County's public school beginning in 1891 and was not phased out until the 1970s. The services at Peabody were expanded in 1927 to include the operation of a four-year high school as well as a boarding school for rural girls living in Georgia. This photograph shows a Peabody classroom in the early 1950s. (Courtesy of Larry Houston.)

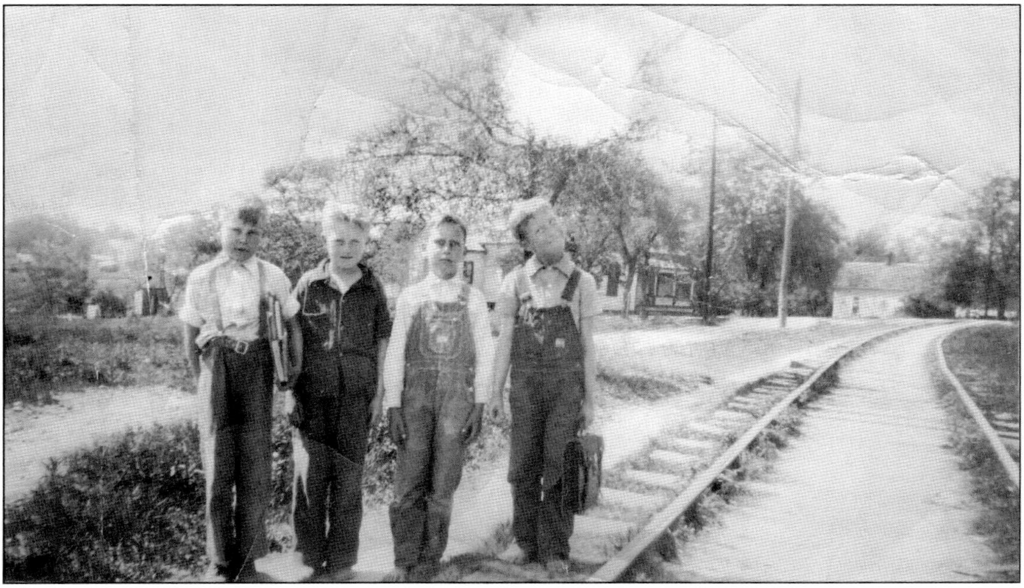

Probably on their way home from school at Midway, these boys are walking somewhere around Irwinton Street in 1942. They are, from left to right, Charles Kemp, Charles Veal, unidentified, and Randall Hattaway. (Courtesy of Buddy Martin.)

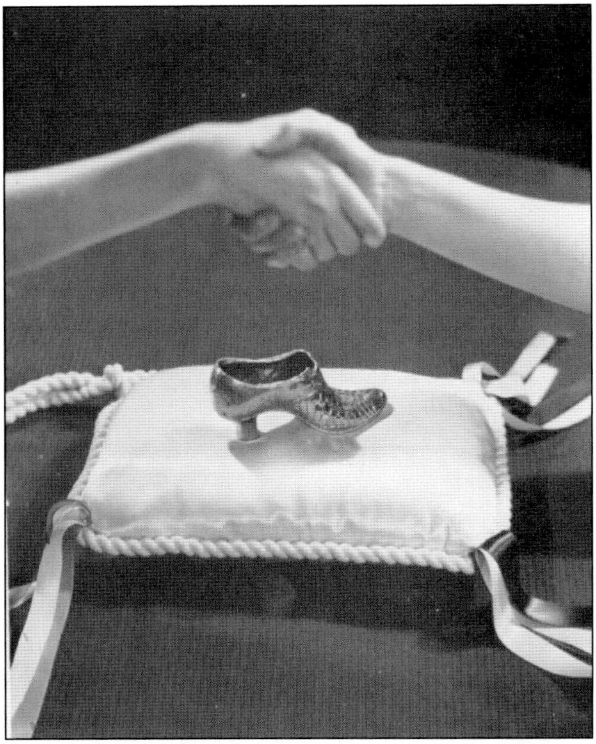

The Golden Slipper was the award given after lively theatrical competitions involving skits, and dance was introduced by Ethel Adams, dean of girls, as a means of boosting the morale of the students. (Courtesy of Larry Houston.)

The tradition of the Golden Slipper began in 1935 and endured until the 1970s. The competition came to embody the spirit of the college and the Jessies, the name given to students attending Georgia State College for Women.

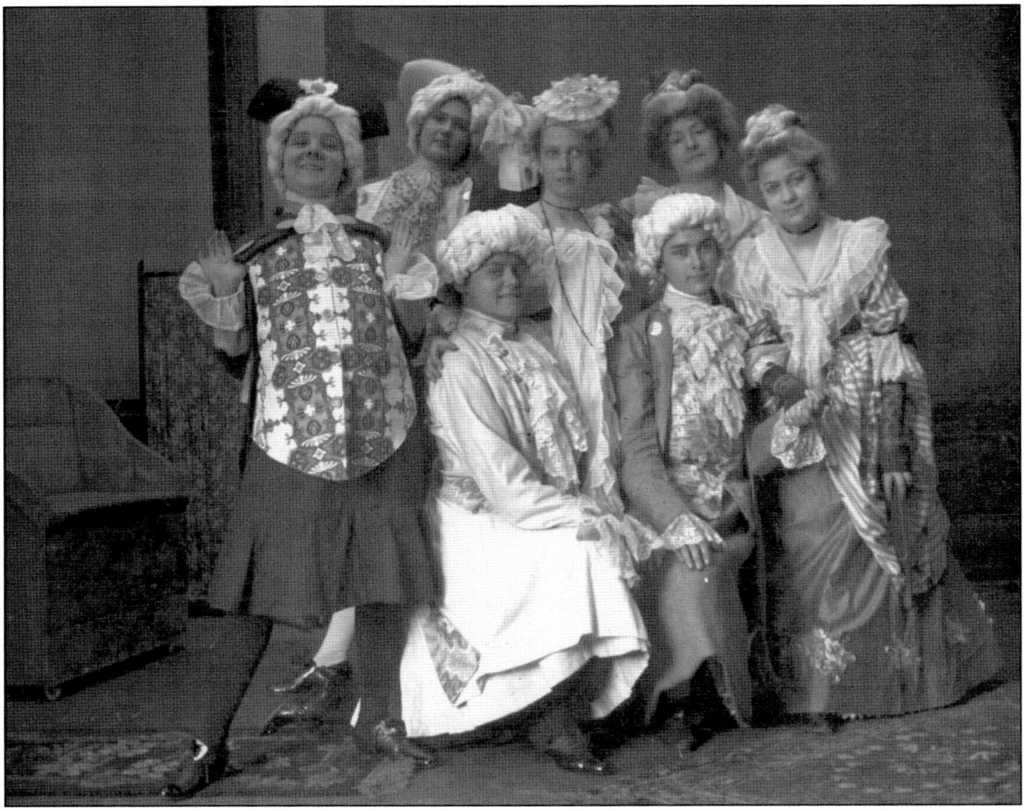

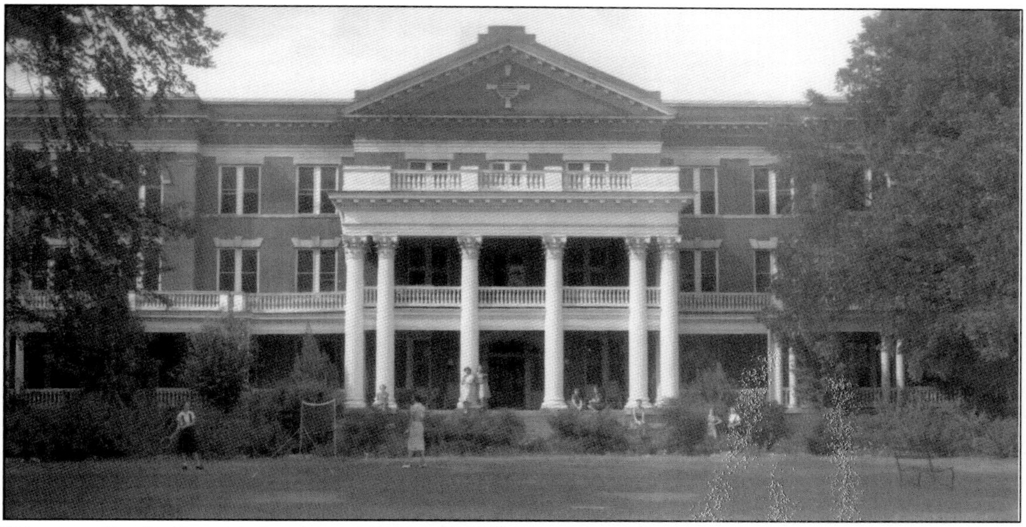

Women play badminton in front of Terrell Hall, constructed in 1908 to serve as a residence hall on the campus of Georgia State College for Women. President Parks changed the dormitory's name, with the support of the board, from Lamar Hall to Terrell Hall in 1913. The name was changed because Lamar was not a supporter of President Parks. The name Terrell Hall was given in honor of the recently deceased Joseph Terrell, who served as Georgia's governor from 1902 to 1907. (Courtesy of the University of Georgia Special Collections.)

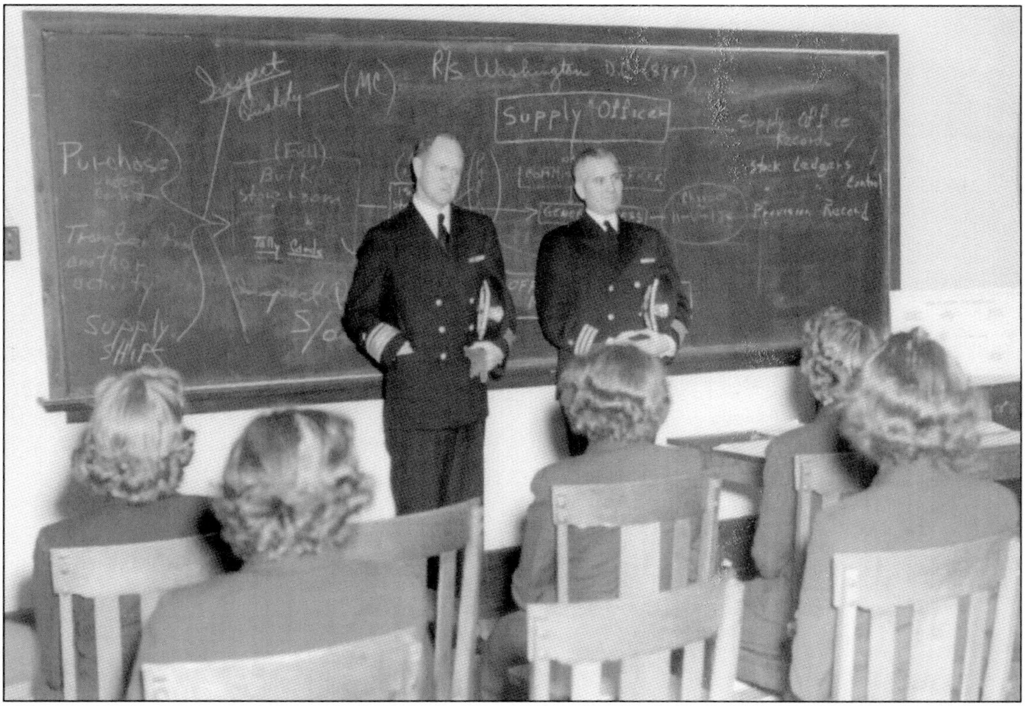

Georgia State College for Women was a WAVES training center. This 1944 photograph shows instruction being given to members, with a flow chart illustrating the chain of command and process for controlling military supply. WAVES members could not serve aboard combat ships or aircraft. They were primarily trained for clerical work, but some did take occupations in the aviation community. (Courtesy of Georgia College and State University Special Collections.)

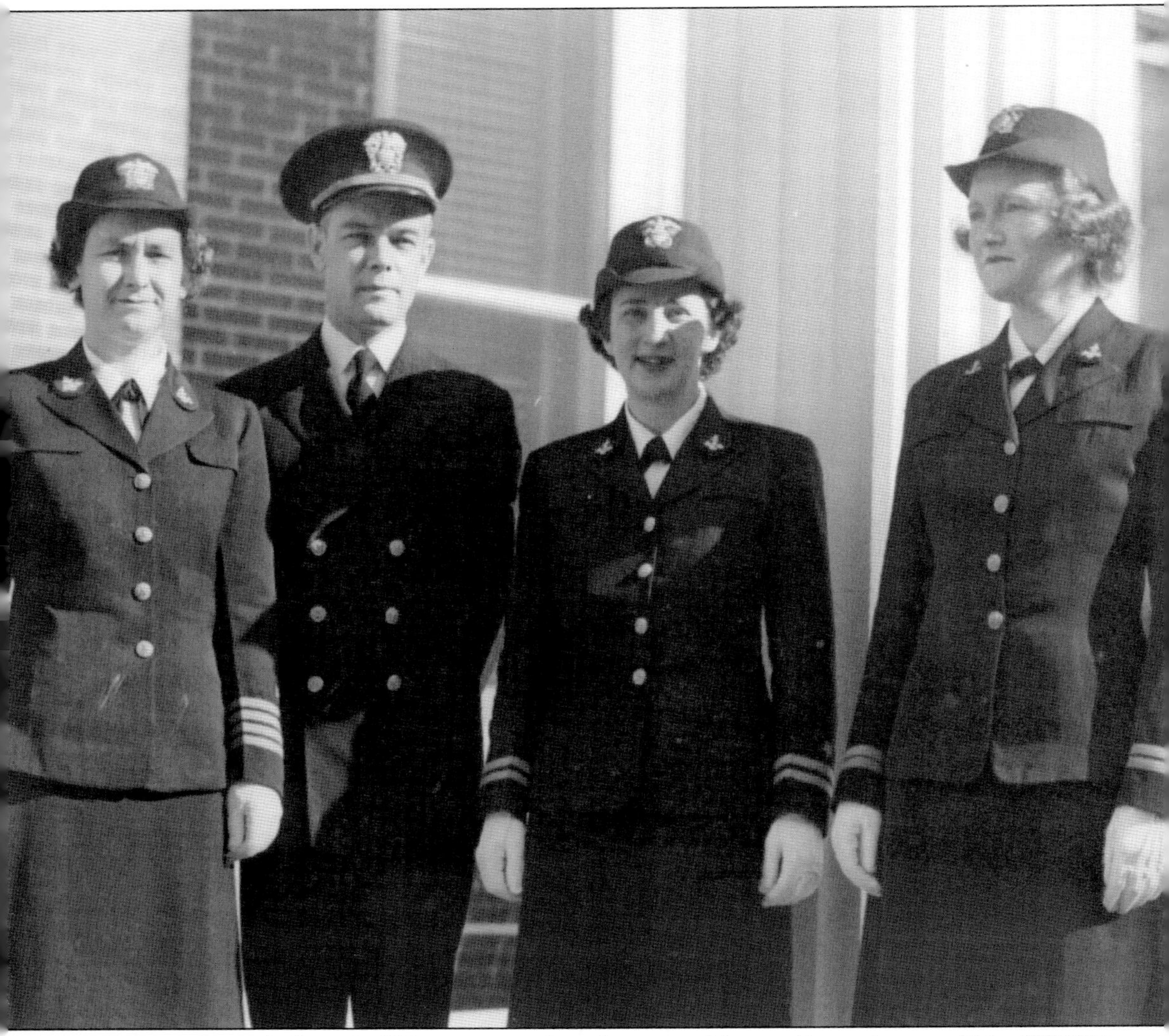

Georgia State College for Women was selected as one of four colleges that would be WAVES training centers. WAVES is the acronym meaning Women Accepted for Volunteer Emergency Service and given to a Navy division during World War II. The interested responses were so numerous from women to join the program that the task of recruitment was more management than undertaking. Before WAVES, women had never held formal officer status. In this photograph, one male and three female officers stand in front of Lanier Hall on the campus of Georgia State College for Women. During two years, about 15,000 women received training on the campus in the WAVES program. At the end of World War II, women made up about 2.5 percent of the Navy's military members. In some places, Waves constituted the majority of uniformed personnel. (Courtesy of Georgia College and State University Special Collections.)

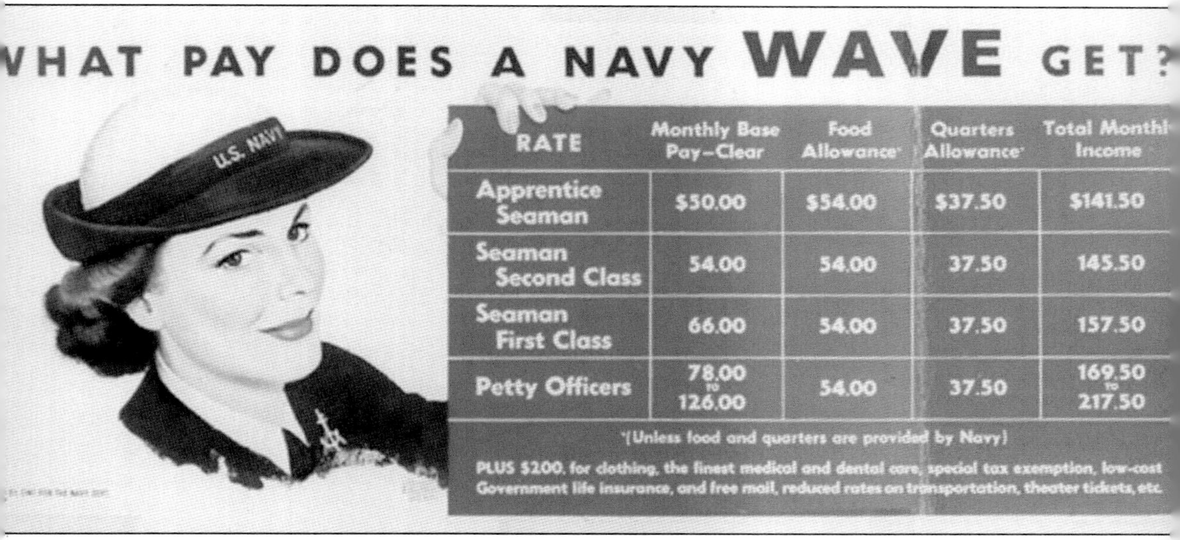

This WAVES recruitment poster appealed to candidates' motivation for higher pay, rank, and additional benefits. A notable distinction of this group compared to others was the members serving in the military and not simply with it. From the beginning, WAVES members held the same rank and pay as male personnel and were subject to the same military discipline. (Courtesy of the United States Navy, Naval History & Heritage Command.)

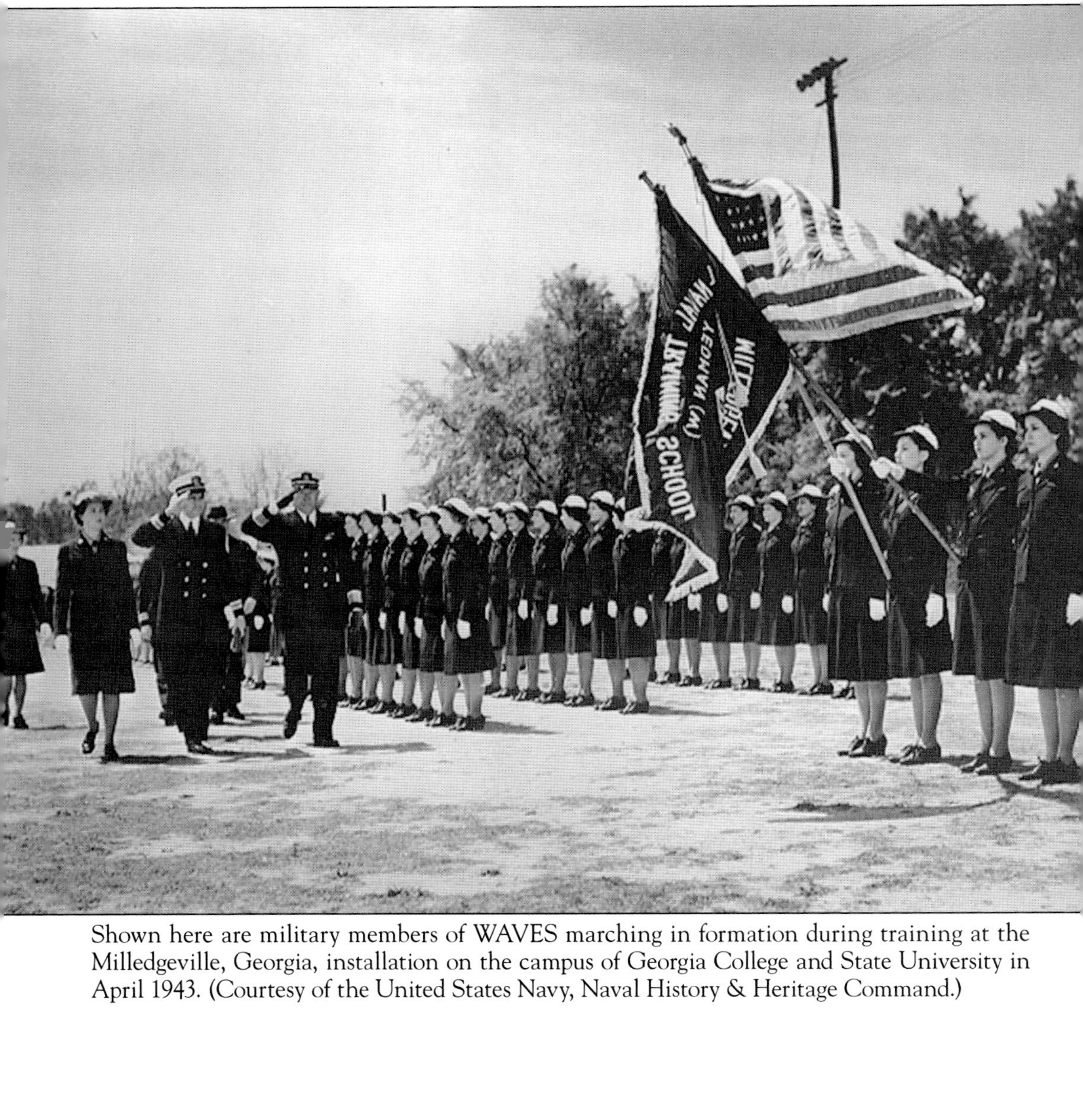

Shown here are military members of WAVES marching in formation during training at the Milledgeville, Georgia, installation on the campus of Georgia College and State University in April 1943. (Courtesy of the United States Navy, Naval History & Heritage Command.)

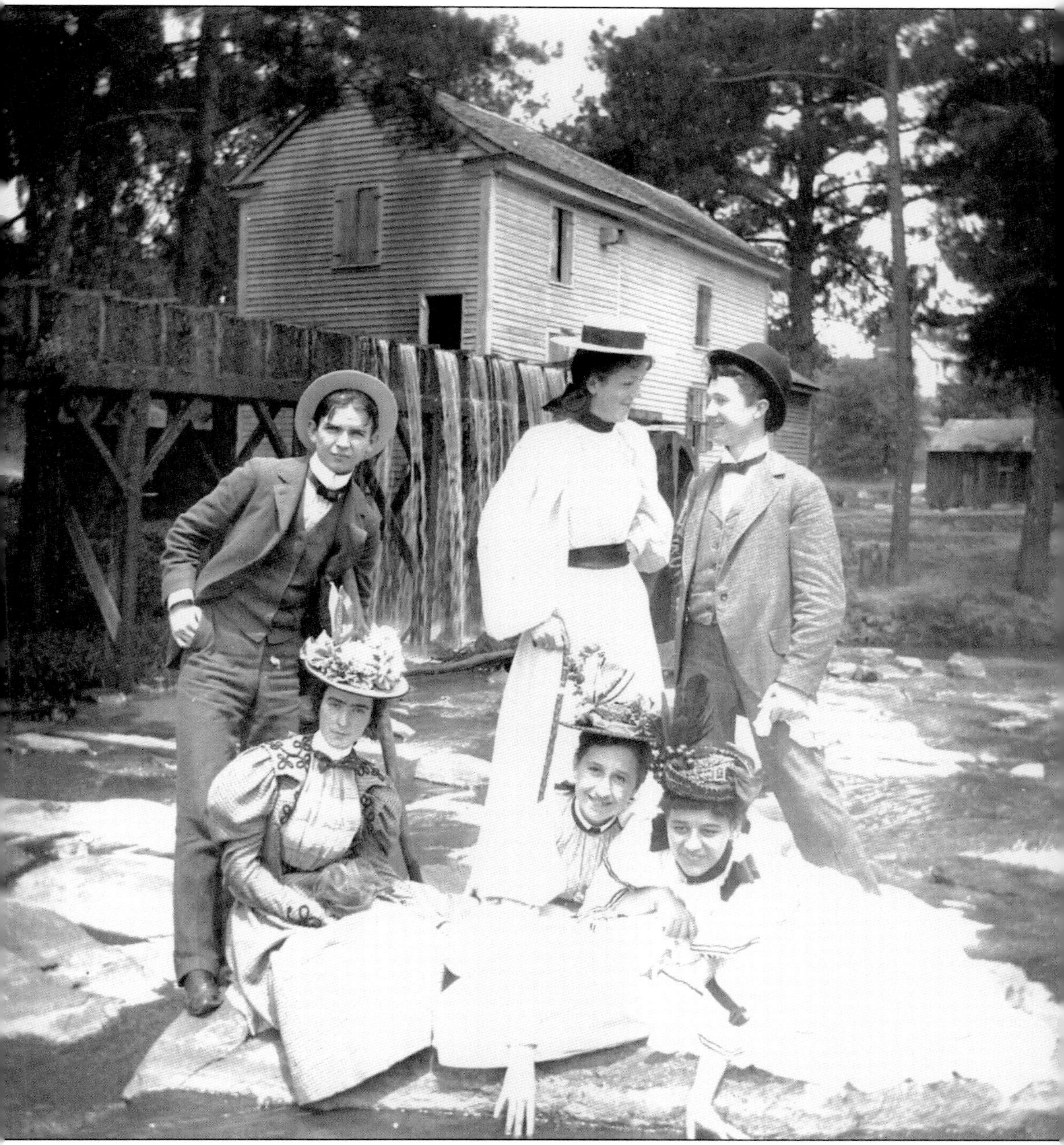

In the early 1900s, river picnics and boating were entertaining diversions for youths, as these young people from Milledgeville show as they pose for this photograph. As printed in the *New York Times* in 1912, "it was customary for those going on the picnic to choose a spot near a river about the size of a creek with many rocks on which young ladies could cross to the other side. In choosing a chaperone, clever picnickers could choose someone about four or five years older and arrange an older brother to come along as a diversion for the chaperone. The day after the picnic, the local newspaper would write it up and close by saying 'a delightful time was had' and that was the truth."

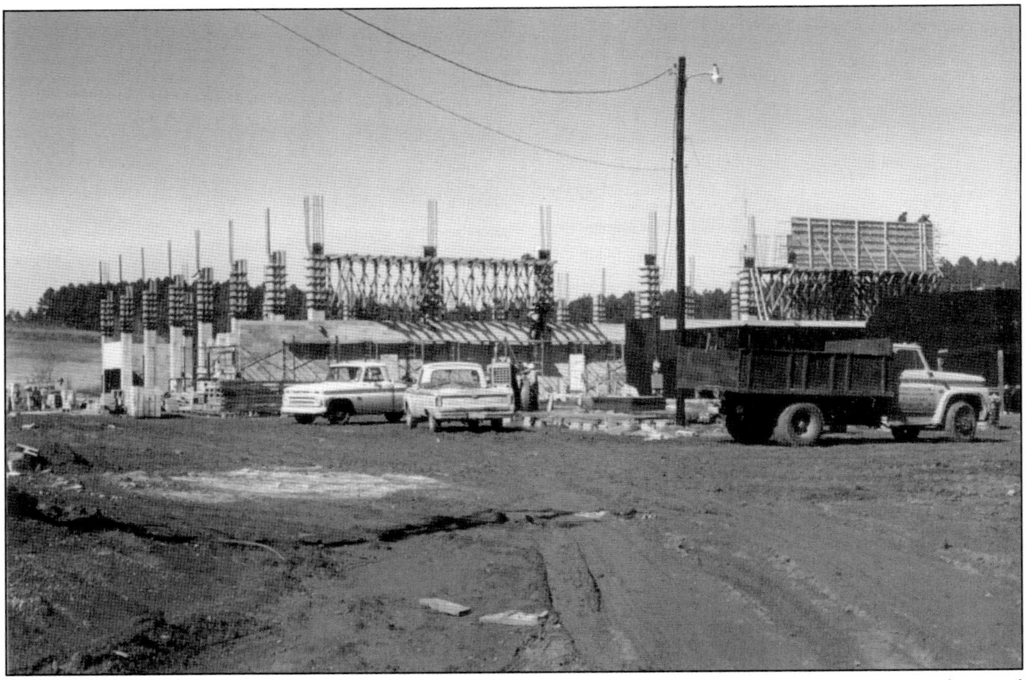

The area of land on which the Milledgeville–Baldwin County Recreation Department is located was originally to be developed by the State of Georgia as Baldwin State Park. When the state failed to proceed with plans to develop the park, 630 acres were acquired by leasing the land from the state to develop what would later become Walter B. Williams Recreational Park, named after the then mayor of Milledgeville. This photograph was taken at the beginning of construction of the facility in 1975. (Courtesy of Barbara and Buddy Martin.)

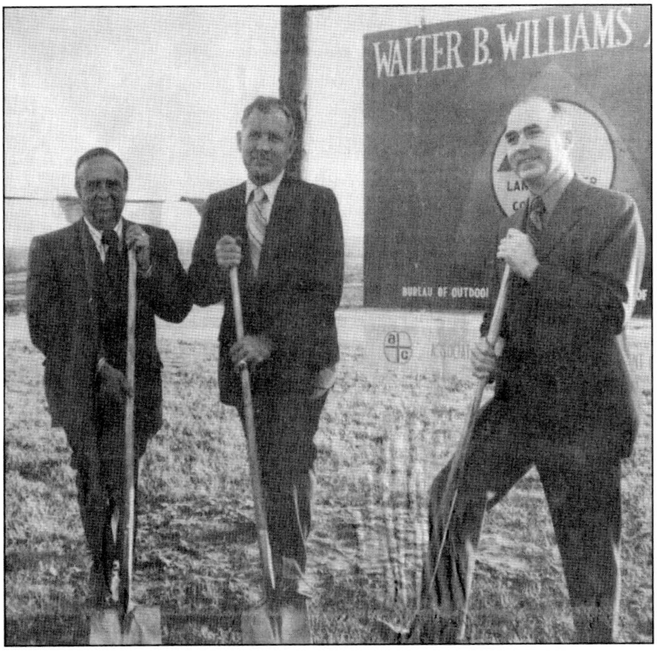

The ground-breaking ceremony took place at the newly named Walter B. Williams Jr. Park in 1975. Digging shovels into the dirt are Mayor Walter Williams (left), Baldwin County Commission chairman Ralph Harrington (center), and recreation commission chairman Buddy Martin. (Courtesy of Barbara and Buddy Martin.)

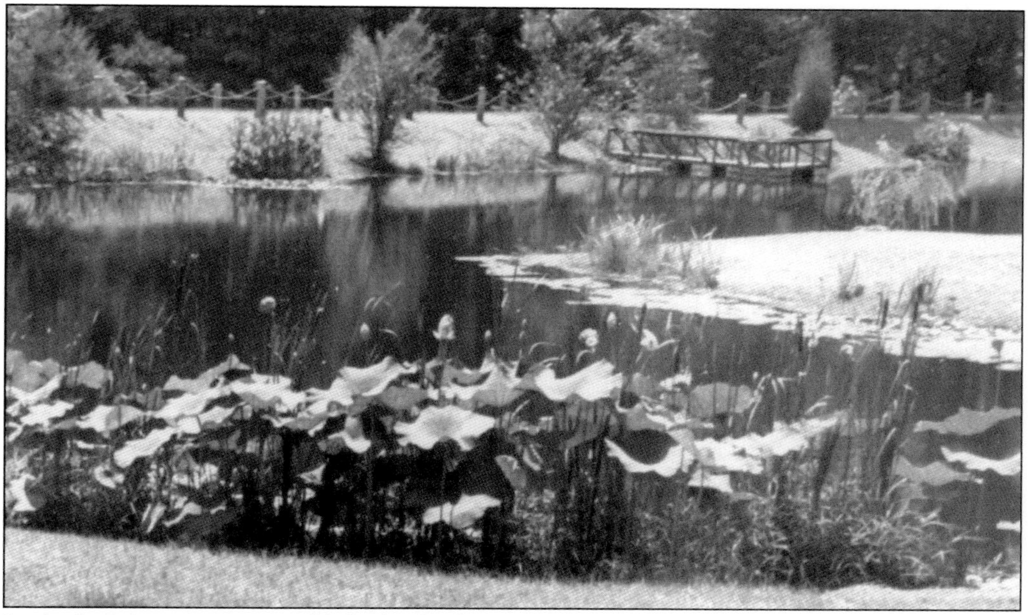

Lockerly Arboretum was established as both an educational resource and public gardens in 1965. The formation of Lockerly is an example of the American environmental movement that began as an upper-class wilderness-centered concept in the 1960s. The movement later transformed to include the urban environment and a more diverse membership. (Courtesy of Lockerly Arboretum.)

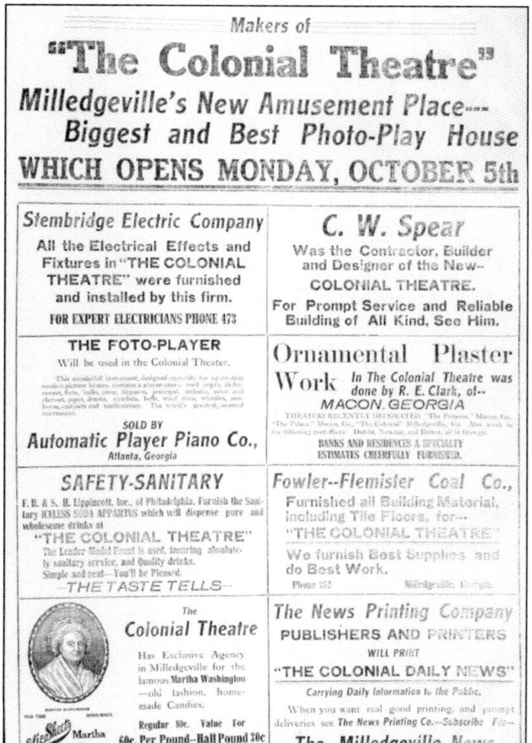

The Colonial Theatre, managed by Edmund Reid, opened its doors on October 5, 1914, and was billed as the new wordless playhouse. This flyer from the theater advertises the opening. The initial presentation was *Love, Luck and Gasoline*. The Colonial Theatre touted itself as being one of only two motion picture places in the state using a Fotoplayer. It offered a soda fountain service, as well as a candy, cigar, and cigarette stand. (Courtesy of author.)

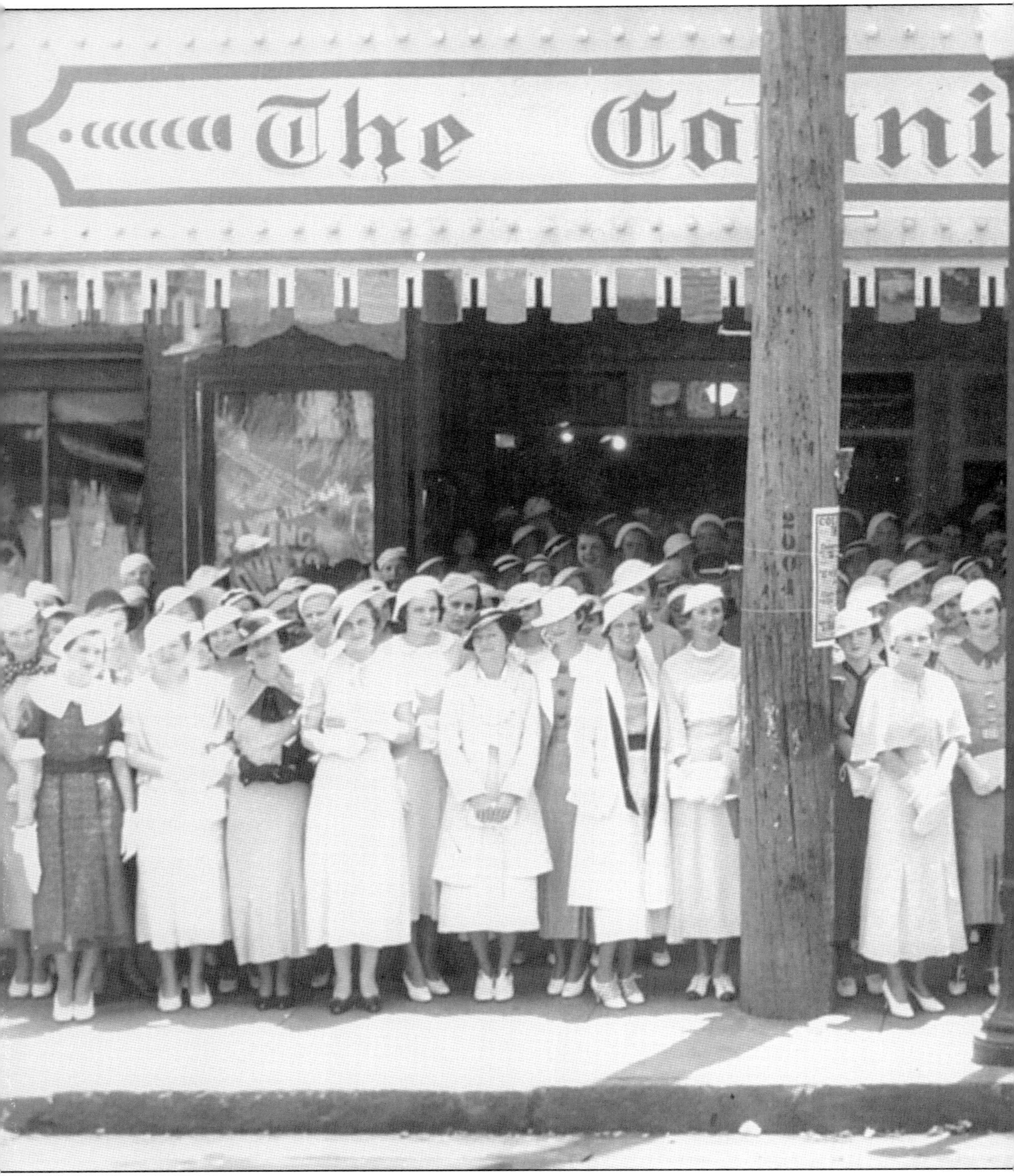

These women pose for a photograph in front of the Colonial Theatre in 1934. The Colonial was located at what is now Dodo's Pool Hall on Hancock Street. It has, at times, been confused as being the same venue as the Campus Theatre. In the background are film posters for *Flying Down To Rio* (1933), starring Fred Astaire and Ginger Rogers, and *Men In White* (1934), starring Clark Gable and Myrna Loy. Between 1914 and 1920, several theaters existed in downtown Milledgeville, with constant fluctuation both theater managers and names and a combination of theaters coexisting. In 1914, the newly opened Star Theatre, in operation at the same time as the Colonial, occupied

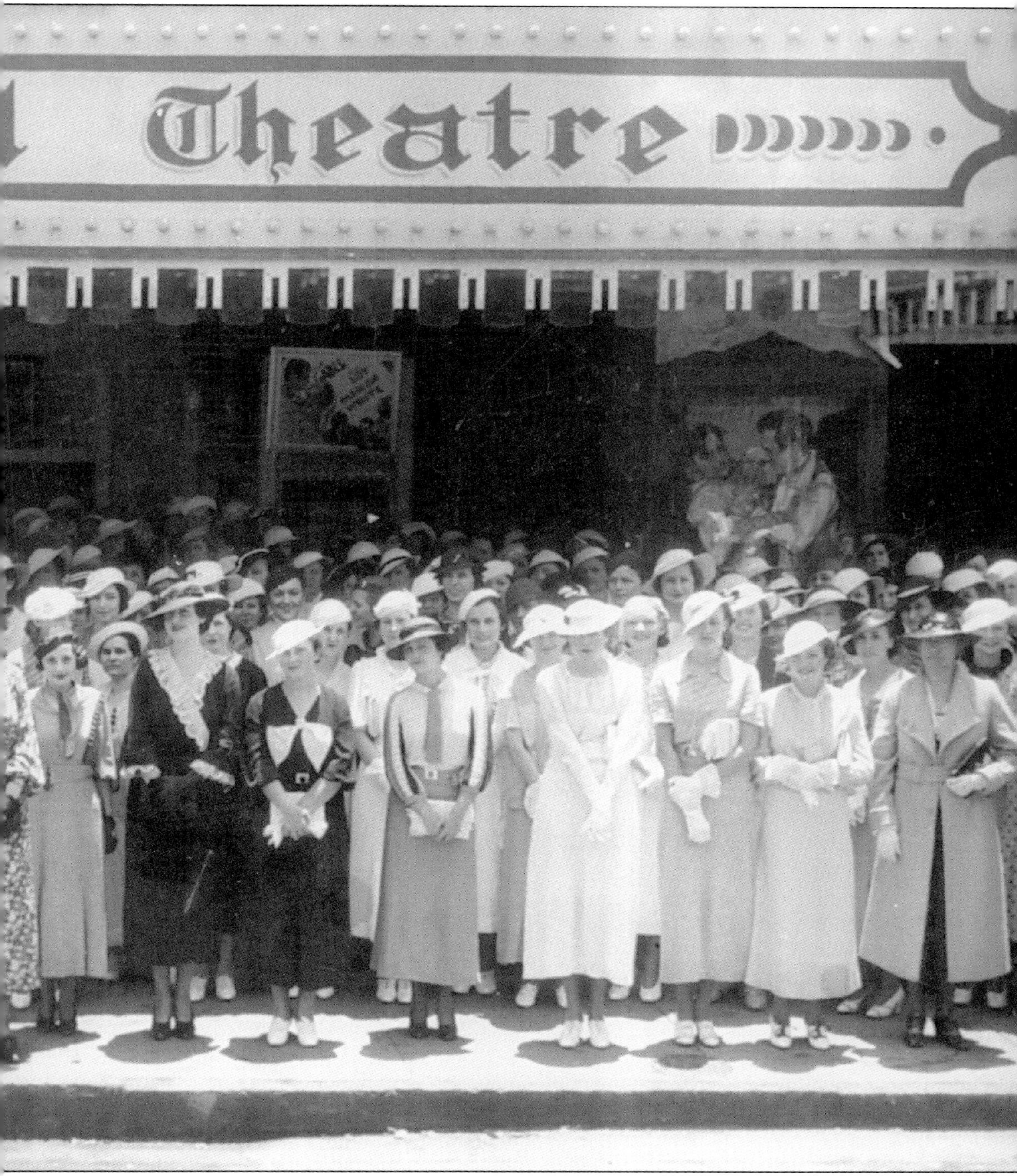

the storeroom next door to Culver and Kidd's. Over the next several years, the theater changed hands, closed, and reopened. It was sold in 1915, and the name changed to the Elizabeth Theatre. It was purchased in 1917, and became the Cozy Theatre. It was bought again the same year and renamed the Star Theatre before closing. The space was remodeled and opened in 1920 as the Dixie Theatre. (Courtesy of the Georgia Archives, Vanishing Georgia, bal-116.)

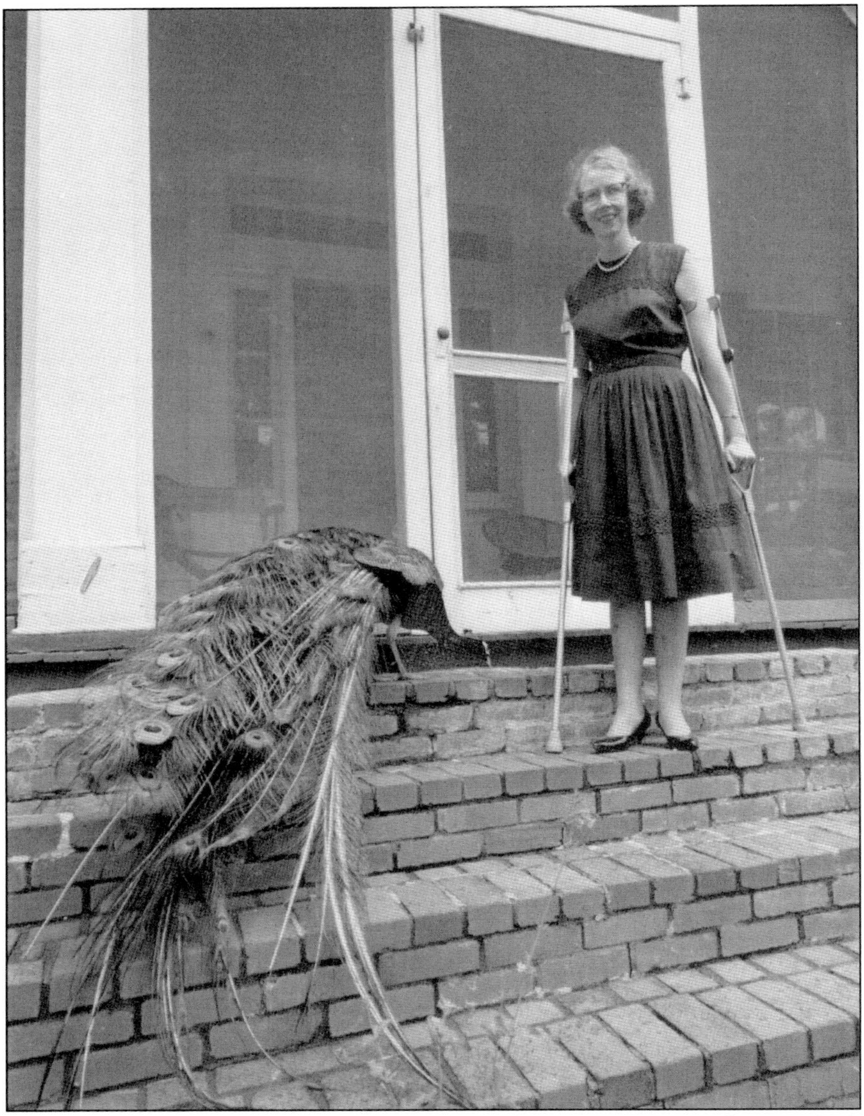

Flannery O'Connor was a notable American novelist and short-story writer whose work challenged traditional categorization. Born Mary Flannery O'Connor in 1925, she grew up in Milledgeville, attended the Peabody School, and graduated from the Georgia State College for Women. She moved to Iowa in 1945, where she attended the State University of Iowa and completed a master of fine arts in 1947. For the next few years, she lived in both New York and Connecticut before returning to Milledgeville after developing lupus, the same disease from which her father had died at a young age. O'Connor lived her remaining years on the family farm, Andalusia, where she continued her writing. She also gave lectures, conducted book readings, and took the time to respond to letters from younger writers. While at Andalusia, she received numerous awards, grants, a fellowship from the *Kenyon Review,* and several O. Henry Awards. In early 1964, a surgery to remove a tumor reactivated her lupus, which had been in remission, and her health declined until she slipped into a coma for several days before dying at the Baldwin County Hospital. She is buried next to her parents at Memory Hill Cemetery. Published posthumously in 1971, *The Complete Stories of Flannery O'Connor* was the winner of the National Book Award for fiction. (Courtesy of Bo Edmonds.)

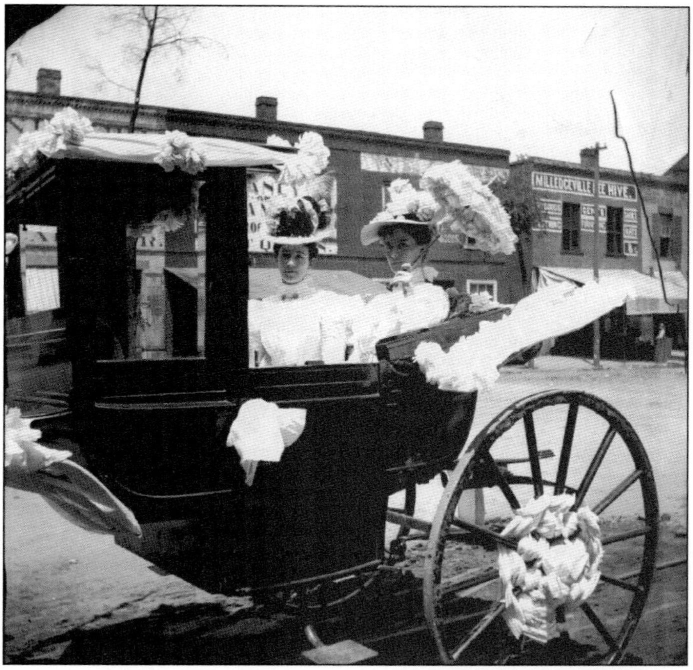

Processing in the Band Tournament and Carnival Parade in June 1898, "Mrs. L.N. Callaway's Victoria carriage is occupied by Mrs. Callaway and Mrs. E. Compton, decorated in yellow," according to *The Union-Recorder.*

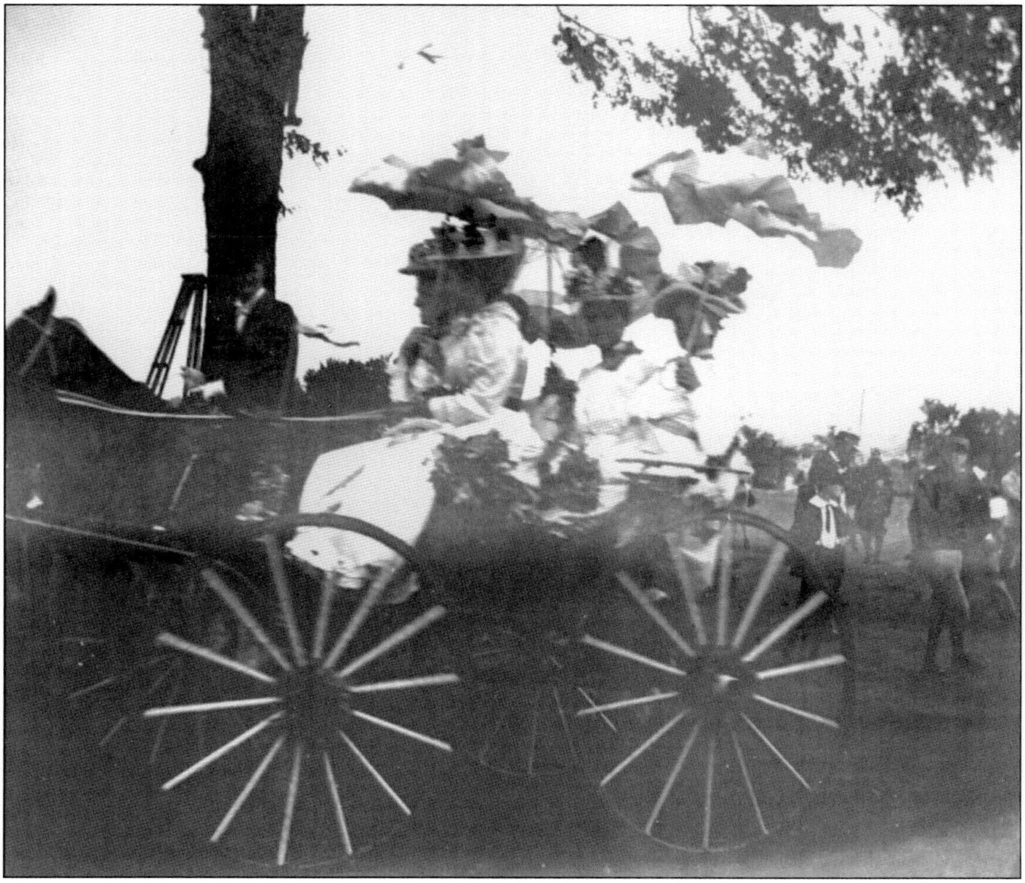

At the Band Tournament and Carnival Parade, as reported in an account by *The Union-Recorder,* Mary Conn, Mabel Hodges, and Louise Edmonson of Eatonton are shown here riding with Mrs. Mark Johnson in her trap carriage, adorned with yellow flowers.

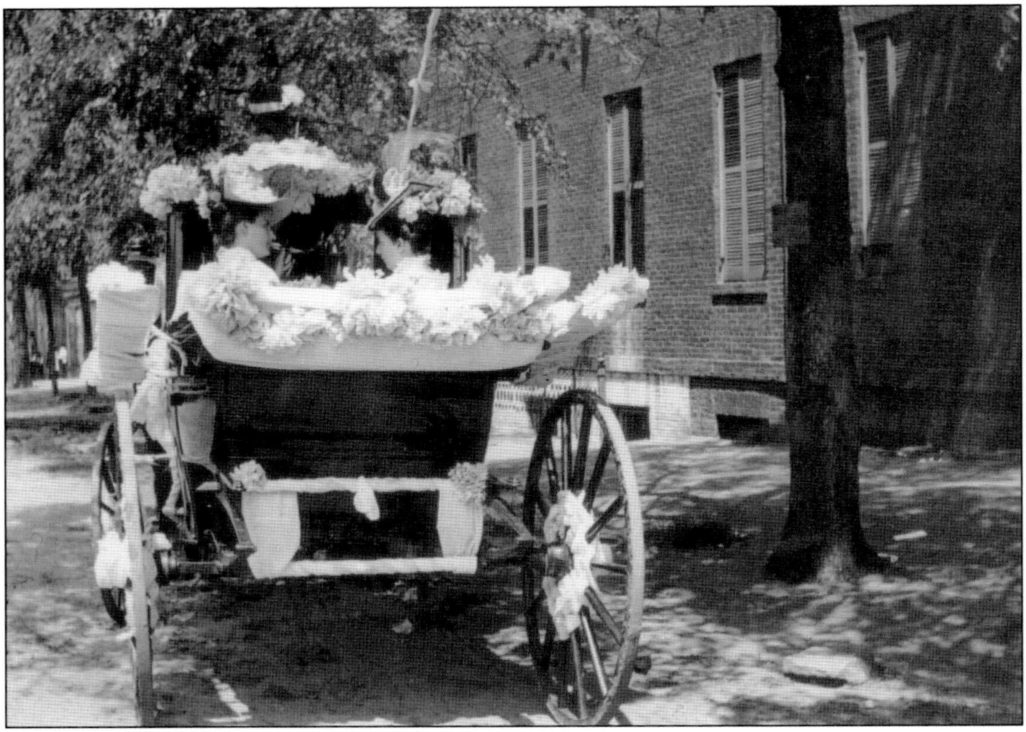

The Victoria carriage of Mrs. L.N. Callaway is shown from the rear in the 1898 Band Tournament and Carnival Parade. The coachman can be seen driving in front of the imperial, or closed-in compartment, of the carriage. The boards projecting out above the wheels, decorated with wrapped fabric and flowers, are called wings and deflect mud, water, and dirt from being flung into the carriage.

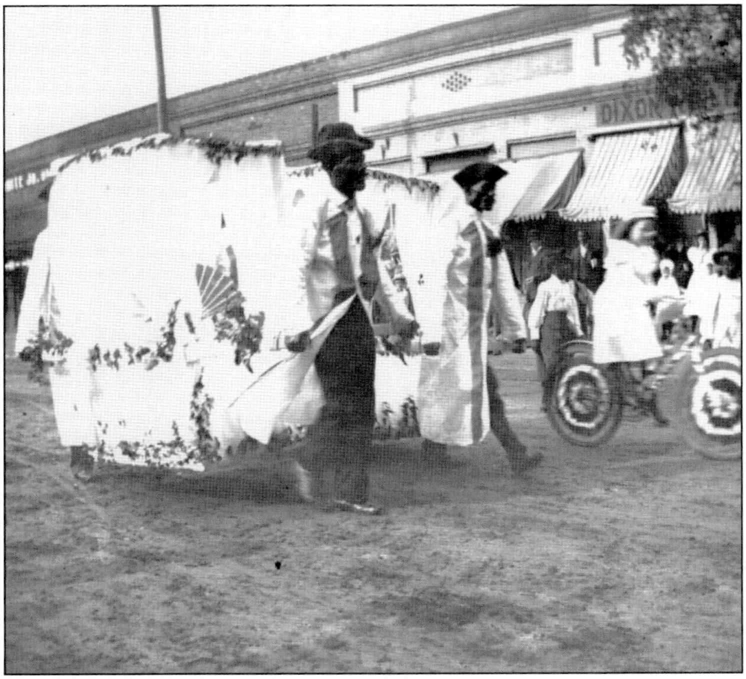

More for display than function, John Callaway and Rufus Roberts occupied the sedan chairs that are being carried in this photograph. Sedan chairs were used for the function of transportation from one's home to around town without getting one's clothing dirty on roads. The roads were unpaved, traveled by carriages and horses, and muddy at times.

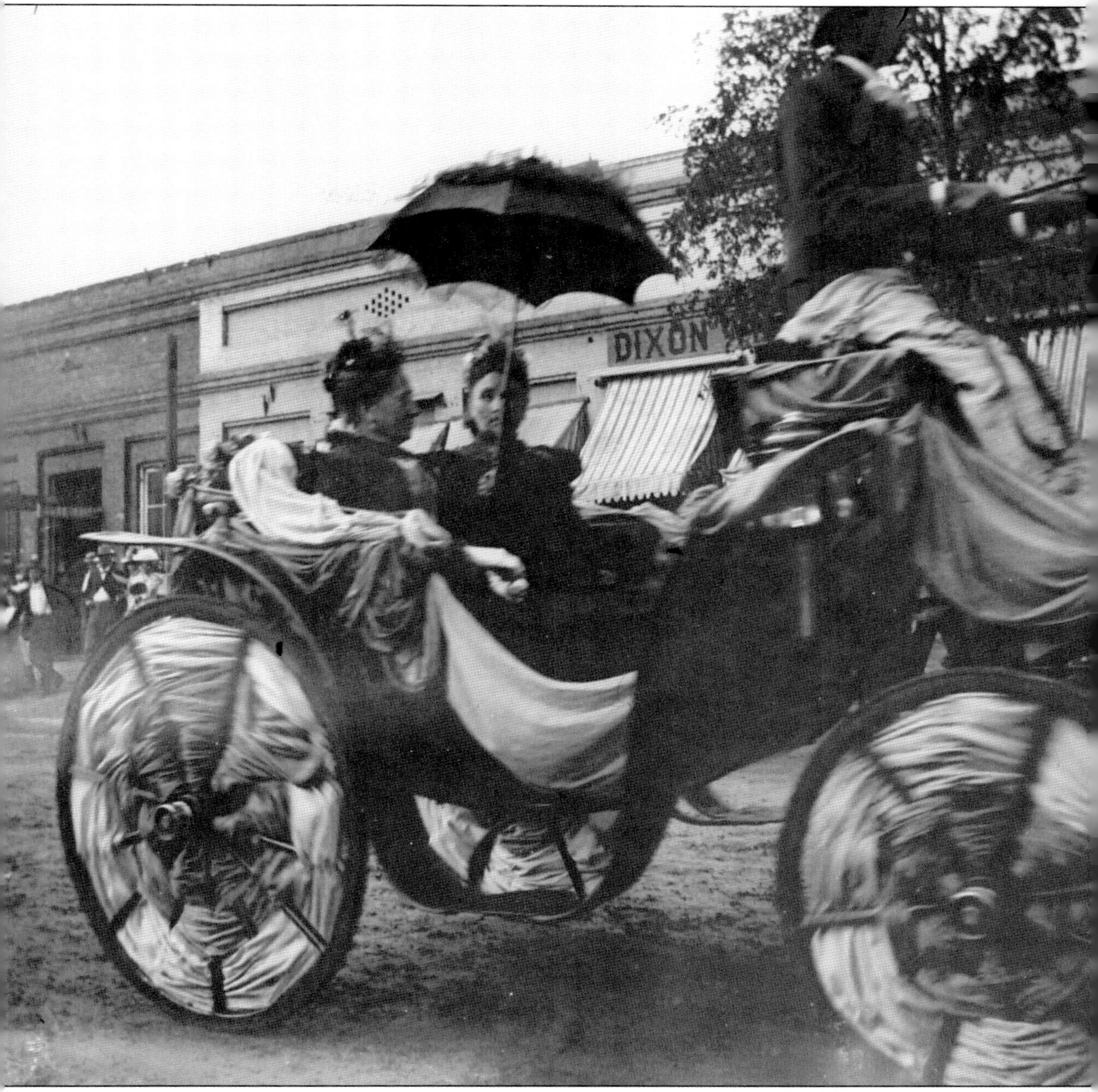

Passing in front of Dixon Williams's jewelry store in the June 1898 Band Tournament and Carnival Parade procession, Mrs. W.A. Walker (left) is accompanied in her carriage by ? Allen. This photograph was made on South Wayne Street between the present-day locations of Grant's Jewelry and Magnolia State Bank.

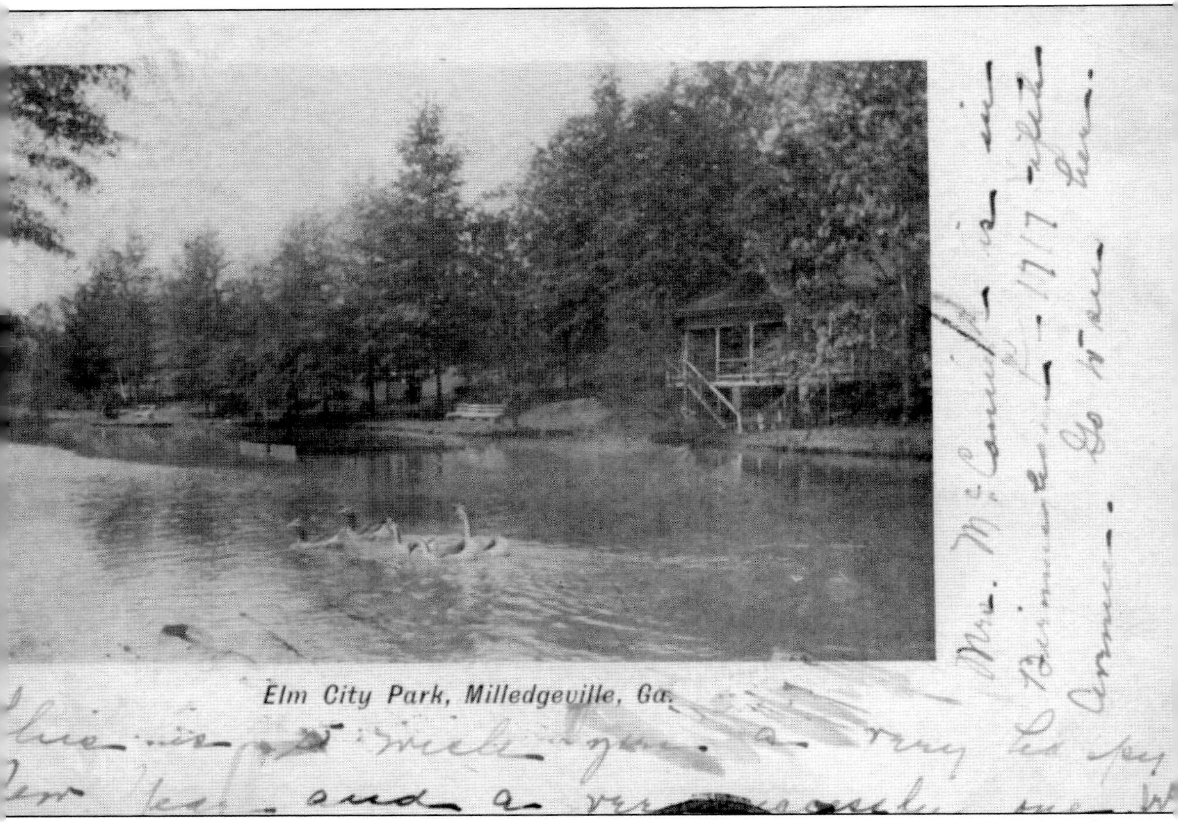

In 1898, the Elm City Garden Club secured the location for the creation of a park, including the old O'Brien Spring near Walker's fishpond, which was formerly owned by Sam Walker. Dr. Robson purchased the property for the development of a natatorium, and the location was described as being in the suburbs of southwestern Milledgeville. The property had three ponds fed by a spring, and the right side of the property was bounded by a high, overgrown embankment. A second lake with a bathhouse was added to the existing bathhouse and boats on the property. Visible in the water on the left, the mid-side is a shallow, floored enclosure in which beginning swimmers could learn to swim. Dr. Robson's intention was to also house ducks, chickens, and rabbits on the property. Geese can be seen in the foreground of the photograph. It is believed to have been located on the property that is currently the Georgia College Centennial Center parking lot, extending down to Franklin Street. (Courtesy of Bo Edmonds.)

Urma Lewis of Vidalia (left) and Irene Powell of Clayton pose for a photograph in their tennis outfits on the campus of Georgia College and State University. (Courtesy of the Georgia Archives, Vanishing Georgia, bal-163.)

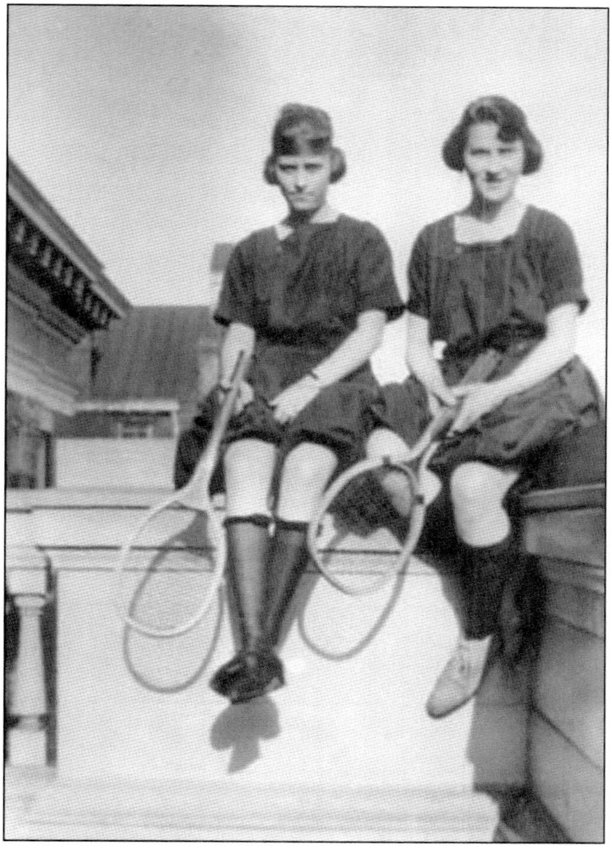

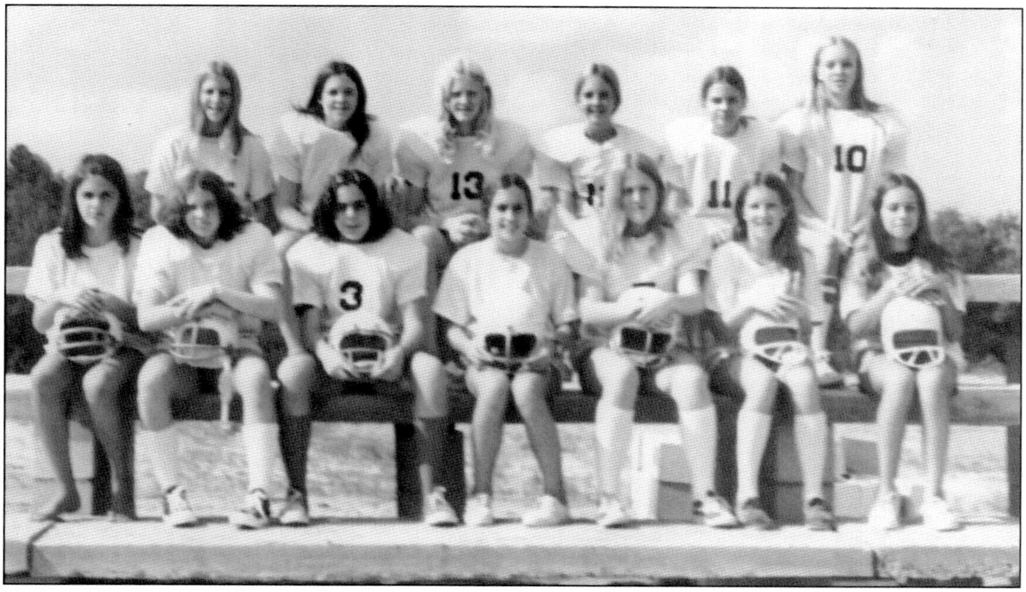

Girls in this picture taken in the early 1970s find entertainment in playing an altered form of the traditionally all-male sport of football. By implication a less physically rough game, the version played by females, came to be called powder-puff football. (Courtesy of John Milledge Academy.)

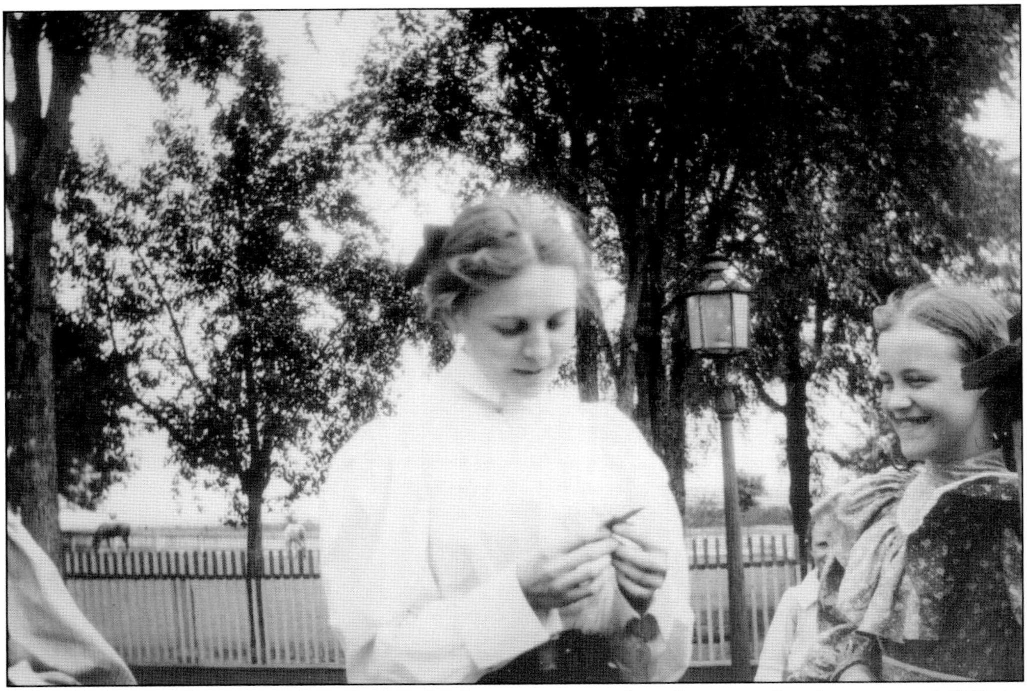

These girls spend some time in each other's company in this photograph taken around 1910 in Milledgeville. They appear to be delighted as they examine an unknown object.

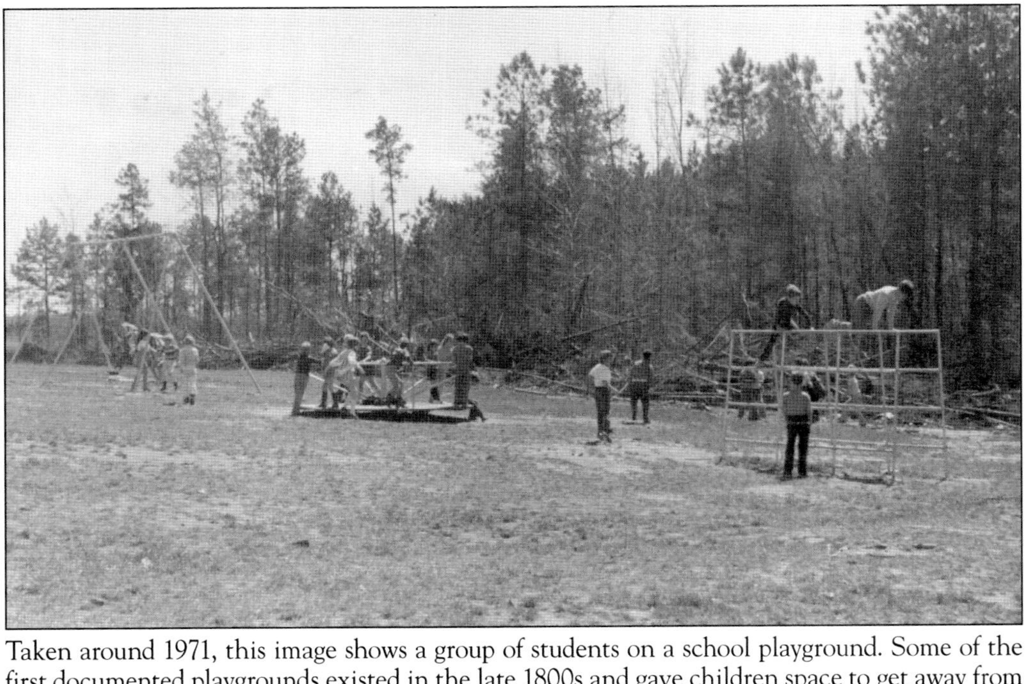

Taken around 1971, this image shows a group of students on a school playground. Some of the first documented playgrounds existed in the late 1800s and gave children space to get away from overcrowded immigrant neighborhoods. They have evolved in more recent times into places where children can go to play and increase physical activity levels reduced by the advent of technology devices. (Courtesy of John Milledge Academy.)

By 1900, around when this photograph was taken, the cost of bicycles dropped, making them affordable for working people. As today, bicycles remained primarily recreational as opposed to functional for transportation. Bicycles were not as practical for transportation because of the poor conditions of roads, mechanical design that made handling difficult, and impracticality for carrying loads. For women, social mores made clothing an impediment to riding.

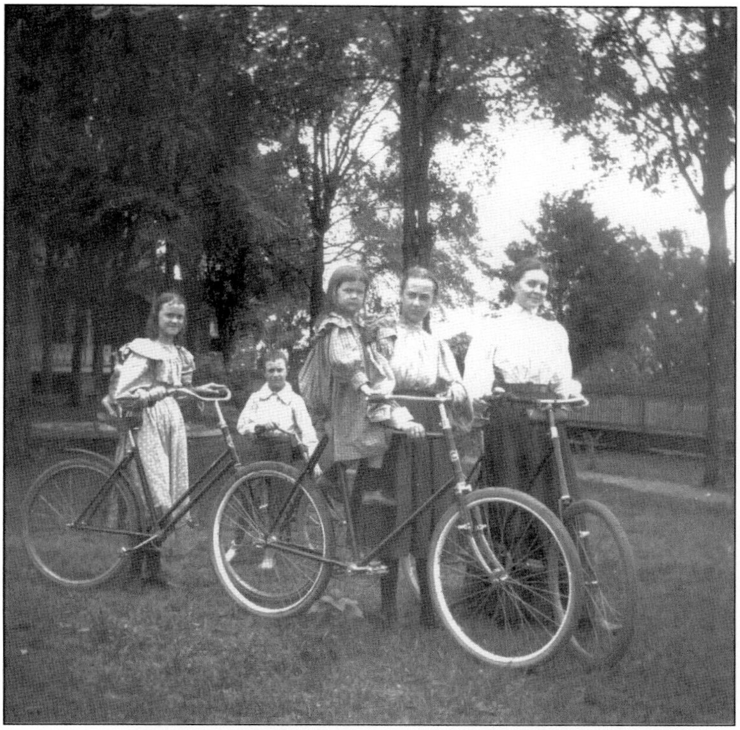

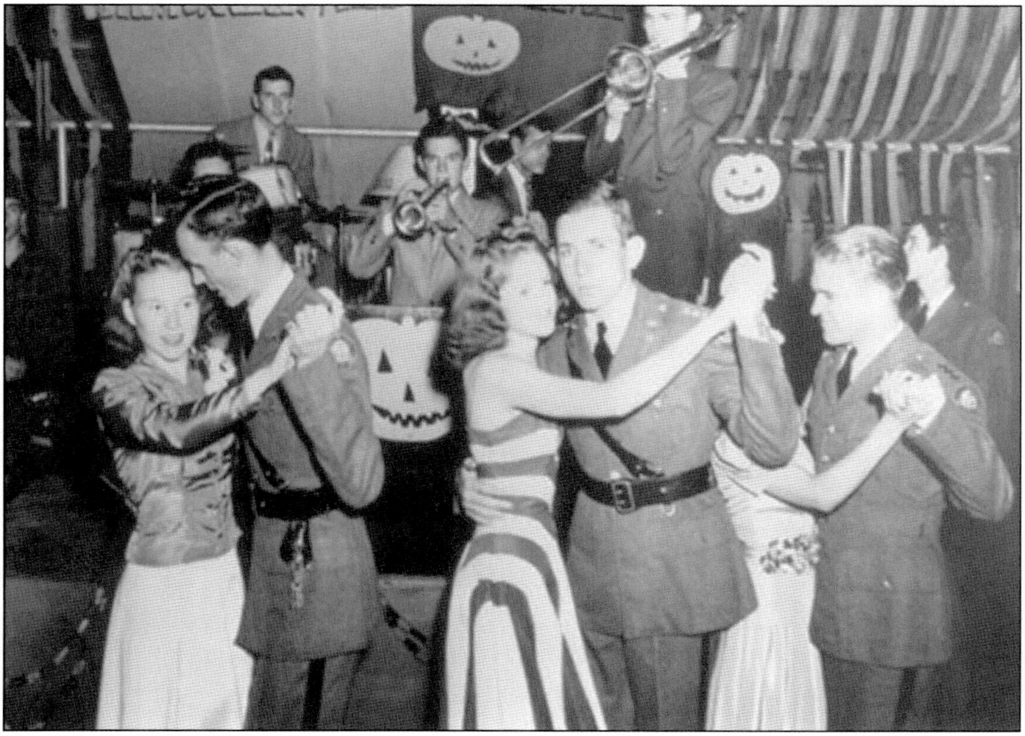

Taken in the 1940s, this photograph shows a Halloween dance at Georgia Military College. Swing music and dancing the swing, Lindy, and jitterbug were popular during this time period. (Courtesy of the Georgia Archives, Vanishing Georgia, bal-161.)

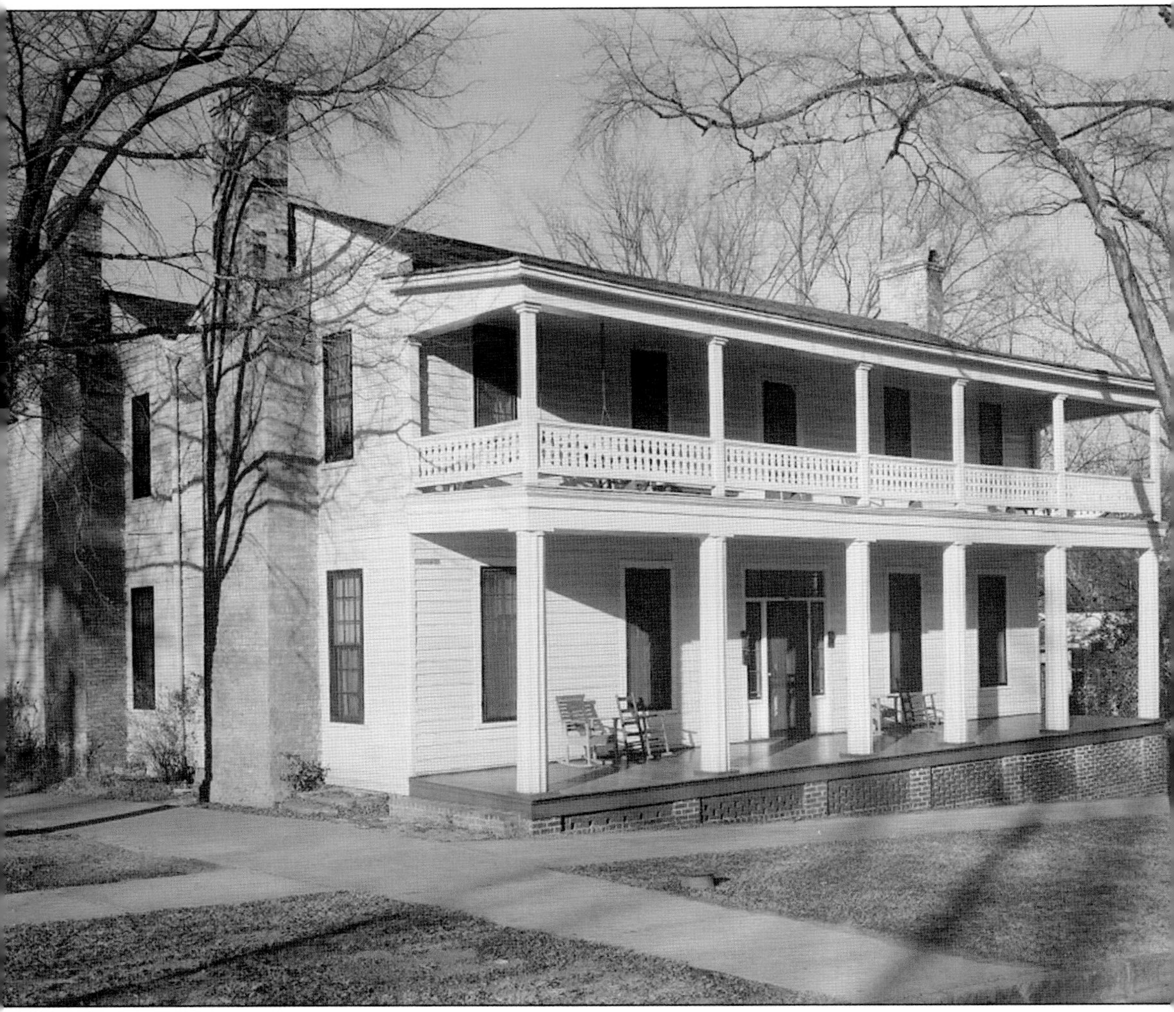

The Tomlinson Fort house is pictured here around 1950. Fort served in the Georgia state legislature as well as the US Congress. He was a physician and authored a book on the practice of medicine. Fort was also largely responsible for the establishment of the Georgia Lunatic Asylum, later Central State Hospital, in 1837. (Courtesy of the Library of Congress, Carnegie Survey of the Architecture of the South, LC-J7-GA-1436.)

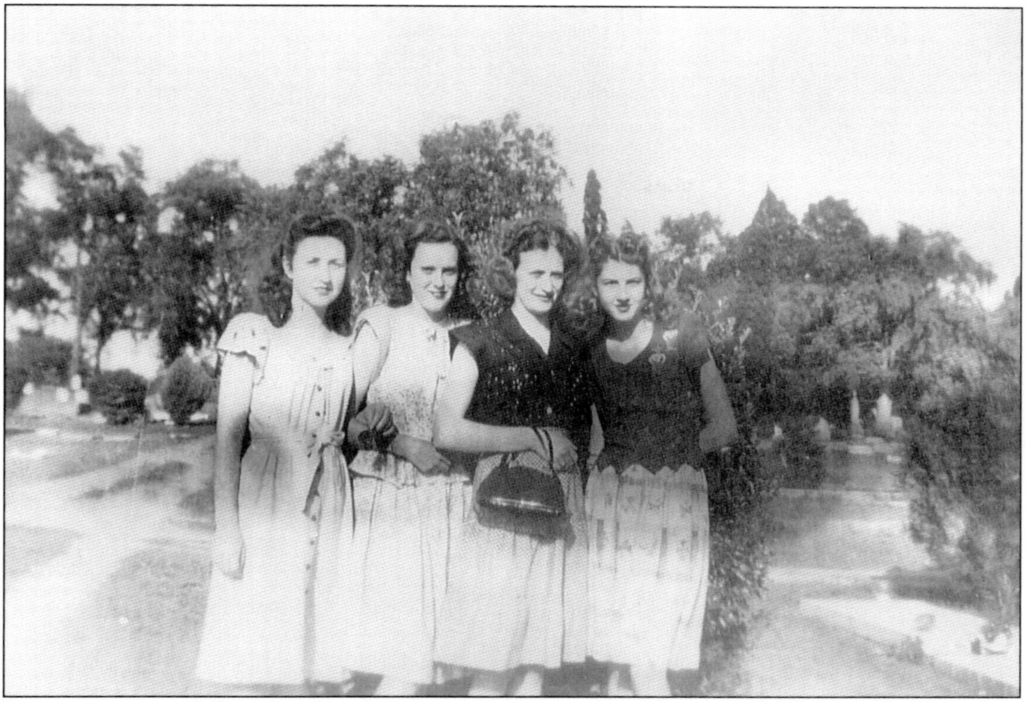

Four women spend their Sunday afternoon visiting sites around town in Milledgeville. Here, they are posing for a photograph at Memory Hill. The women are, from left to right, Emma Batson, unidentified, Ann Ward, and Carolyn Robinson. (Courtesy of Kay Ward Johnson, Terri Spires Wall, and the Gilman/Ward family.)

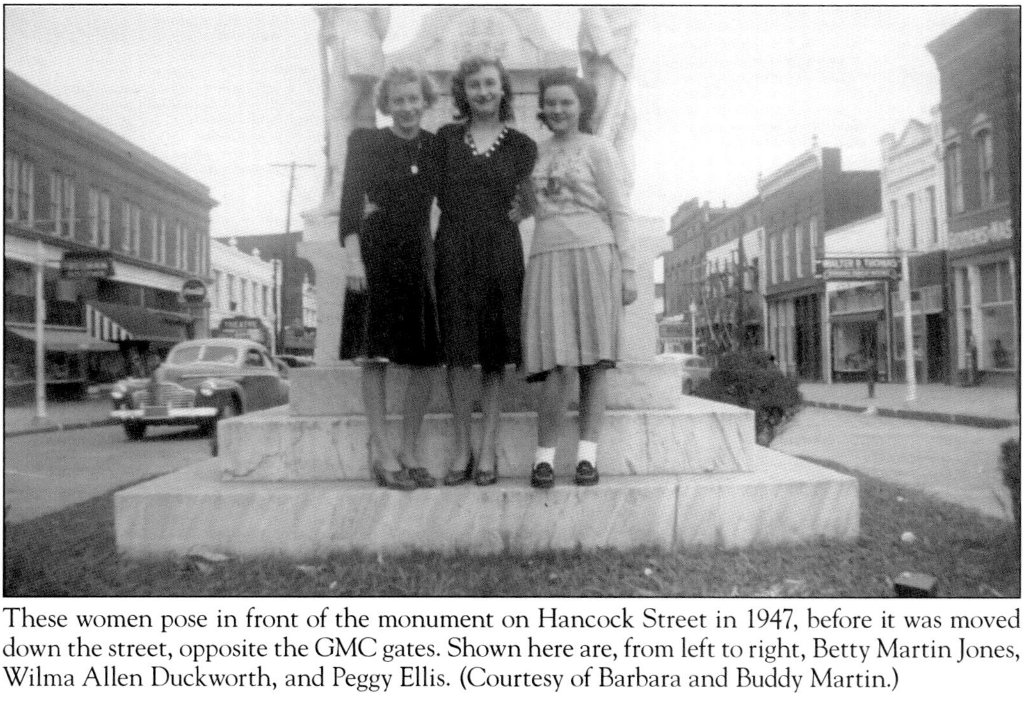

These women pose in front of the monument on Hancock Street in 1947, before it was moved down the street, opposite the GMC gates. Shown here are, from left to right, Betty Martin Jones, Wilma Allen Duckworth, and Peggy Ellis. (Courtesy of Barbara and Buddy Martin.)

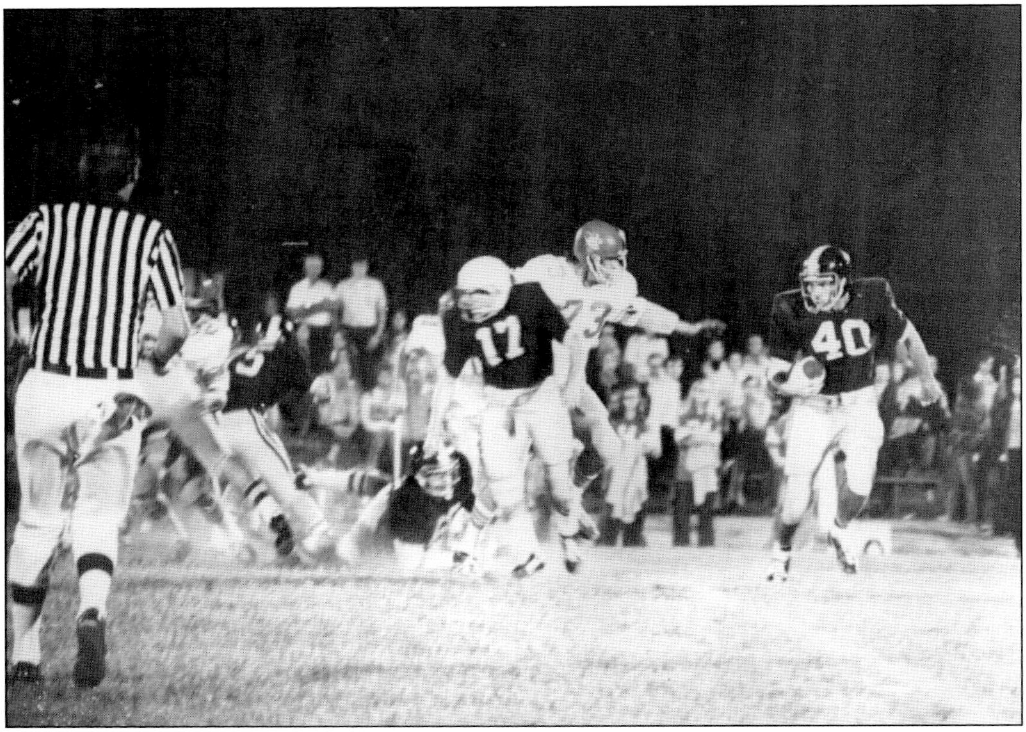

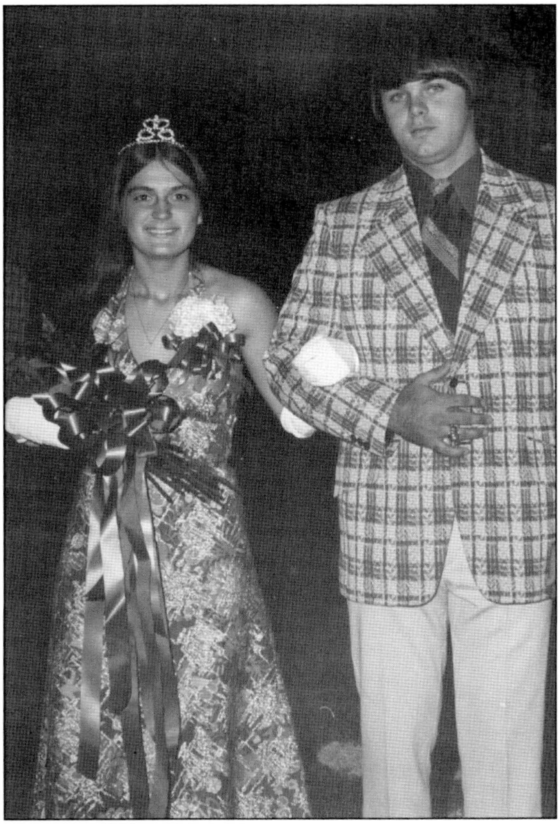

The homecoming football game and the corresponding crowning of homecoming king and queen have become American staples of school spirit. These late-1970s images show a game and the unidentified homecoming queen and her escort. (Courtesy of John Milledge Academy.)

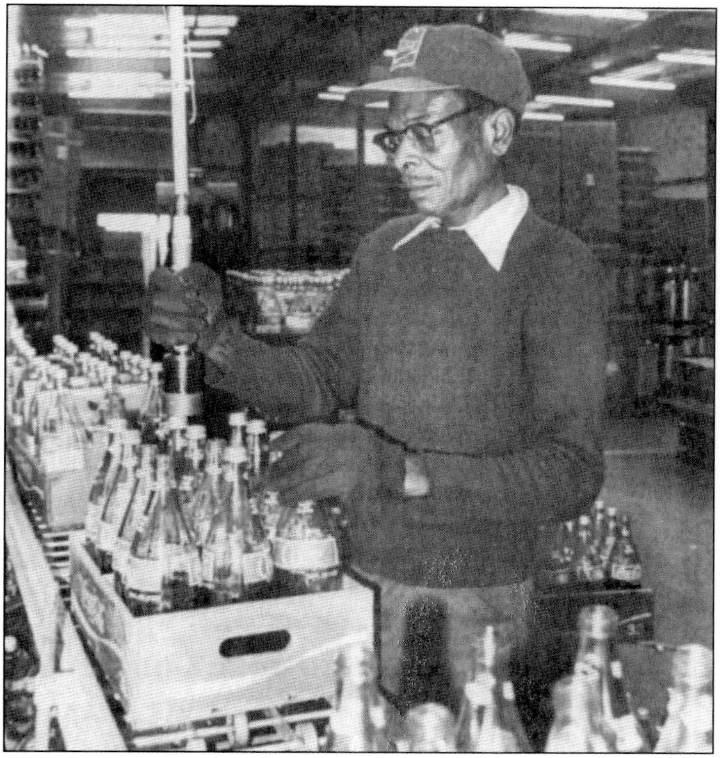

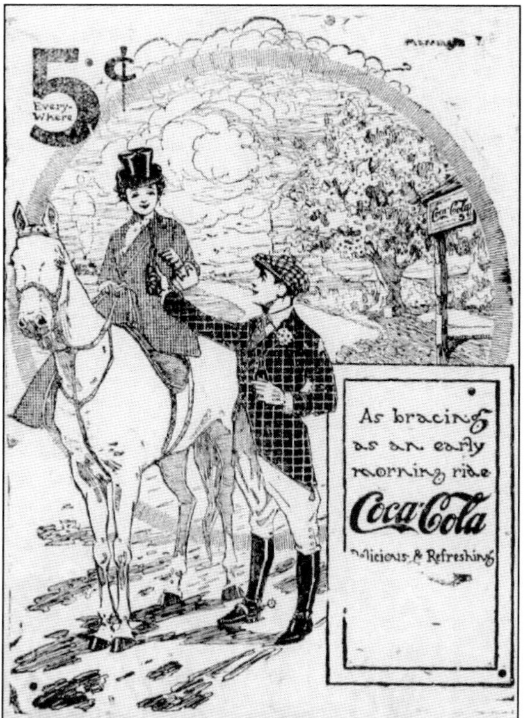

In 1913, the Macon Coca-Cola plant opened a bottling plant in Milledgeville called the Milledgeville Coca-Cola Company. Initially, the plant was located on Hancock Street, and it later moved to the industrial park off of Highway 441. It was the smallest Coca-Cola bottler in the state of Georgia and, in later years, became a privately owned franchise that distributed the product. Advertisements for Coca-Cola were prominently displayed in the downtown area on signs, in theater programs, and even on the side of the Culver and Kidd Drugstore. Sodas were originally served inside a pharmacy or store. A server would pull a lever to dispense the soda to the client and, by doing so, earned the name soda jerk. Since soda is an item many people have grown up with, feelings of nostalgia have been a major factor in product marketing and sales. (Courtesy of *The Union-Recorder.*)

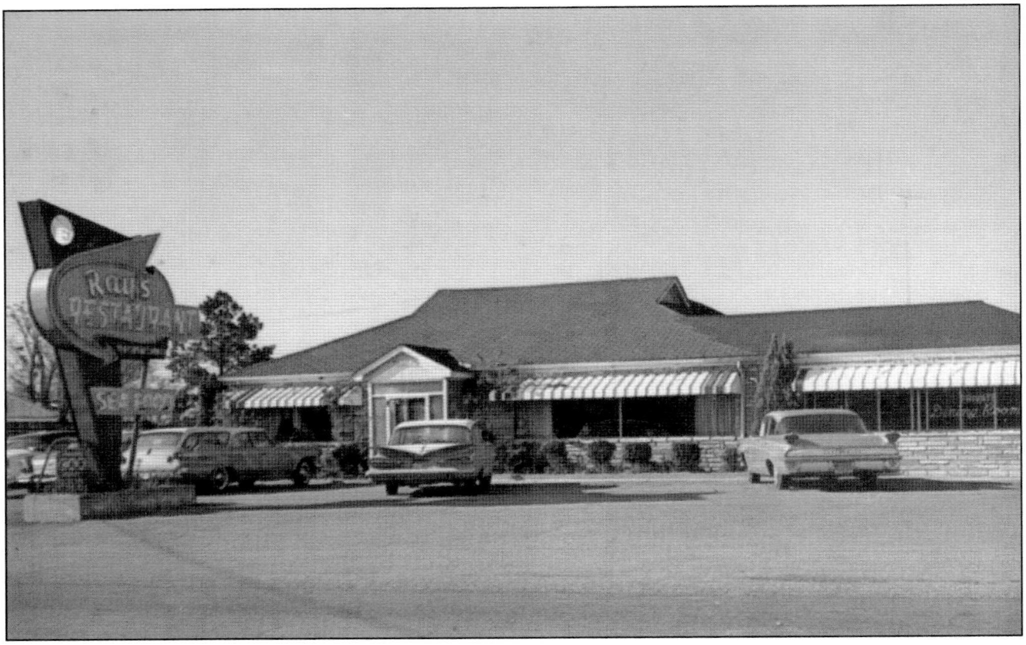

Beginning in the 1950s and 1960s, the increasing ease of transportation and the availability of refrigeration techniques allowed restaurant dining to become popular. These restaurants were made further profitable by the expansion of advertising. The steak houses that were popular in the 1950s and 1960s, such as the Steak & Ale chain in the United States, served beef and a limited number of simple side dishes, which were easily prepared by semiskilled labor. Seen above is Ray's Seafood Restaurant, and below is the Steak Out Steakhouse; both were formerly located in Milledgeville. (Both, courtesy of *The Union-Recorder*.)

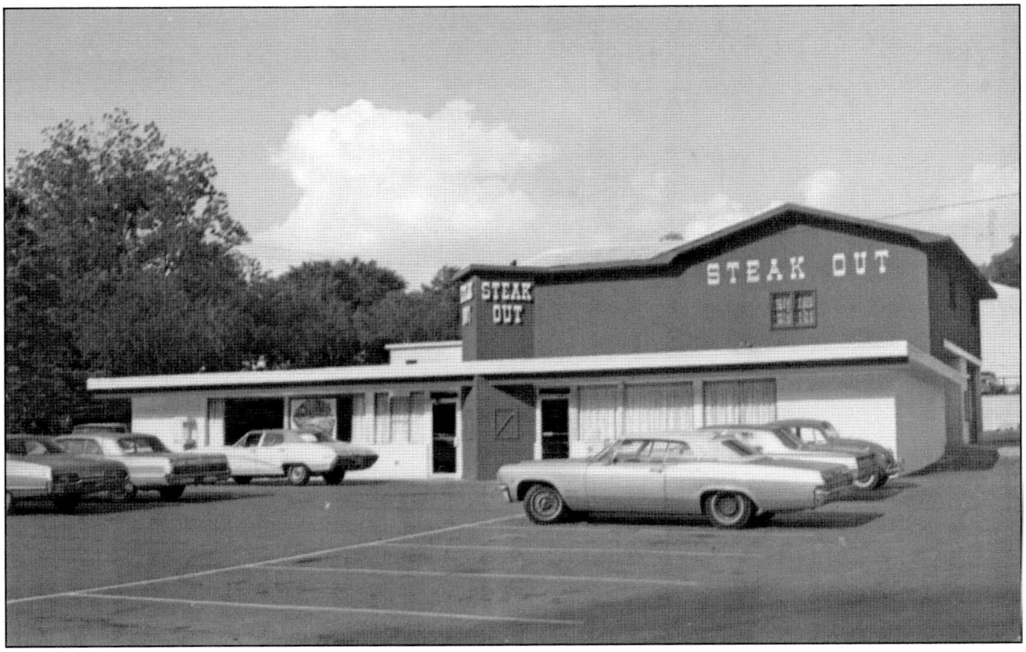

Five

Science and Technology

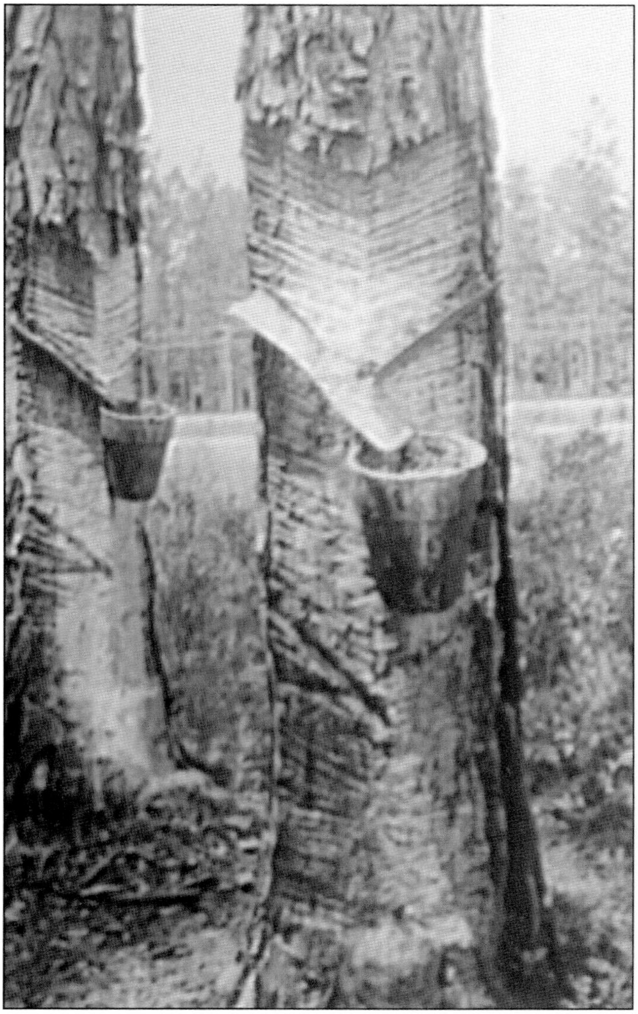

Charles Holmes Herty revolutionized the turpentine industry in the United States. In 1903, Herty patented a simple cup and gutter method of harvesting pine tree resin by making shallow cuts that did not kill the tree. (Courtesy of the Chemical History Foundation.)

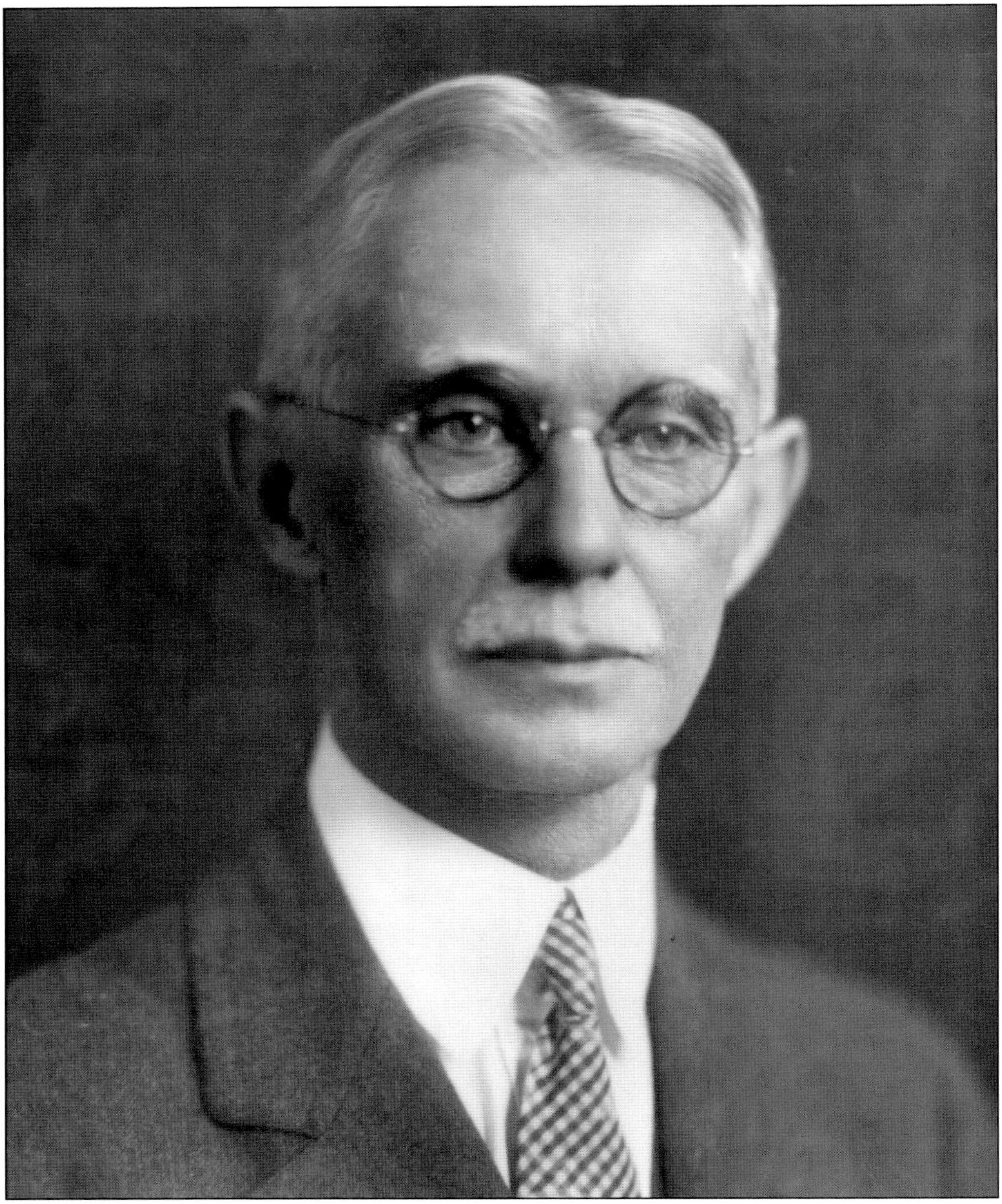

Esteemed and visionary chemist Charles Holmes Herty was born in Milledgeville on December 4, 1867. His aunt, who was a schoolteacher, raised him after he was orphaned at age 11. Herty secured employment as a chemistry professor and director of physical culture at the University of Georgia, where he founded the athletic program. He later left the university for a position with the United States Bureau of Forestry as an expert studying the problem of killing trees by the turpentine industry. His developments and research led to the creation of the southeastern United States pulp industry. He was also instrumental in the formation of the National Institutes of Health. (Courtesy of the Chemical History Foundation.)

This advertisement from 1903 is representative of the layman's understanding, during the time period, of malaria and how it was contracted. Instead of being connected to mosquitoes and their breeding grounds, malaria was associated with bad air being inhaled from sewers, damp places, and marshy regions, which was said to cause poisoning of the blood. (Courtesy of *The Union-Recorder*.)

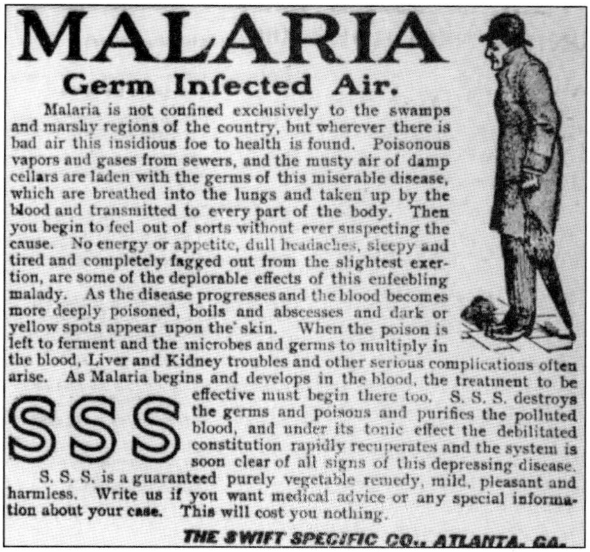

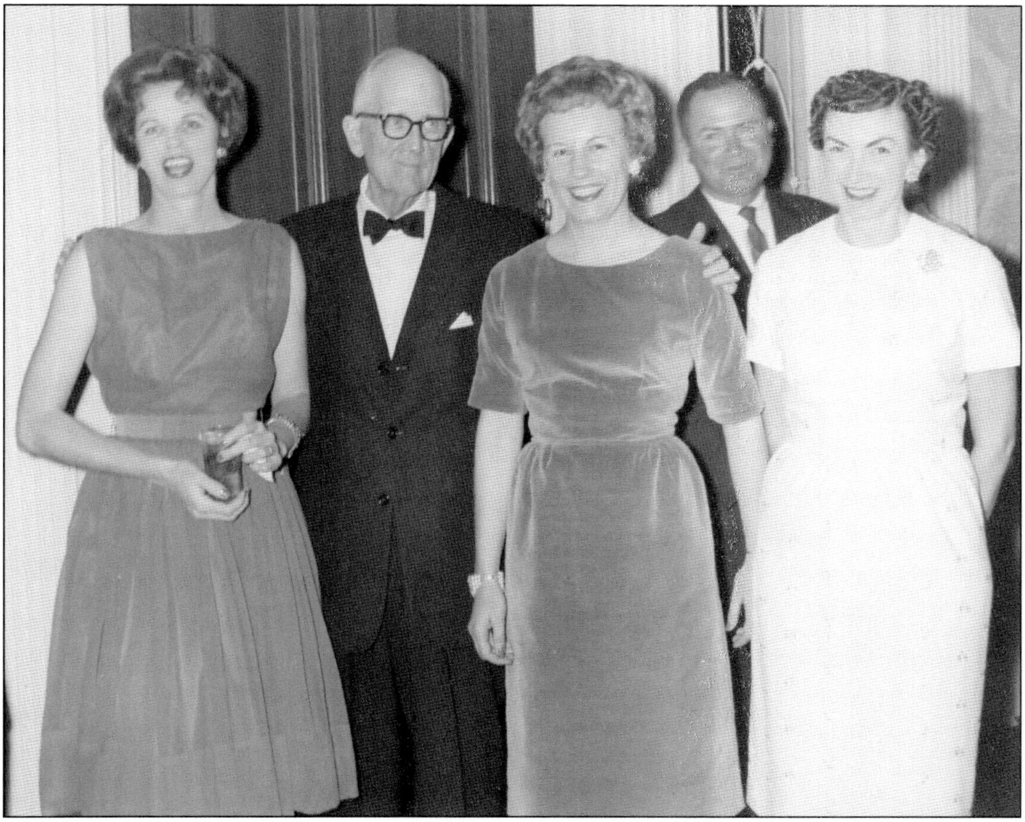

Although not shown in this photograph, Lawrence Welk attended this reception, held in his honor at the home of Frank E. Bone, around the late 1950s to early 1960s. Pictured are, from left to right, Ruth Cransford, Frank Edgar Bone, Betty Jones, John Williams, and Elizabeth Williams. The house where the reception was held later became Georgia College's Cathy Alumni Center. Lawrence Welk was in Milledgeville for the purpose of a fundraiser and had served as the marshal of the Milledgeville Christmas Parade. (Courtesy of Barbara and Buddy Martin.)

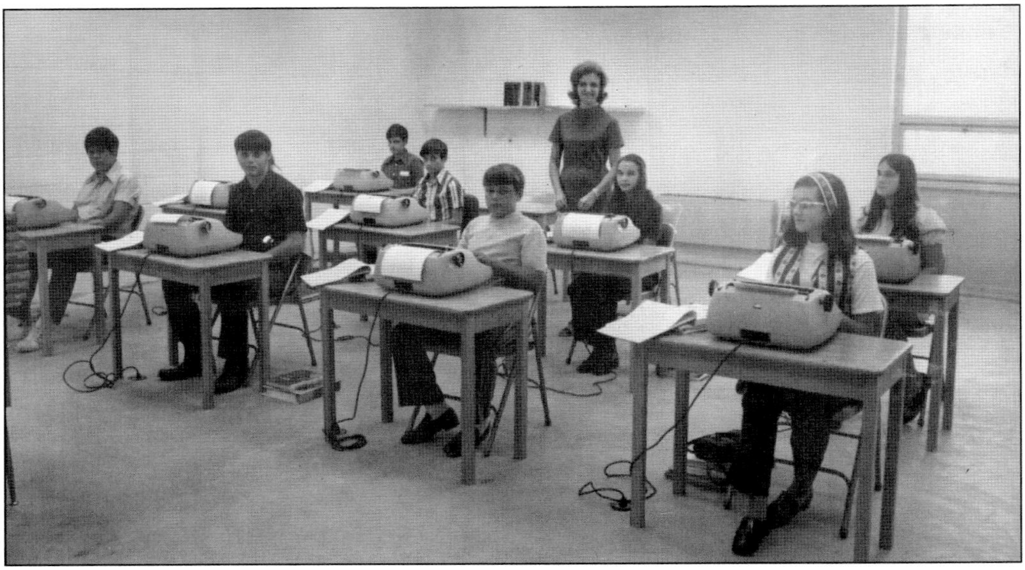

In this 1970s image, a high school class learns and practices typewriting skills in the years before personal computers came into use. Around the same time as this image was made, word processors, which allowed the typist to correct mistakes and move words around without endless retyping required on a typewriter, began to compete with typewriters. (Courtesy of John Milledge Academy.)

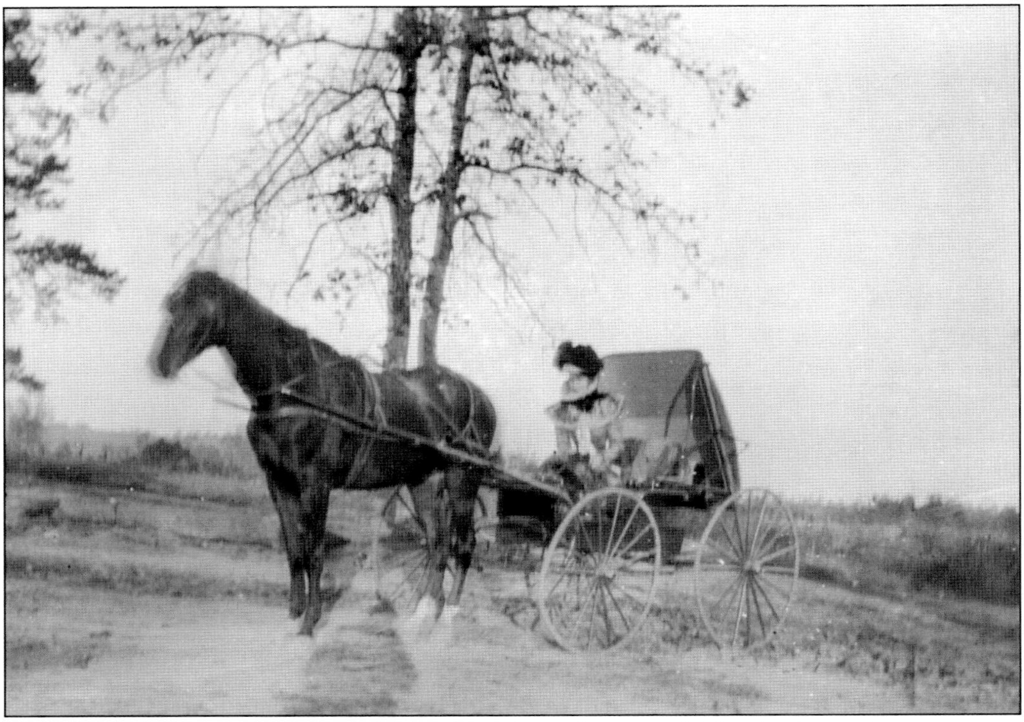

Seen at an unidentified location in Milledgeville in the early 1900s, this horse-drawn carriage would have been common transportation at the time. In later years, carriages and coaches began to disappear as use of steam propulsion generated more and more interest and research. Steam power quickly won the battle against animal power.

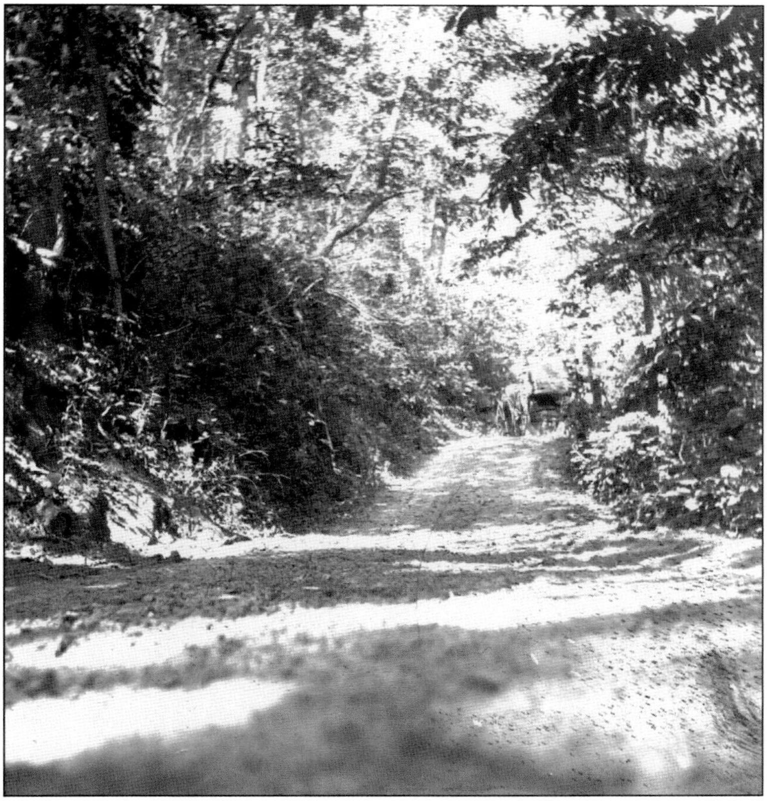

This photograph was taken of an unknown dirt road in Milledgeville in the 1890s. The development of roads facilitated travel between settlements and expanded trade as well as increased the exchange of knowledge. Many of the roads followed already existing Indian trade routes, and they also contributed to the removal of the Native Americans from their lands.

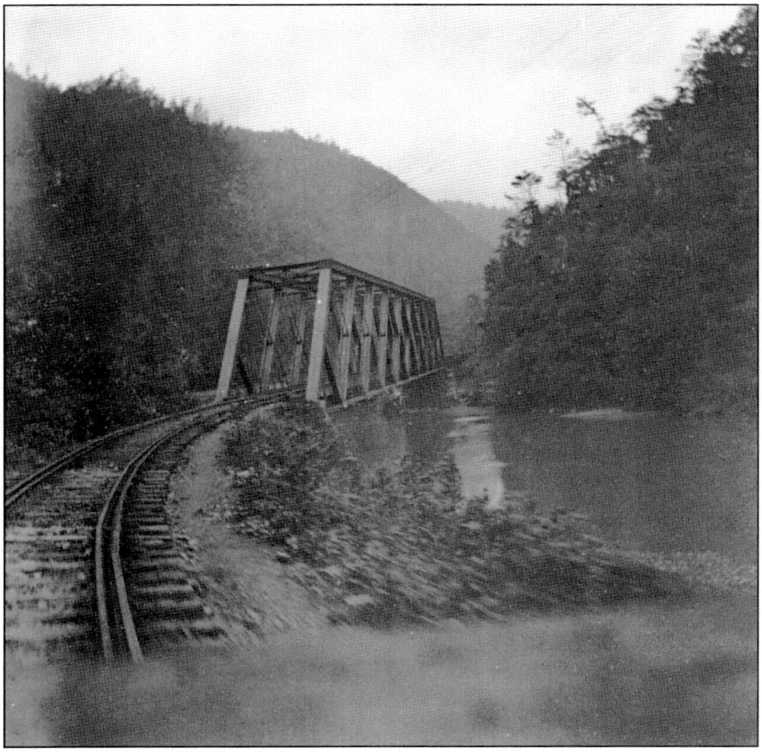

Between 1860 and 1890, the miles of operational railroad tracks in the state of Georgia tripled. The building and expansion of railways in Milledgeville allowed for faster, more efficient transportation of people and goods. Railroads were faster than any other form of transportation and were not subject to restriction due to weather. The railroads provided for economic growth by opening the market for goods nationally.

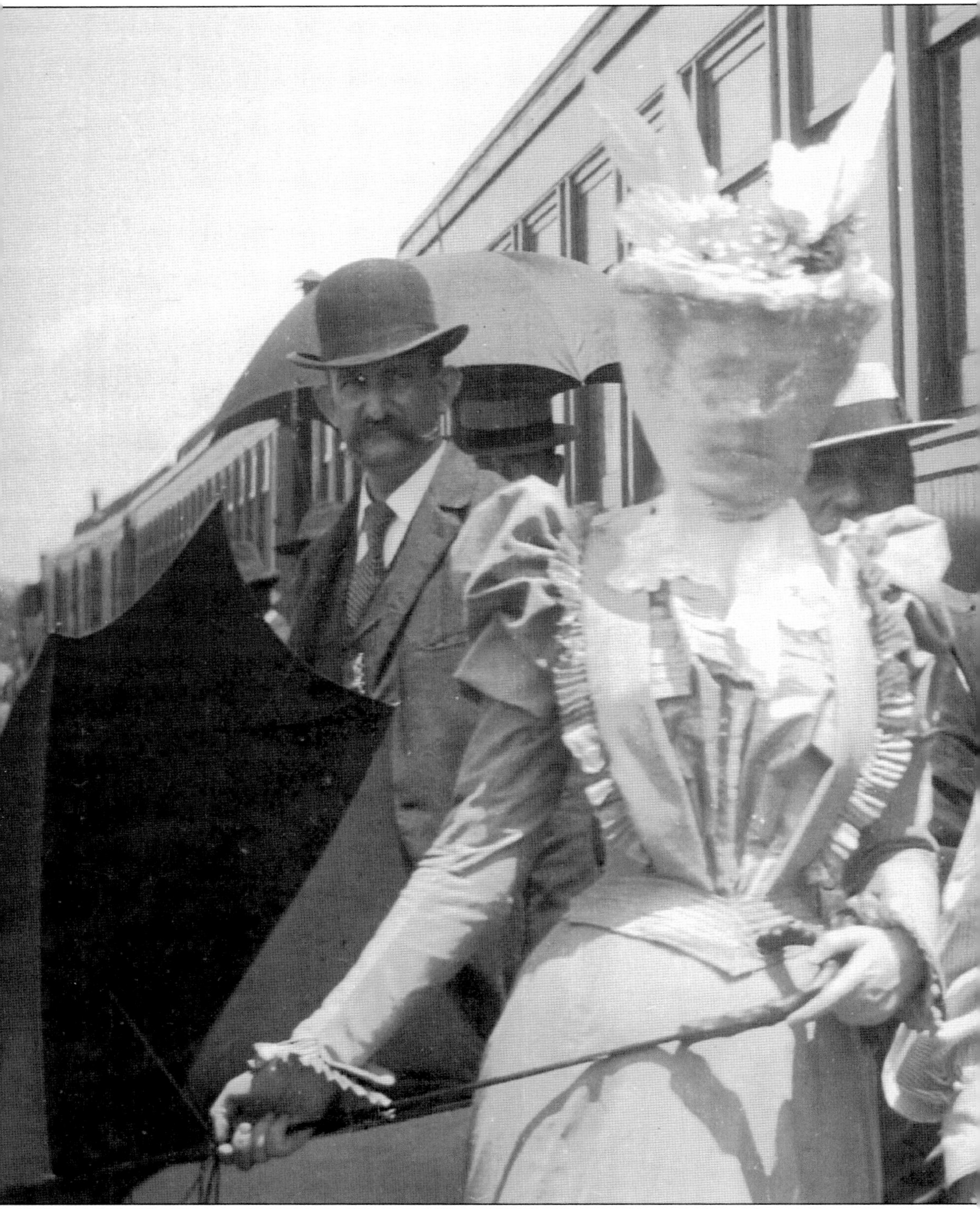

In this c. 1900 image, these passengers are either arriving or departing on a passenger train running on the Milledgeville-Eatonton line of the Central of Georgia Railroad. The Central later bought the Middle Georgia and Atlantic Railway in a foreclosure sale and continued operation of the line between Milledgeville and Covington. The Central was one of the most significant railways

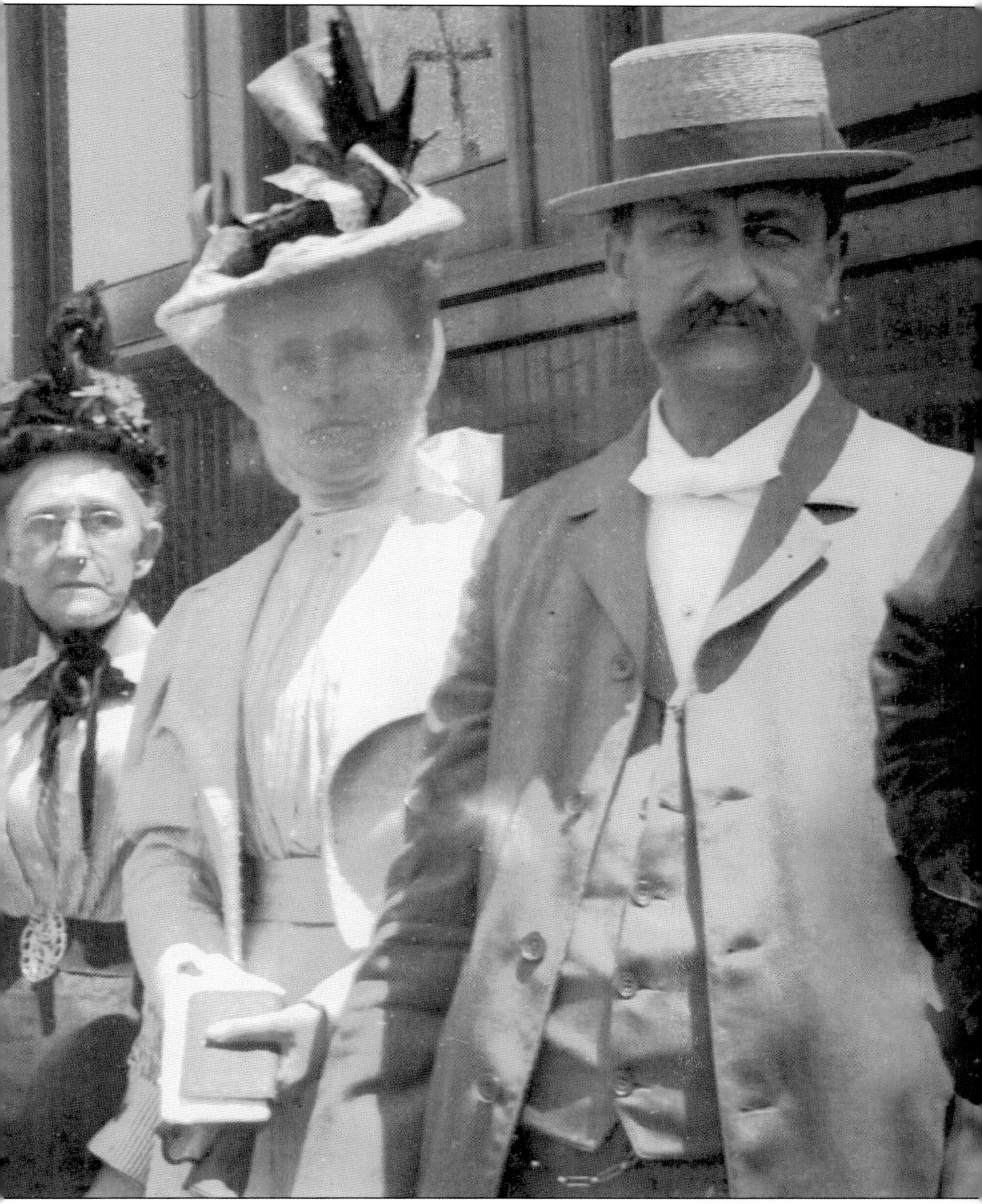

in the southern United States. It was vital to the cotton economy of Milledgeville and, in later years, as cotton declined in economic importance, the railway encouraged the industries of clay, textiles, and timber to move development into Georgia. Central of Georgia currently continues to operate as a unit of Norfolk Southern Corporation.

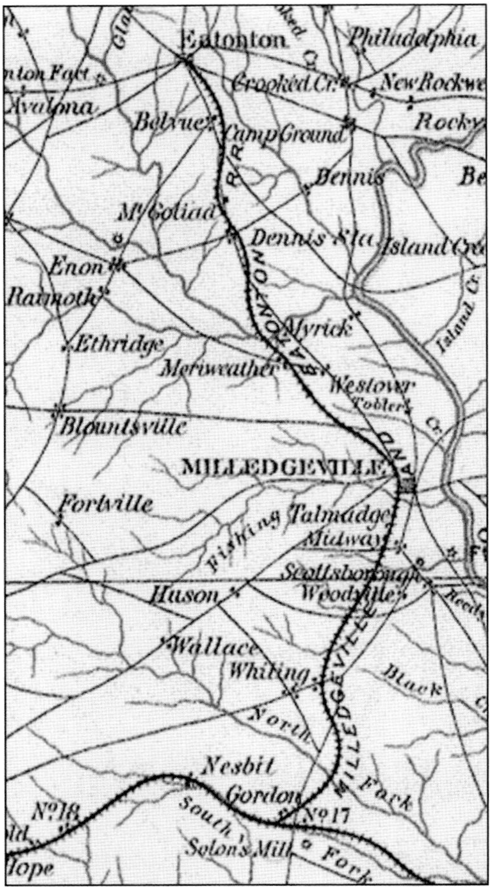

The Middle Georgia and Atlantic Railway incorporated in 1889, and a 64-mile rail line was built from Milledgeville to Covington. A 22-mile line also connected Milledgeville to Eatonton. The Milledgeville-Eatonton segment was connected to the main line at Gordon. (Courtesy of the Georgia Department of Transportation.)

Seen here is a postcard from the perspective of looking north from the south end of Wayne Street. On the corner in the right foreground is the Milledgeville Hotel, also known as the Baldwin Hotel. From 1891 to 1896, a streetcar line, called the Milledgeville and Asylum Dummy Line Railroad, ran down Wayne Street. Accounts have been given of the streetcar having earned a place in the Guinness Book of World Records for being the only one to stop for a traffic light, but no documentation can be found to confirm the stories. (Courtesy of Bo Edmonds.)

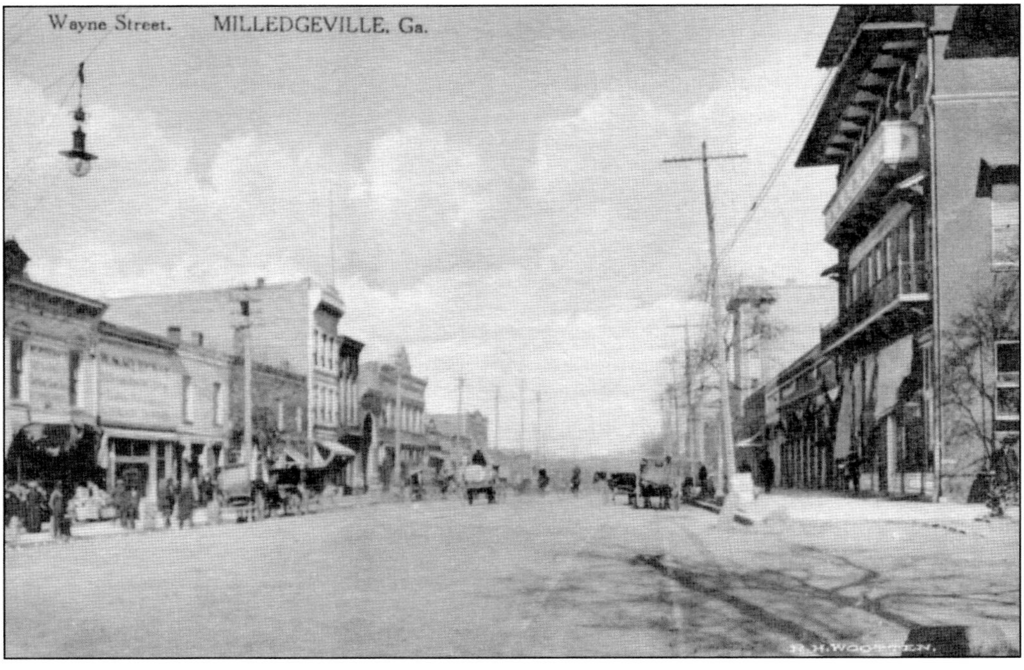

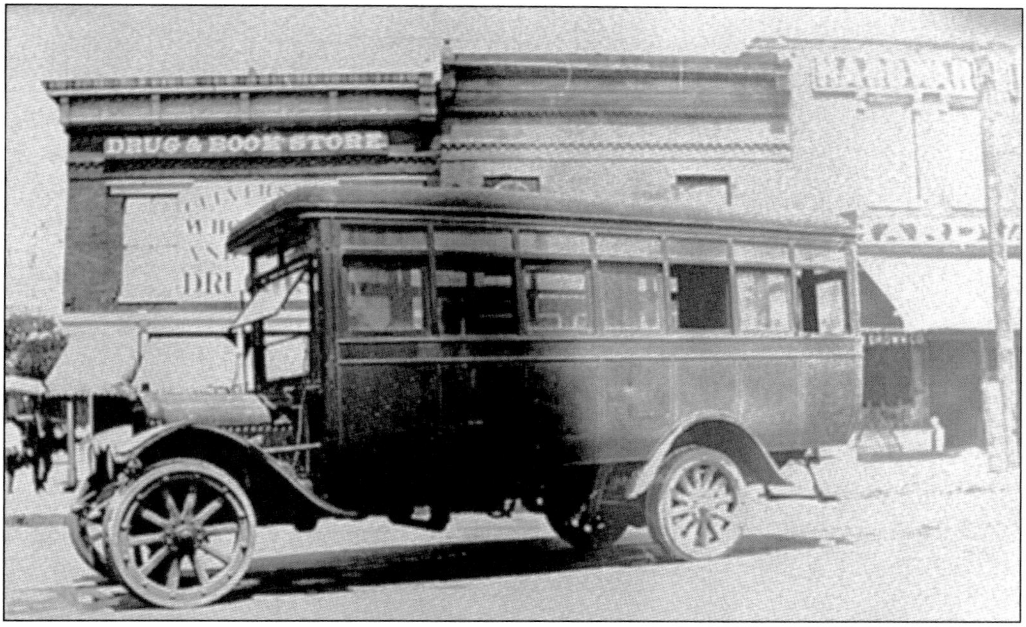

A school bus is parked in front of Culver and Kidd Drugstore on South Wayne Street in the 1920s. In the right background is Brown's Hardware. This bus has a rear entryway like older kid hacks, which were horse-drawn carriages that transported children to school. The rear door prevented startling the horses with the loading and unloading of passengers. (Courtesy of the Georgia Archives, Vanishing Georgia, bal-145.)

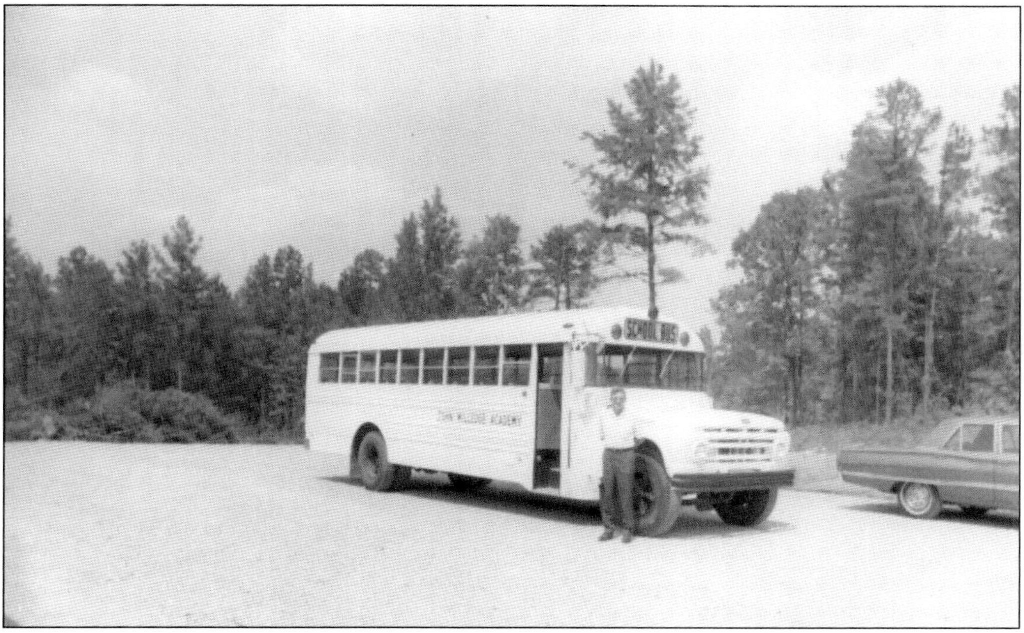

As buses waned as the public transportation of choice, there was still a small group of consistent travelers who preferred bus transport because of its affordability. For some passengers, air travel was not desirable. As shown here in the 1970s, buses have remained the most viable option for schools transporting students for daily education as well as for special events. (Courtesy of John Milledge Academy.)

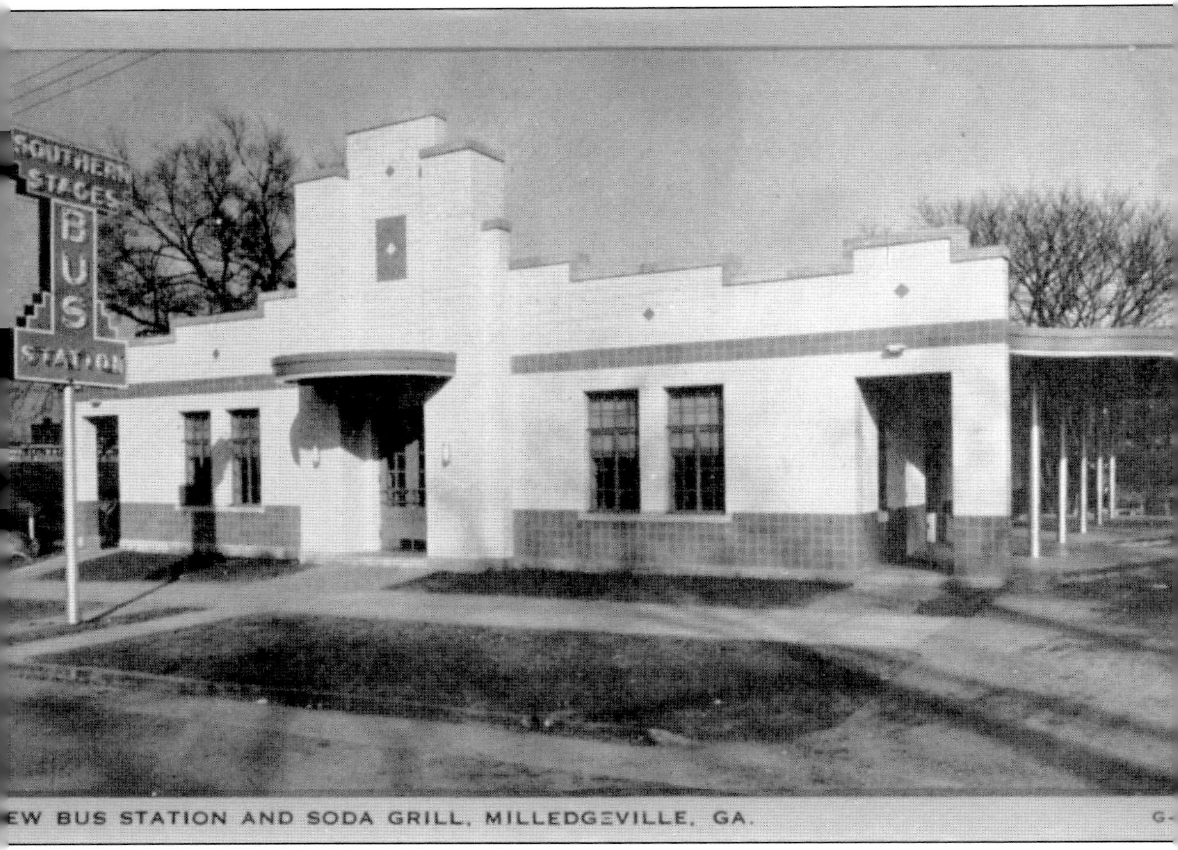

The bus station and Soda Grill was located at the corner of Wilkinson and McIntosh Streets in Milledgeville. Because of buses being the cheapest and relatively slowest form of transportation, bus travel, in the past, became generally associated with the poor, minorities, women, elderly, and young. Passenger travel by bus peaked during the World War II era, but it steadily declined in the decades after, as unemployment caused ticket sales to decline with the inability of people to afford travel. In the 1960s, airplanes offered a faster, more comfortable option for travelers. (Courtesy of Bo Edmonds.)

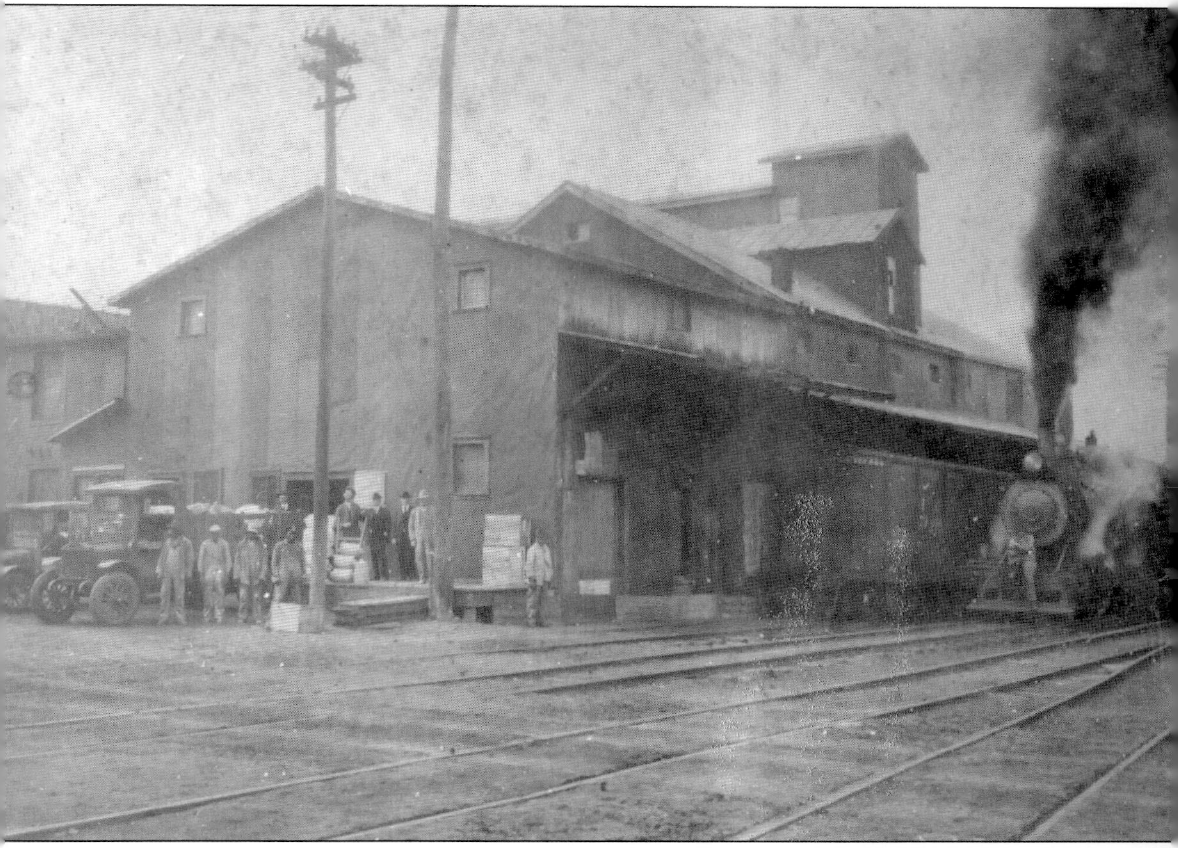

This photograph, taken between 1910 and 1920, shows Whitfield Warehouse, a well-known wholesale grocery business, which was located on North Wayne Street. The business was an establishment for the shipping and receiving of goods using the railroad system. The men standing beside the cars are most likely waiting to handle a shipment, while the men standing on the platform oversee operations.

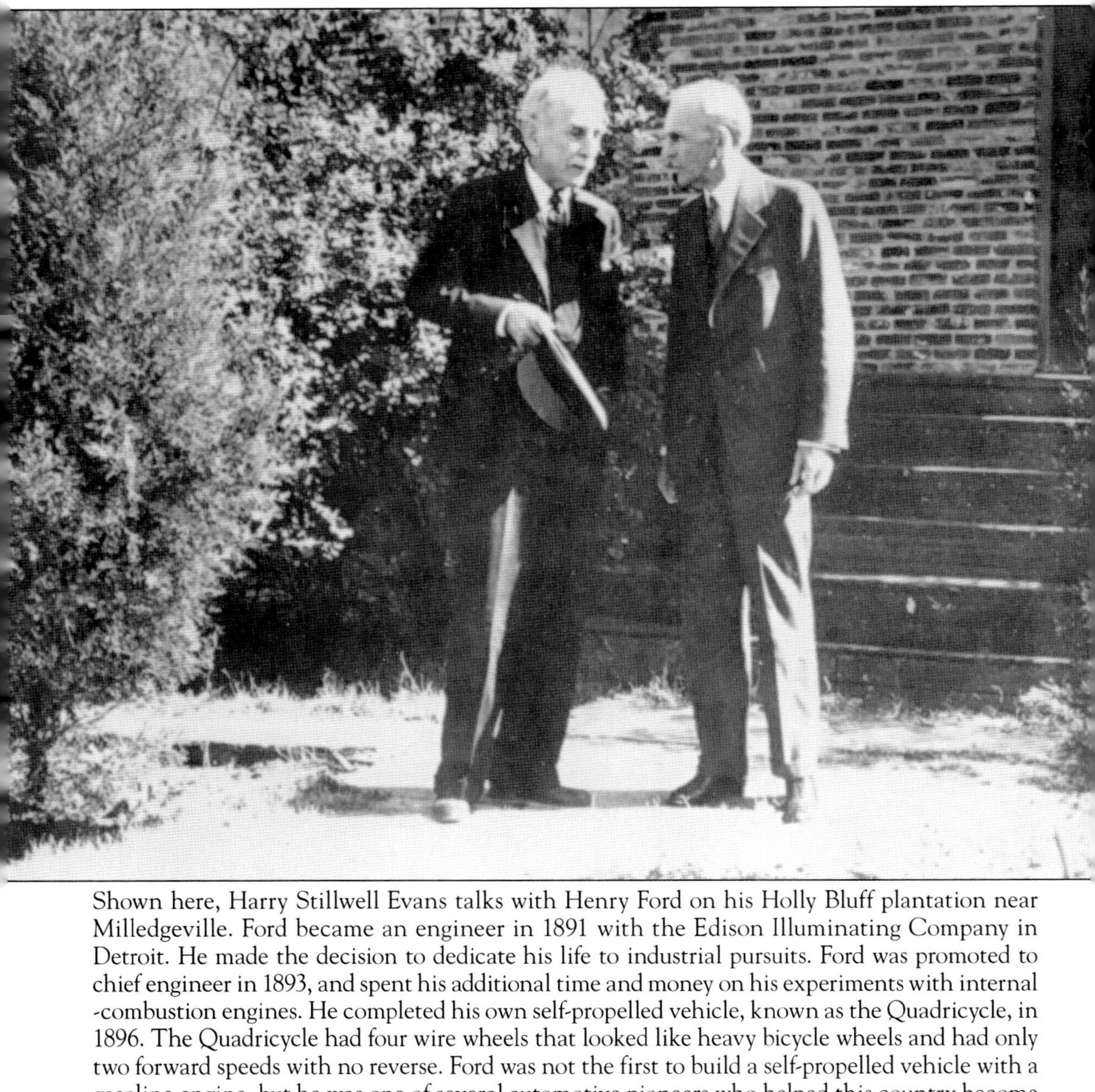

Shown here, Harry Stillwell Evans talks with Henry Ford on his Holly Bluff plantation near Milledgeville. Ford became an engineer in 1891 with the Edison Illuminating Company in Detroit. He made the decision to dedicate his life to industrial pursuits. Ford was promoted to chief engineer in 1893, and spent his additional time and money on his experiments with internal -combustion engines. He completed his own self-propelled vehicle, known as the Quadricycle, in 1896. The Quadricycle had four wire wheels that looked like heavy bicycle wheels and had only two forward speeds with no reverse. Ford was not the first to build a self-propelled vehicle with a gasoline engine, but he was one of several automotive pioneers who helped this country become a nation of motorists. (Courtesy of the Georgia Archives, Vanishing Georgia, bib-182.)

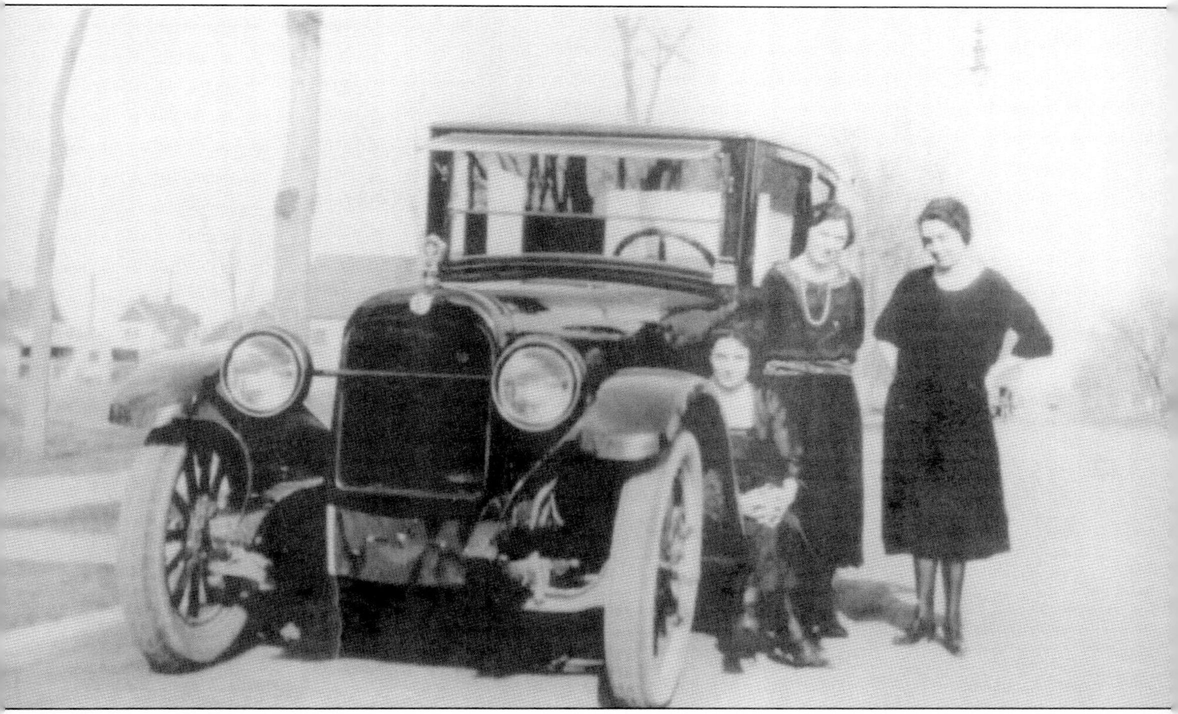

The changes allowing people more freedom to travel also changed the way people perceived their environment, how they utilized the land on which they lived and worked, and how they developed both personal and business relationships. In this image taken in the 1920s, Charles Smith's Aunt Marnie, of Milledgeville, is seen here with two of her friends. With the advent of electric-start automobiles (instead of crank engines), women became less reliant on men and more mobile.

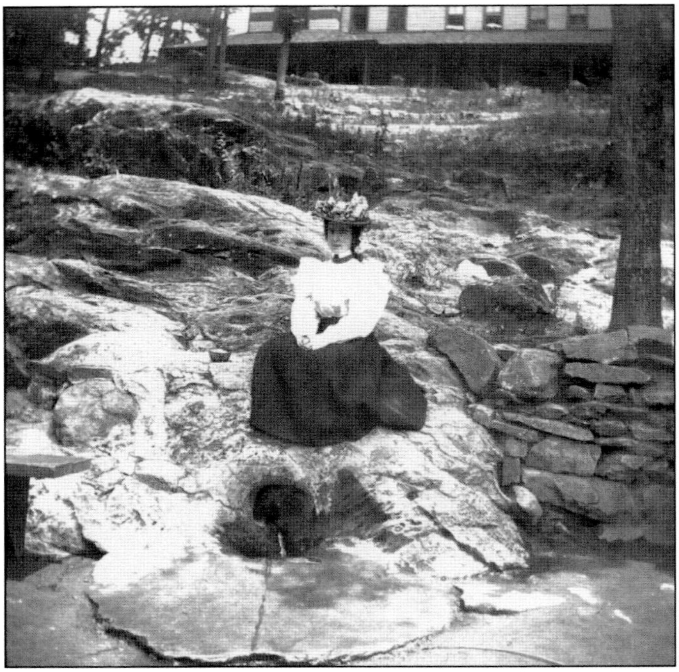

This young woman, seen here around 1910, is photographed with one of the many natural springs in Milledgeville. The numerous springs were a deciding factor in developing a city at this site. Although most are not accessible, several of the springs in Milledgeville have been identified and marked.

Seen in the Old Town Creek, also called Fishing Creek, in Milledgeville in the early 1900s, the object floating in the water has not been positively identified. It could be a type of pole boat or hand-pulled barge.

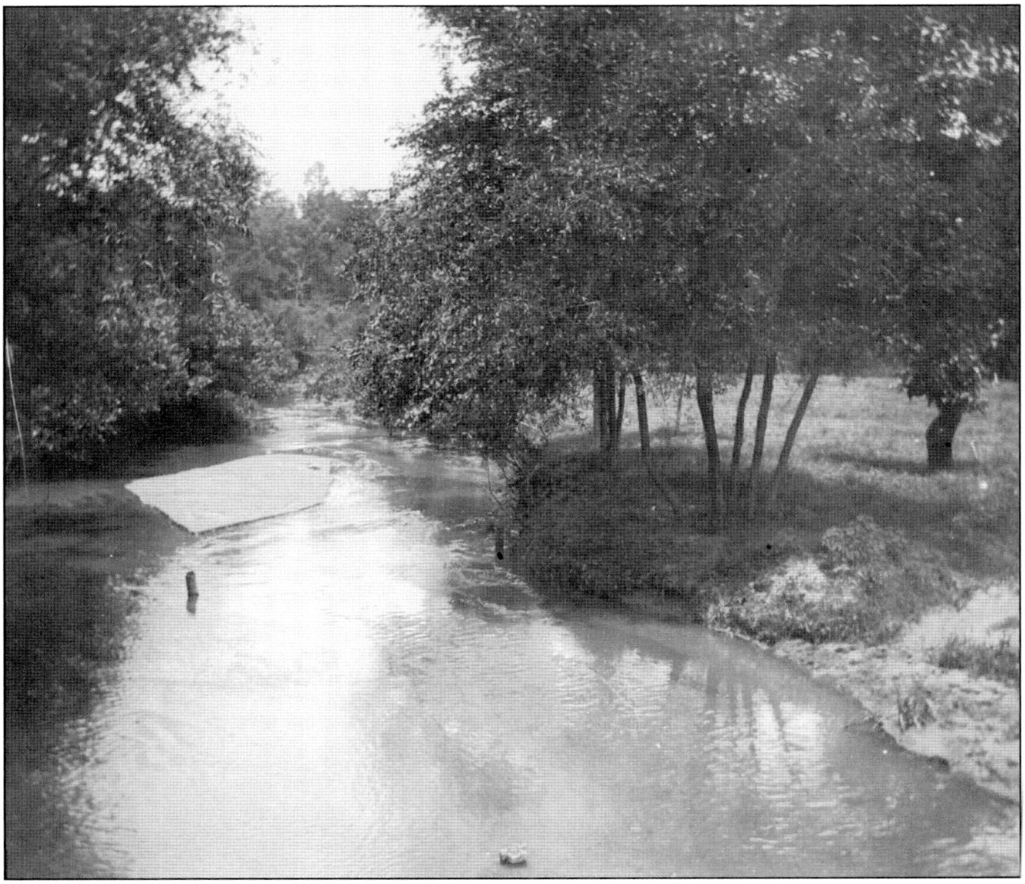

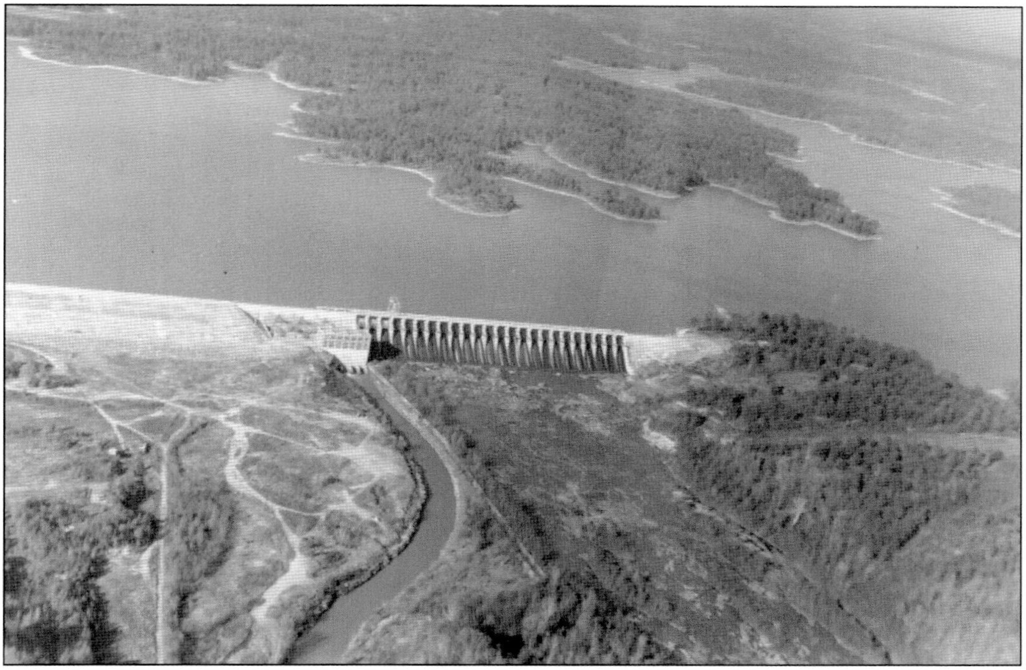

In the 1950s, Georgia Power at Furman Shoals constructed a dam, creating a reservoir called Lake Sinclair. Electricity is generated by water at Sinclair Dam, and Georgia Power pulls water from the lake to serve as a coolant in their condensers. Local economy and society were both impacted by activity in and around the lake. (Courtesy of Georgia Power.)

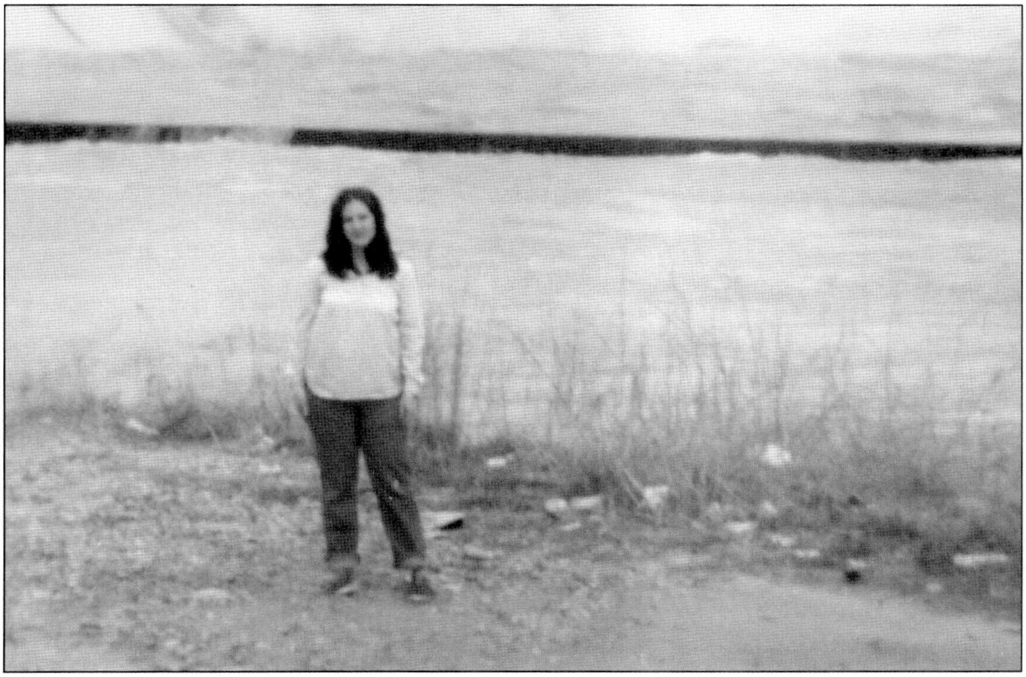

Milledgeville resident MaryLou Hauser is seen in the early 1970s with the open floodgates of the dam in the background. All of the floodgates were opened after a year of record-high water levels, which was a rare event. (Courtesy of MaryLou Hauser.)

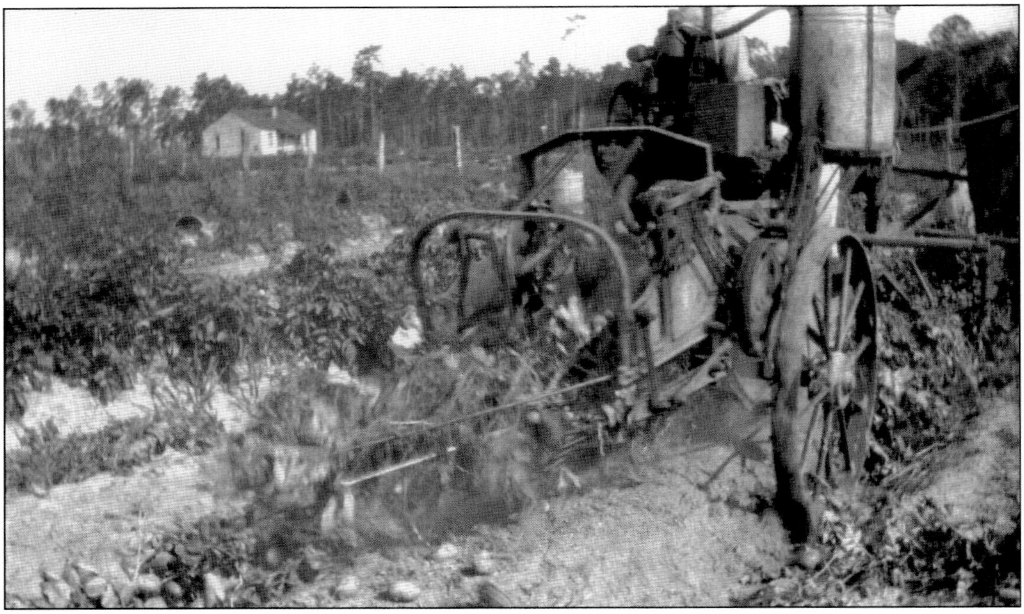

These farmers, photographed in the 1910s in Milledgeville, are using the Irish method of planting, harvesting, and preserving potatoes. When the potatoes were dug, they would have immediately been picked up and piled in a pyramidal form, with straw and soil placed over them. The straw and soil prevented air and sunshine from reaching the potato tubers. In Georgia, as well as other Southern states, the method was used for the farmer to get two harvests of potatoes, sustaining the family's need for the year.

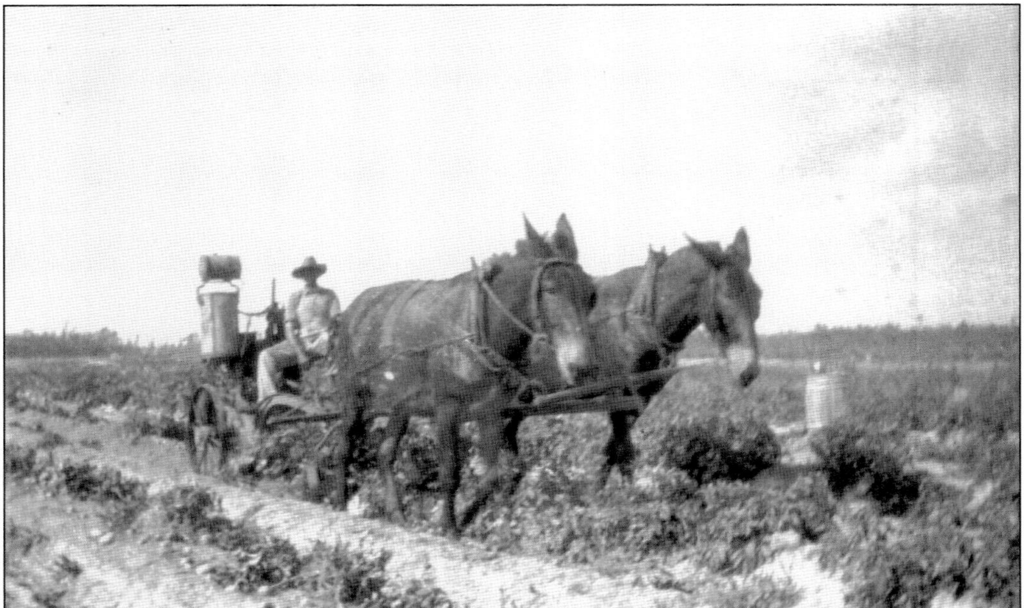

Two unidentified men are shown sitting inside Joseph Staley's Hardware, Cutlery and House Furnishing Goods. This store was located on Wayne Street in downtown Milledgeville in the early 1900s. New Jewel gasoline stoves and ranges, kettles, serving ware of various types, crystal, and many other household goods from the time period are shown. Three important factors that set the stage for industrialization were the expansion of transportation, increased efficiency of harnessing electricity, and improving the process of refining and producing products such as those shown in these photographs.

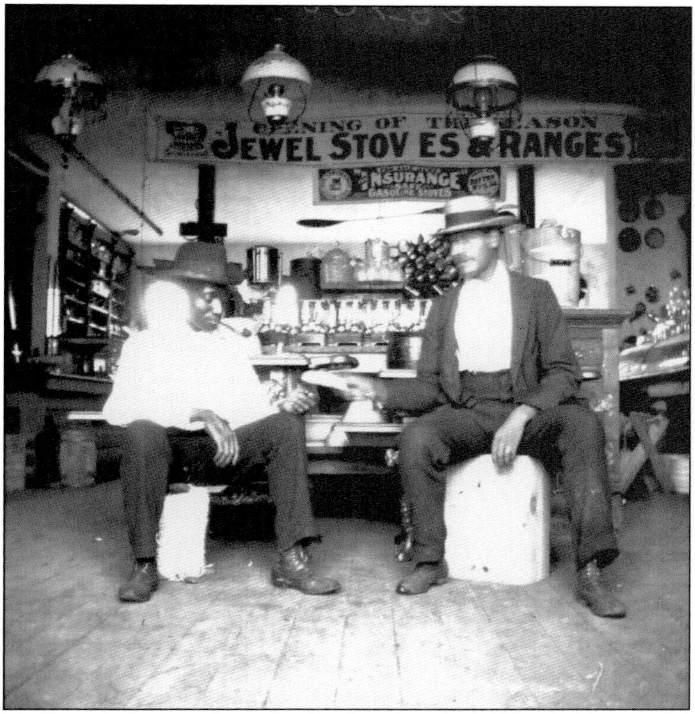

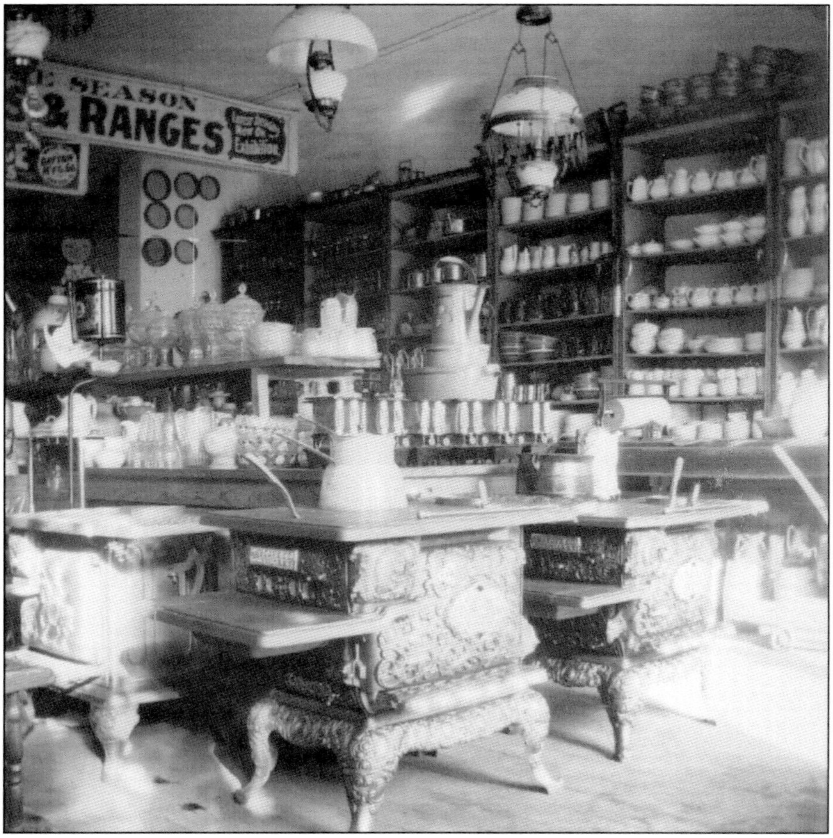

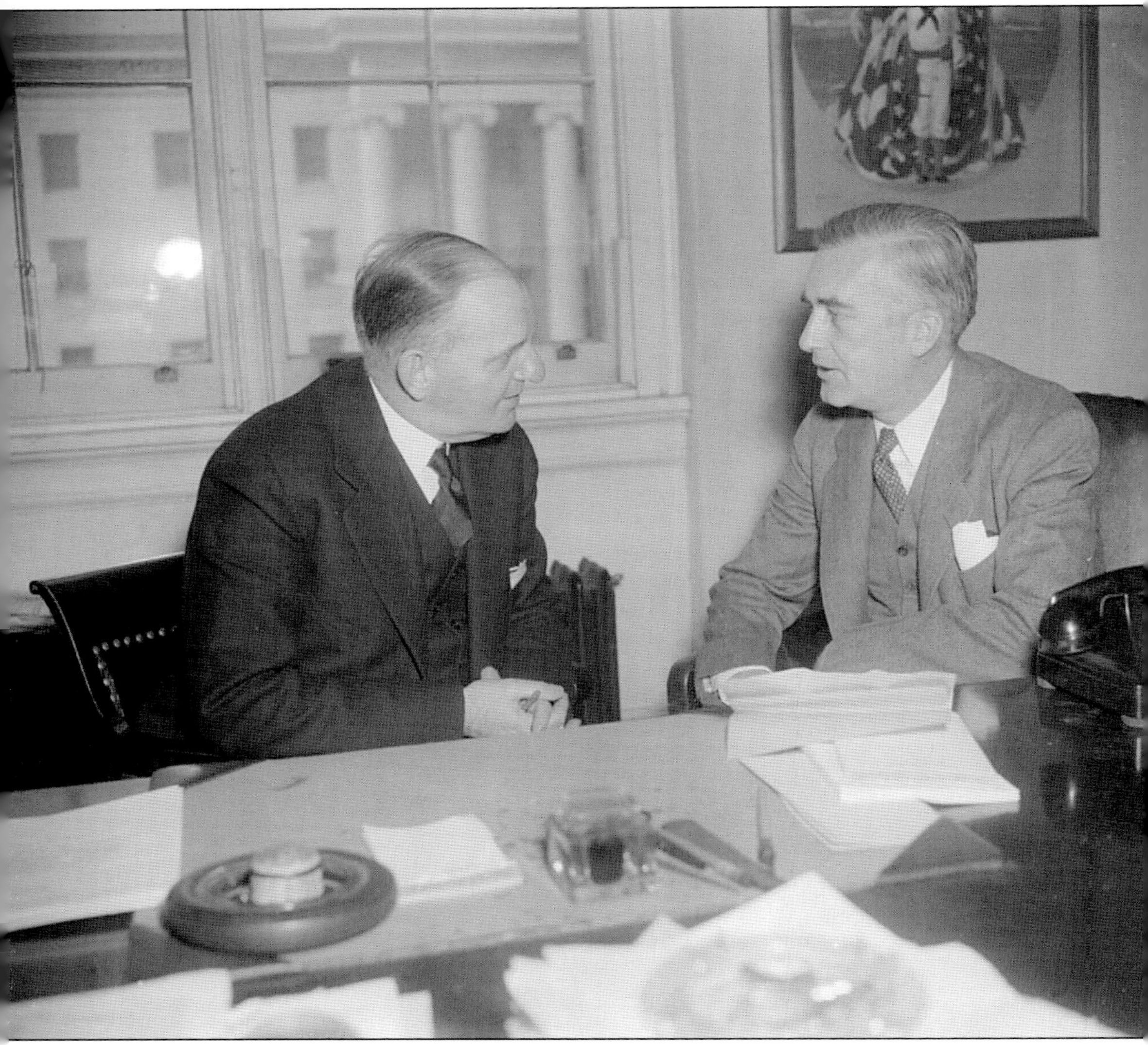

Carl Vinson (left) was born in Milledgeville on November 8, 1883. He was, in the words of Pres. Richard Nixon, "a legendary figure to those who did not know him, and one who is a loved figure for those like me who have had the privilege of knowing him." At the age of 31, Vinson was the youngest member to serve in Congress. He served for a total of 26 terms in the House of Representatives. His interest in national defense and military power on the sea earned him a seat on the House Naval Affairs Committee. During his first nine years on the committee, the House defeated only one bill he sponsored. Vinson retired in 1965, after spending 59 consecutive years in public service. (Courtesy of the United States Navy, Naval History & Heritage Command.)

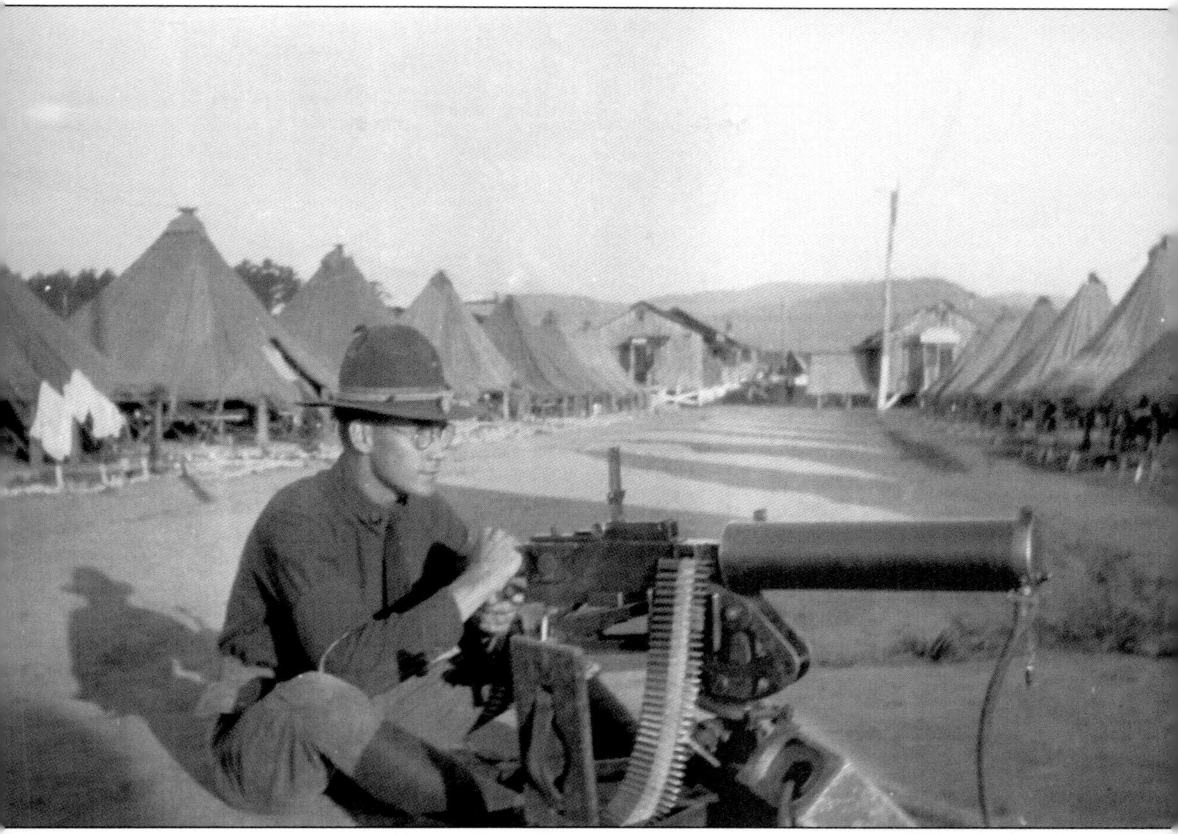

Charles Williams, who was a Milledgeville resident, is shown with a Browning M1917 machine gun that was used in World War II. The barrel of the gun was water-cooled and the ammunition belt fed left-to-right. It was capable of firing about seven rounds a second. During initial demonstrations, John Browning test fired the gun continuously for 48 minutes before it stopped due to a broken firing pin, which was still considered a success to the Army. This photograph was taken in the early 1900s, but it is unknown where this camp was located.

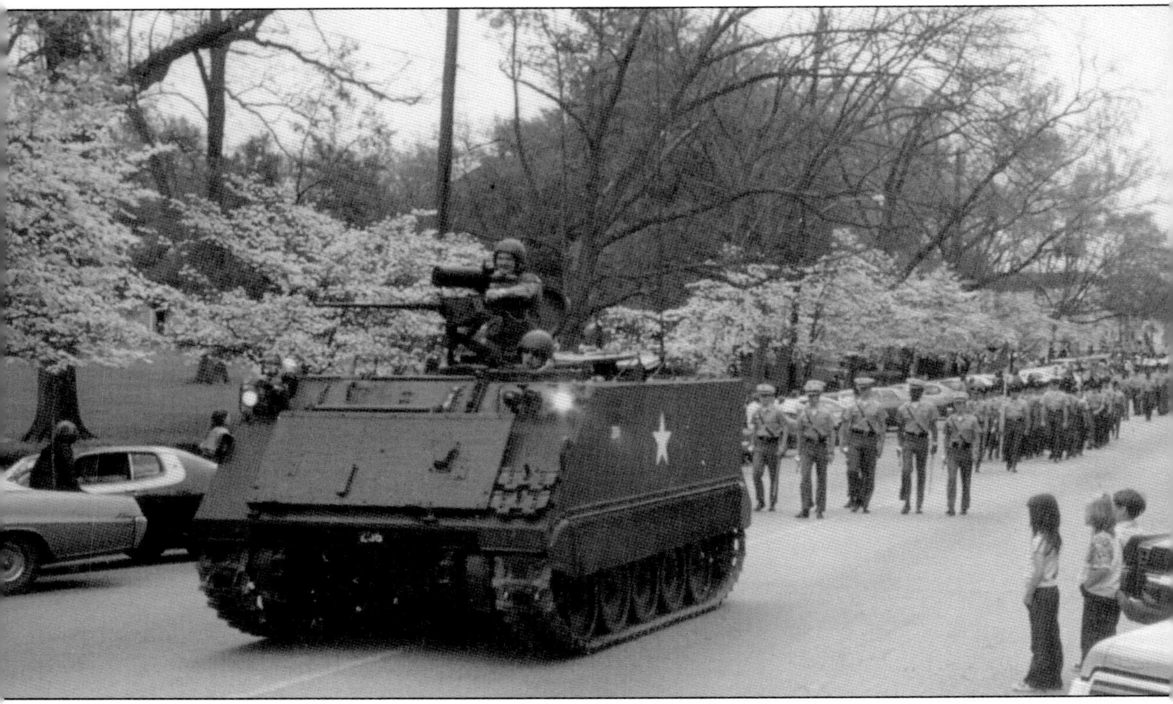

In this photograph taken in the late 1960s, a tank is shown in a Milledgeville parade. The use of the tank began in World War I, when it was deployed in response to the use of trench warfare. The tank's utilization began an era of mechanized warfare. Tanks eventually became predominant in ground wars, and by World War II, tank design had been significantly improved. The Cold War precipitated modern tank use and the general-purpose main battle tank. In the 21st century, the tank is the backbone of land-combat operations. (Courtesy of Barbara and Buddy Martin.)

Six

An Evolving Society

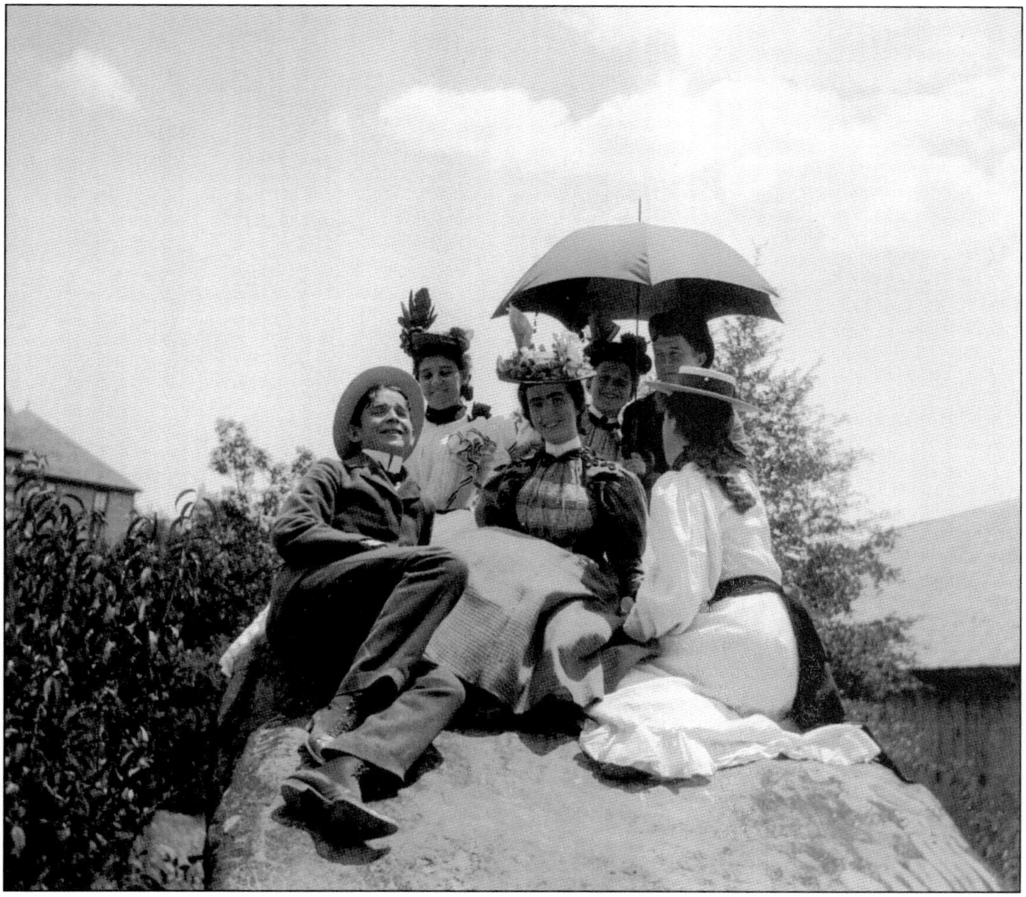

This photograph represents the Victorian attitude about the process of dating, in practice from the mid-1800s to the early 1900s. Etiquette, respectability, and manners were of primary importance. A gentleman had set rules he was expected to follow for receiving a favorable response from a proper young lady. There was a process of calling on a young lady followed by a formal visit, typically at her house under the supervision of her parents. These unidentified Milledgeville youths are pictured on an outing around 1910.

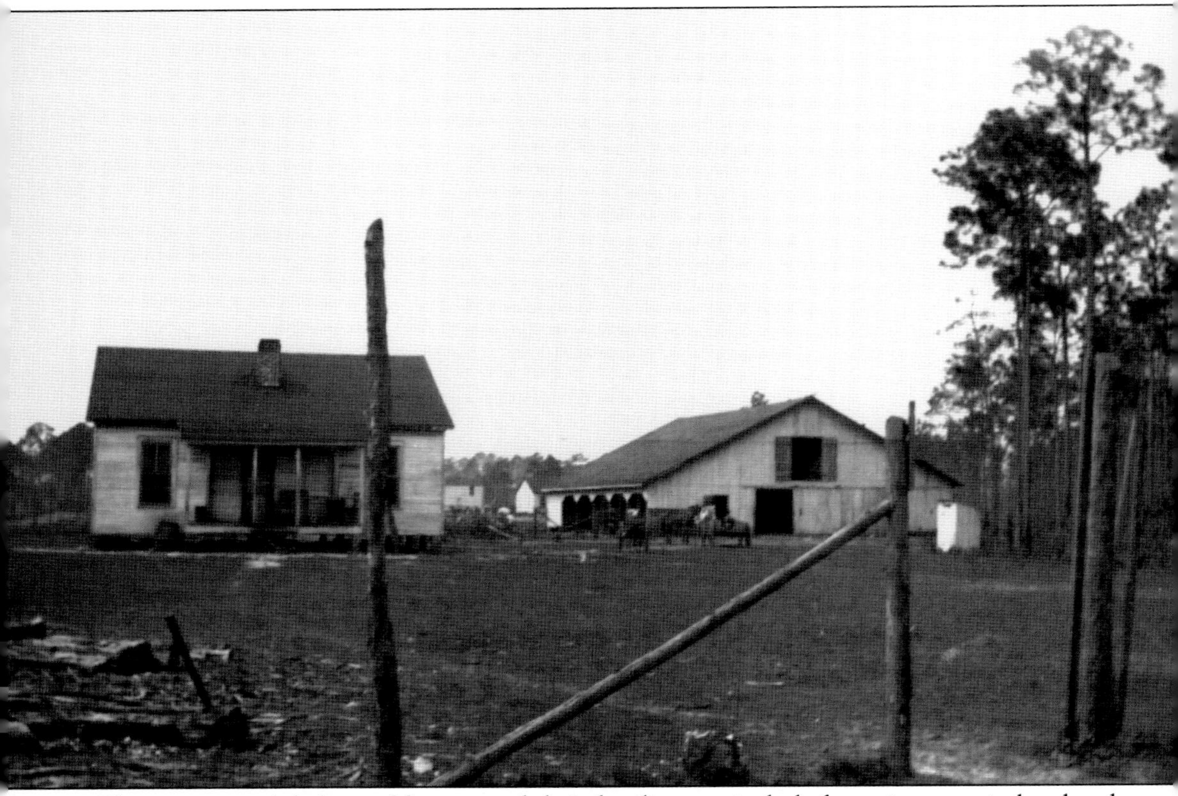

The pre-automobile lives of farmers and their families, particularly farmwives, was isolated and lacked regular social interaction. In 1928, some 70 percent of farming families lived more than five miles from the nearest town—as reported by the *Yearbook of Agriculture*, and as shown in this photograph of an unidentified farming family in Milledgeville in the early 20th century.

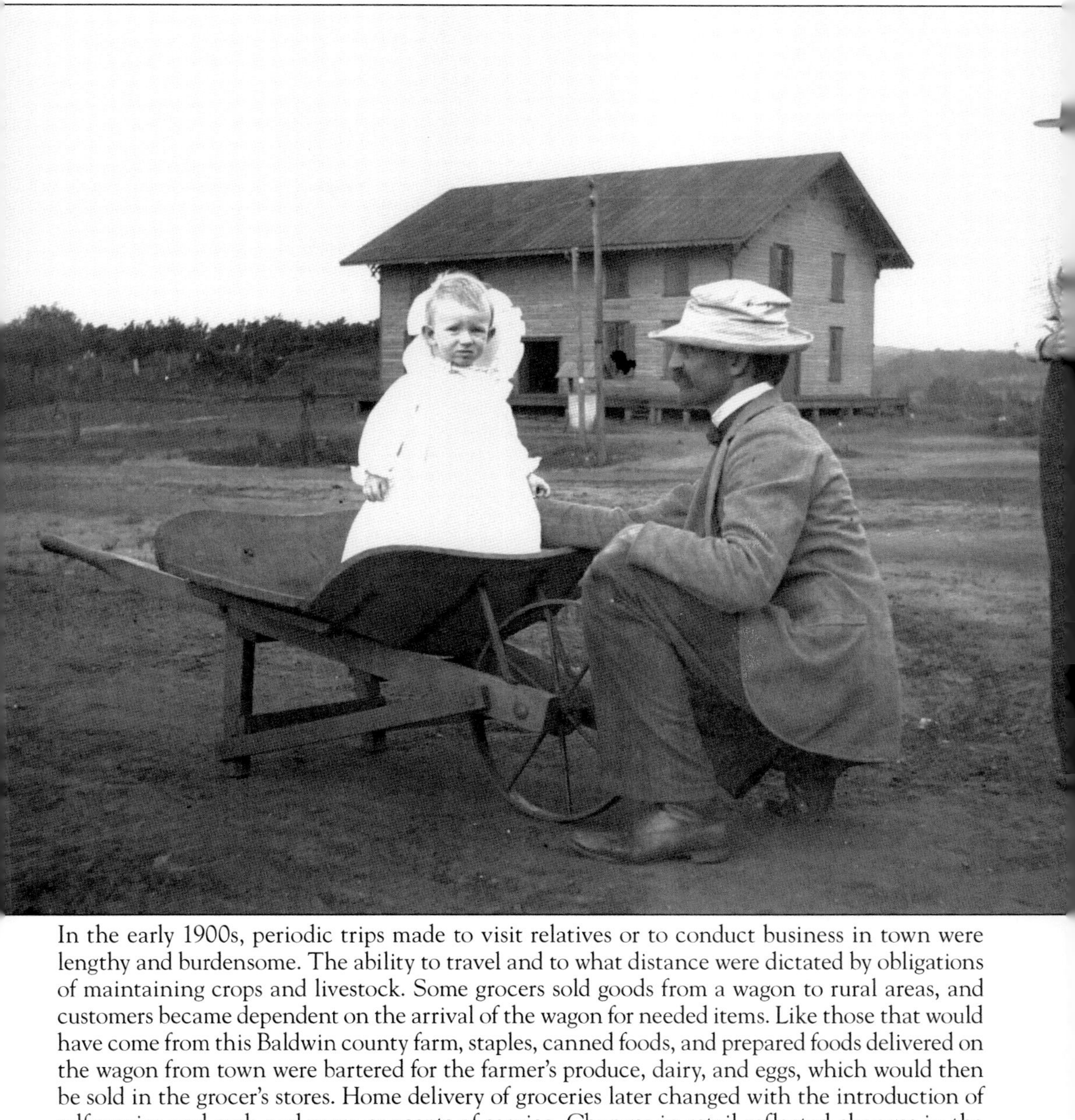

In the early 1900s, periodic trips made to visit relatives or to conduct business in town were lengthy and burdensome. The ability to travel and to what distance were dictated by obligations of maintaining crops and livestock. Some grocers sold goods from a wagon to rural areas, and customers became dependent on the arrival of the wagon for needed items. Like those that would have come from this Baldwin county farm, staples, canned foods, and prepared foods delivered on the wagon from town were bartered for the farmer's produce, dairy, and eggs, which would then be sold in the grocer's stores. Home delivery of groceries later changed with the introduction of self-service and cash-and-carry concepts of service. Changes in retail reflected changes in the economy, moving away from lines of credit, or putting it on the books when the finances of many families were failing.

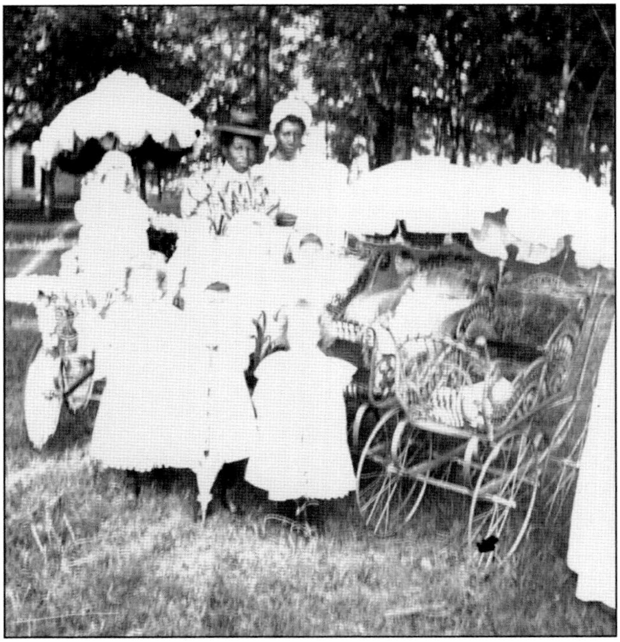

In this c. 1900s photograph, two mammies in Milledgeville stand with the children for whom they care. The role of mammies in the South can provoke mixed feelings and ideas associated with the stereotype. Through the years, black women fed and raised many white children, and they served as an intermediaries between blacks and whites. These women were loved and highly regarded by the families they served—especially the children, for whom they were primary caregivers. Author Lewis Blair writes that he remembers "up to the age of 10 [I] saw as much, perhaps more, of the mammy than of the mother."

This photograph of two women and a baby was taken in Milledgeville around 1908. It would have been common during the time period for multiple generations to live in the same household, helping share in work and raising children. Siblings often lived in the same town, close to each other and family. The family structure changed as automobiles became more affordable and use increased beginning around the 1910s. Greater mobility expanded the pool of potential relationship partners to include those farther away from the family household, and it created the opportunity for adult children to settle father away.

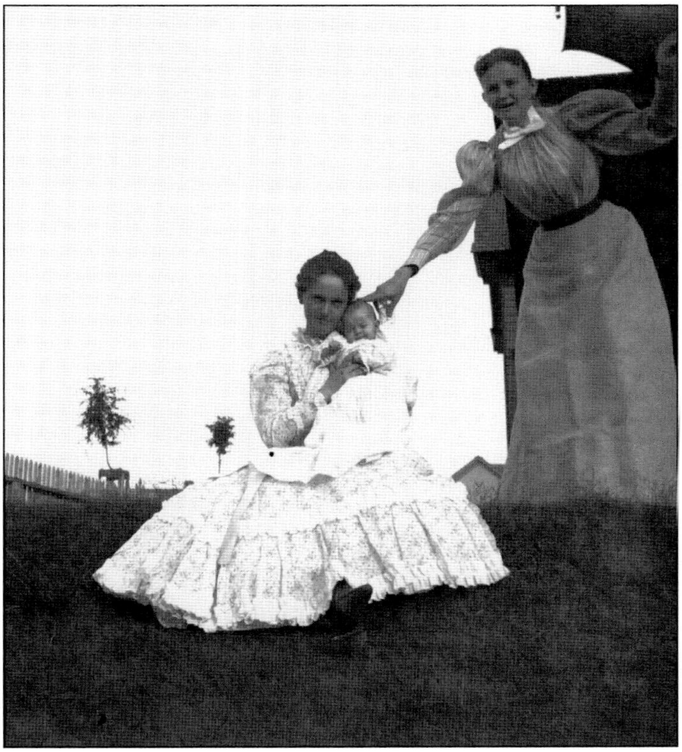

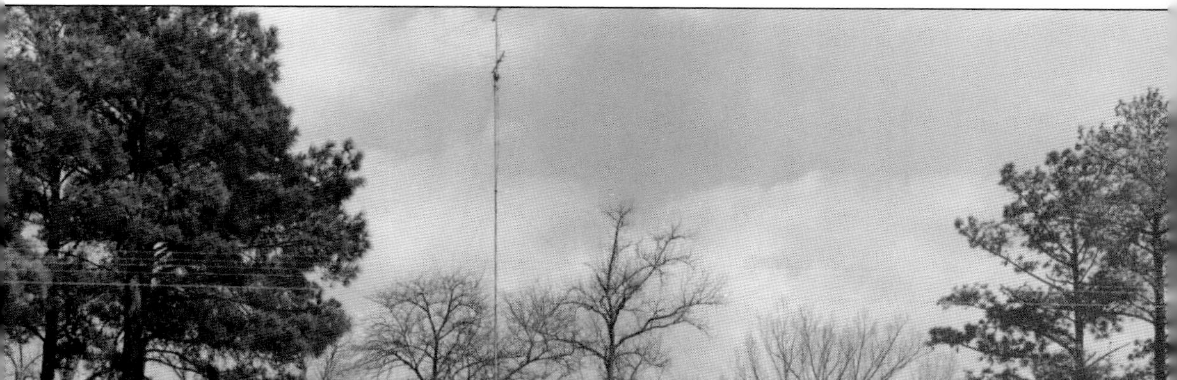

Photographed here in the mid-1900s, Pat's Place was a restaurant owned by Phyllis and Lewis Patrick that served patrons of all races, but it was segregated, as was common to public areas at the time. In the 1890s, Jim Crow laws were enacted in Georgia to segregate public facilities, services, and transportation. The laws were so named for a minstrel character popular in the 1820s and 1830s. Although the United States Supreme Court ruled that "separate educational facilities are inherently unequal" in the case of Brown v. the Board of Education in 1954, the ruling did not abolish segregation in other public areas. Execution of the ruling was also stalled by several states due to the court's vague time line definition of "all deliberate speed." Additional social and legal obstacles enacted by some states to thwart desegregation were the catalysts launching the civil rights movement. (Courtesy of Cynthia Chipman.)

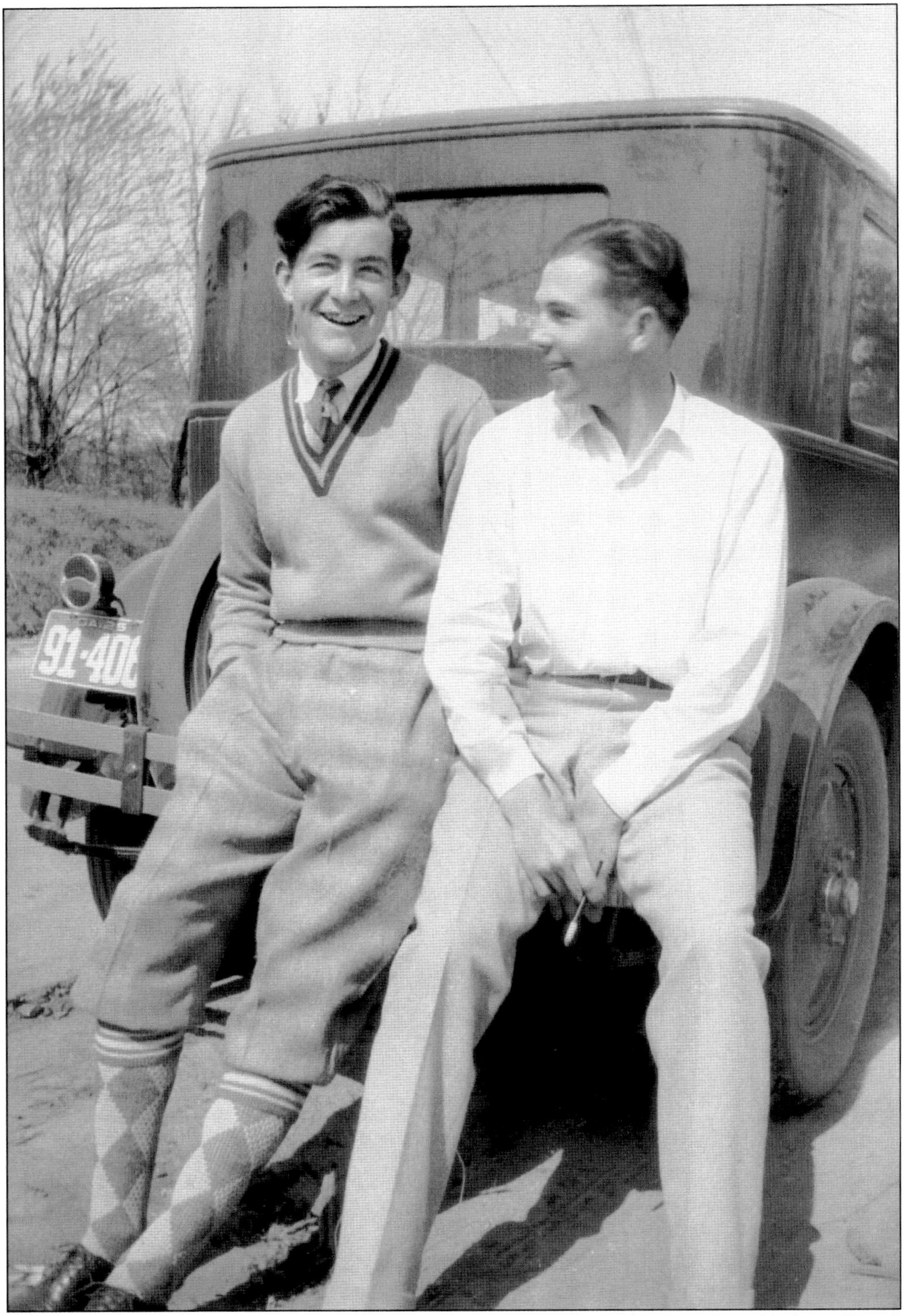

By the time these two young men were photographed around 1925 in Milledgeville, the automobile had emerged after wartime and during the Prohibition era to become an expression of independence and defiance. Leisure activities gained popularity as people sought enjoyment when a lack of resources made life a daily struggle.

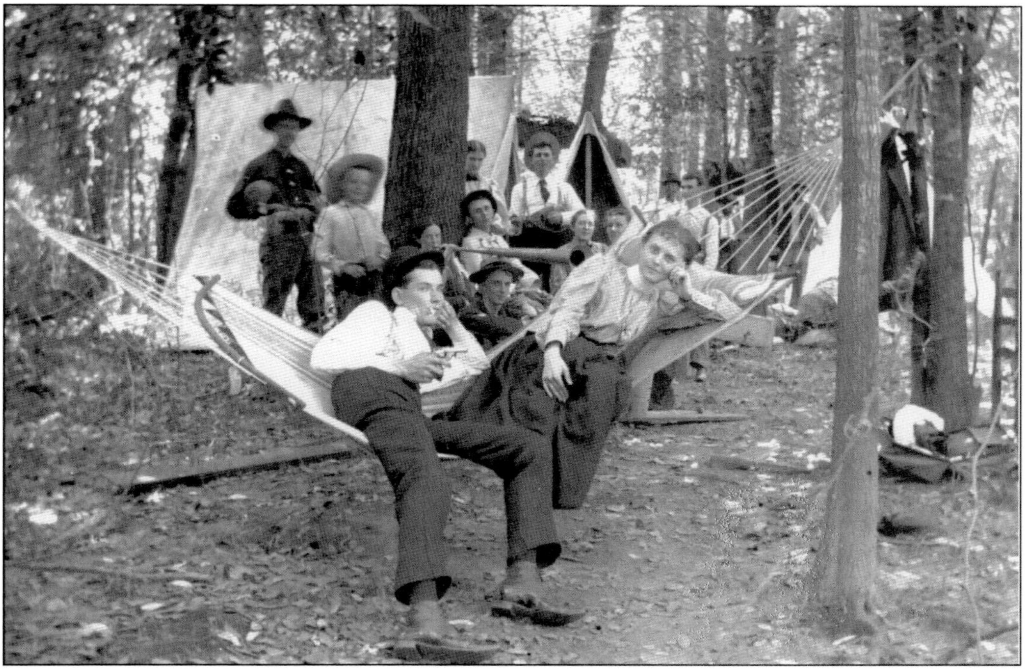

The early 1900s brought a change to America. The increasing popularity of automobiles increased the number of people traveling, and travelers needed places to stay. Motels did not yet exist, and it was common practice to camp for the night along the route being traveled.

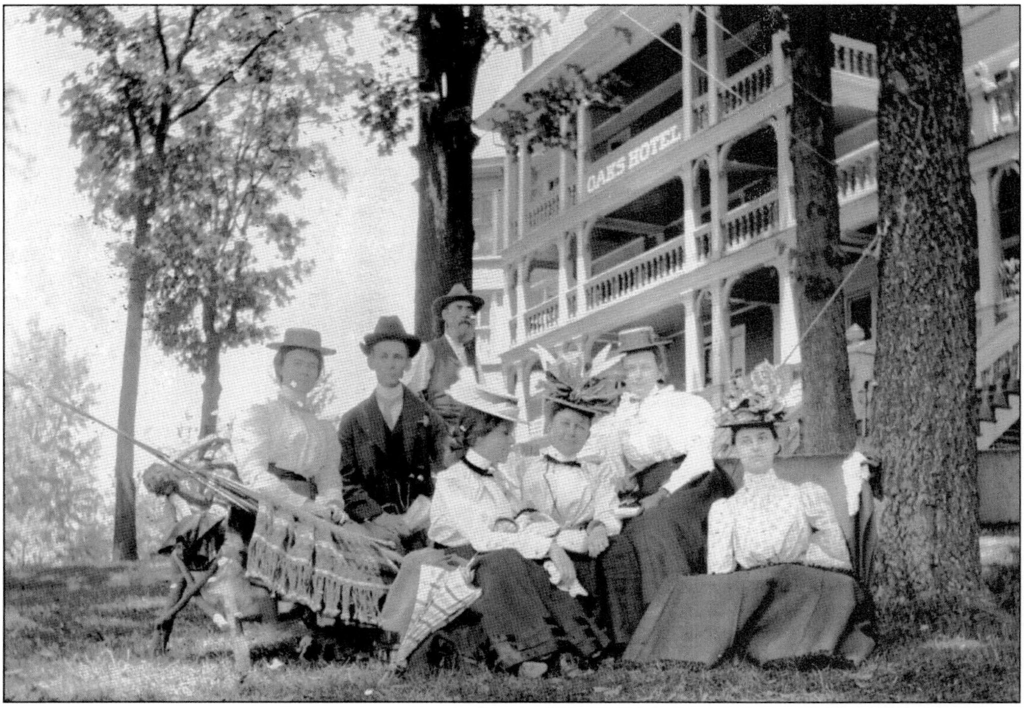

While staying at the Oaks Hotel, which can be seen in the background, this group of unidentified 1920s travelers from Milledgeville would come into contact with more diverse people, who were of varying populations and experiences.

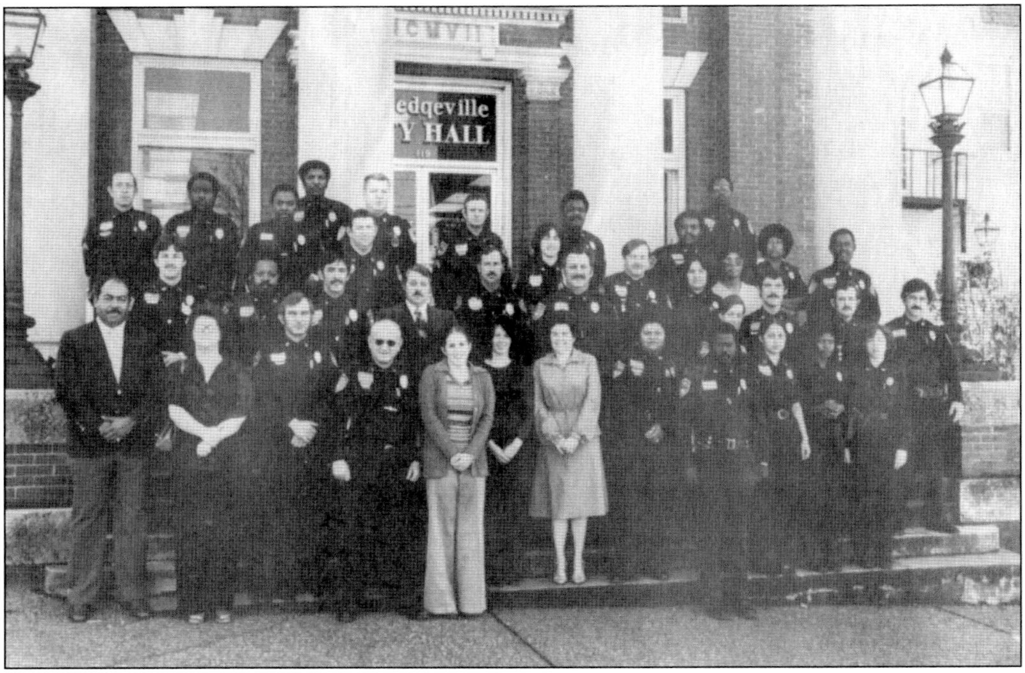

Pictured here are the officers of the Milledgeville Police Department in the late 1970s. They are standing in front of City Hall. Formerly located next to the city hall building, the police department was relocated to a new structure on West McIntosh Street. (Courtesy of Milledgeville Police Department.)

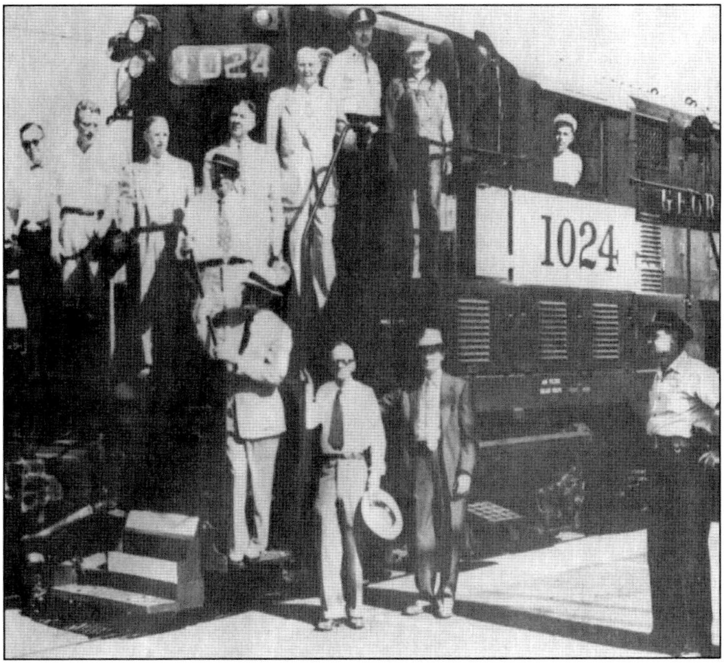

Milledgeville's city officials are shown here with the first diesel engine used by Georgia Railway in the late 1970s. Rail transportation for cargo, as well as people, was revolutionized by the development of the diesel engine. They were superior to and quickly replaced the steam engines. Diesel trains were easier to start, faster, cheaper to operate, and caused less pollution. (Courtesy of *The Union-Recorder.*)

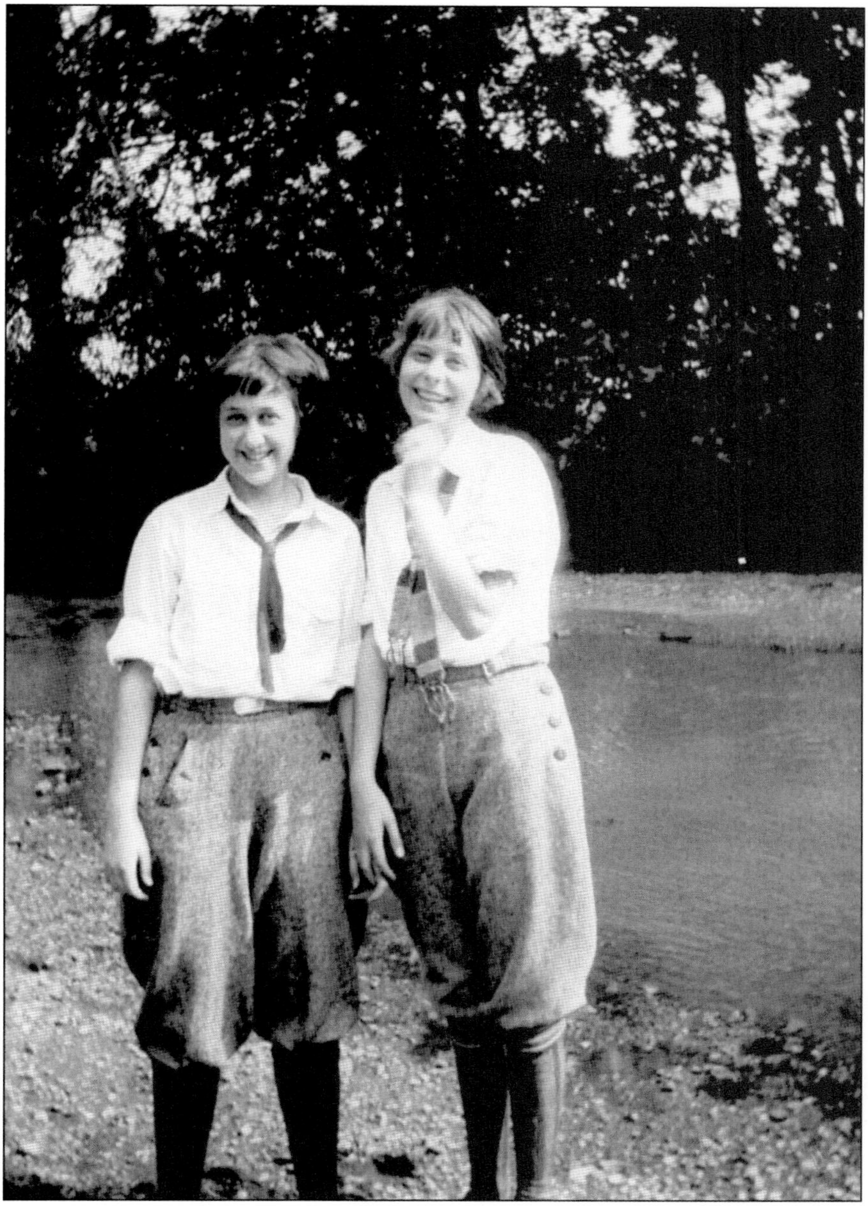

Unidentified Milledgeville women are shown in the 1930s. Leading up to societal changes in women's roles in the 1930s, the creation of the Gibson Girl in the 1890s began a long fascination with idealized types of feminine beauty in America. The era of the new woman in the 1910s saw increasing numbers of women pursue higher education, romance, marriage, and leisure activities with a sense of individuality and greater independence. In 1920, the 19th Amendment giving women the right to vote was ratified, and the League of Nations was established. The Equal Rights Amendment was introduced to Congress in 1923. The 1930s were years of fierce class struggle and great advances for the working class. From the beginning, women were deeply involved in these struggles. At that time, women made up 25 percent of the workforce, but their jobs were more unstable, temporary, or seasonal. There was also a decided bias and cultural view that women did not work, and, in fact, many who were employed full-time often called themselves homemakers. In the South, both black and white women were equally unemployed at 26 percent.

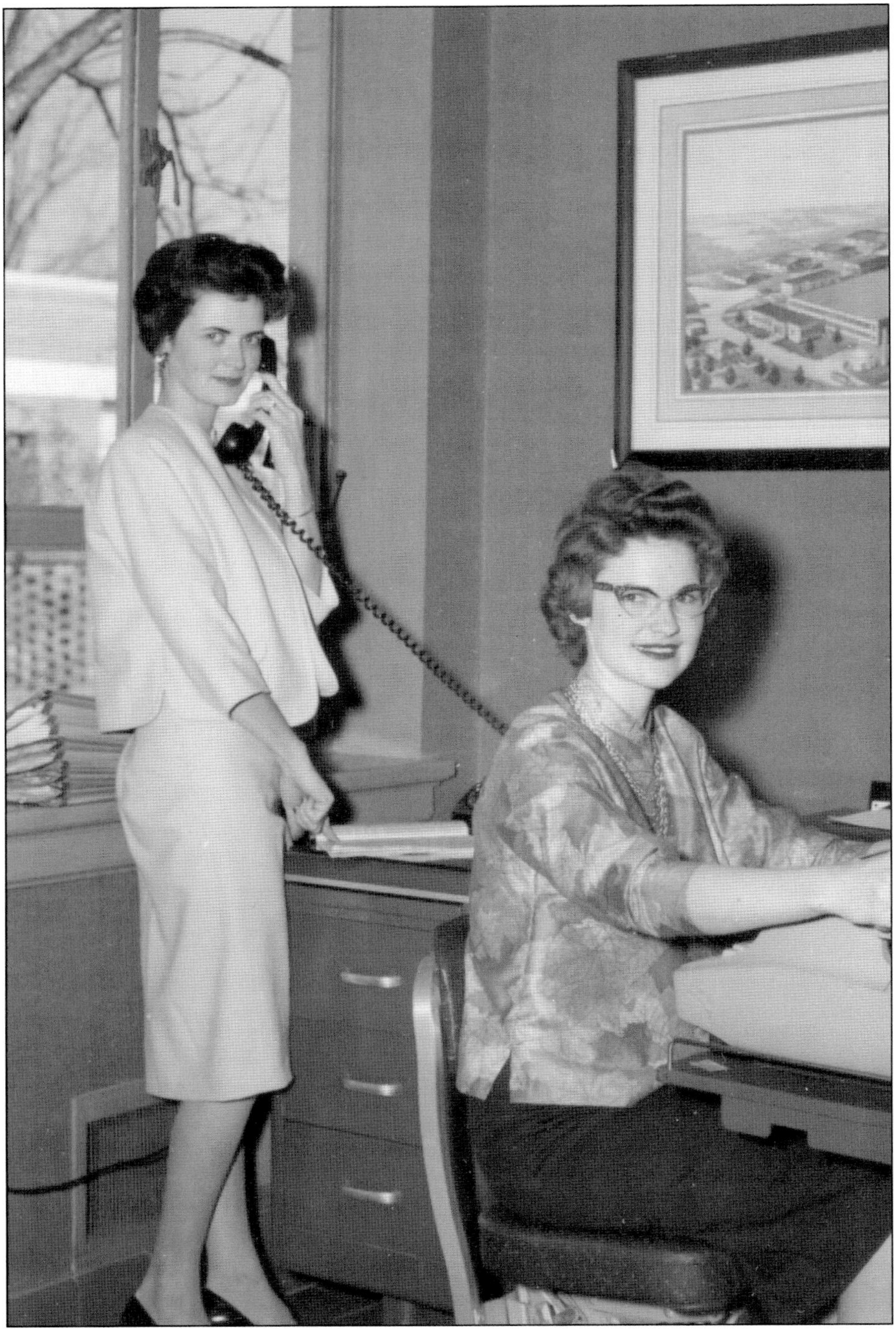

Prior to the 1960s, opportunities for women in the workforce were scarce, and it was not yet accepted by the majority of society for women to have careers outside the home. Jobs available to women were usually as librarians, secretaries, teachers, or in factories. Companies were still normally run by men, and a female boss would have been considered absurd. Photographed here are two women who worked office jobs at Oconee Clay Products in the 1950s. Seated is Barbara Martin, and standing is Patricia Brooks Ivey. (Courtesy of Barbara and Buddy Martin.)

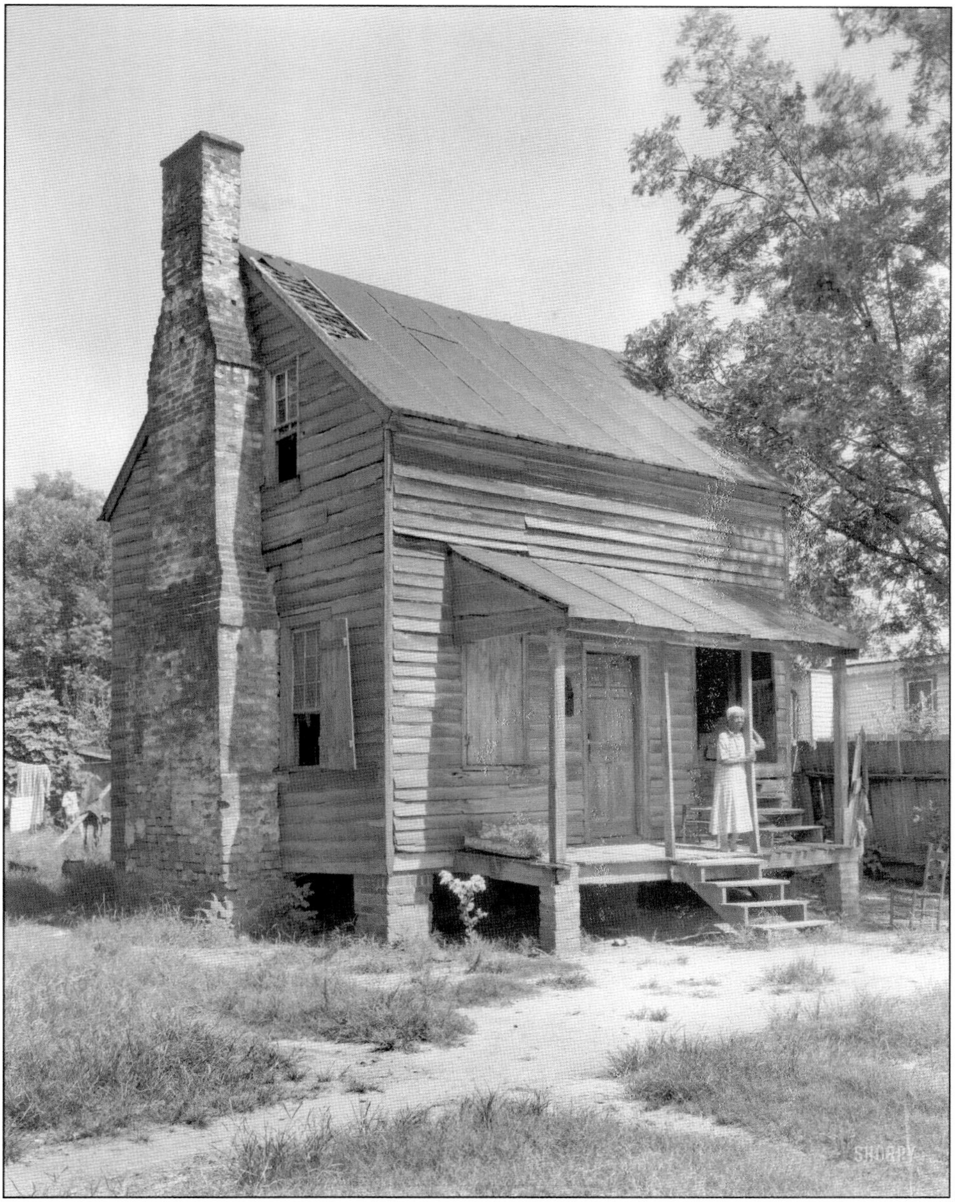

The woman in this photograph is former slave Aunt Carrie Mason. She was interviewed in July 1937 as part of the Federal Writers' Project, in which former slaves were subjects. In her account, Carrie recalls being one of 10 children, working from sun up until after dark, beds made of sacks stuffed with straw or cotton supported by rope on the bed frame, her mother using sand to scrub the floor, working in the fields, and cooking dinner for her master's family. Carrie said that her family never had land of their own and, at the time of the interview in 1937, she reported the land that she lived on belonged to a Mr. Cline. She was meeting her family's needs with the help of charity from Cline and from the Red Cross. (Courtesy of the Library of Congress, Carnegie Survey, LC-J7-GA-1439.)

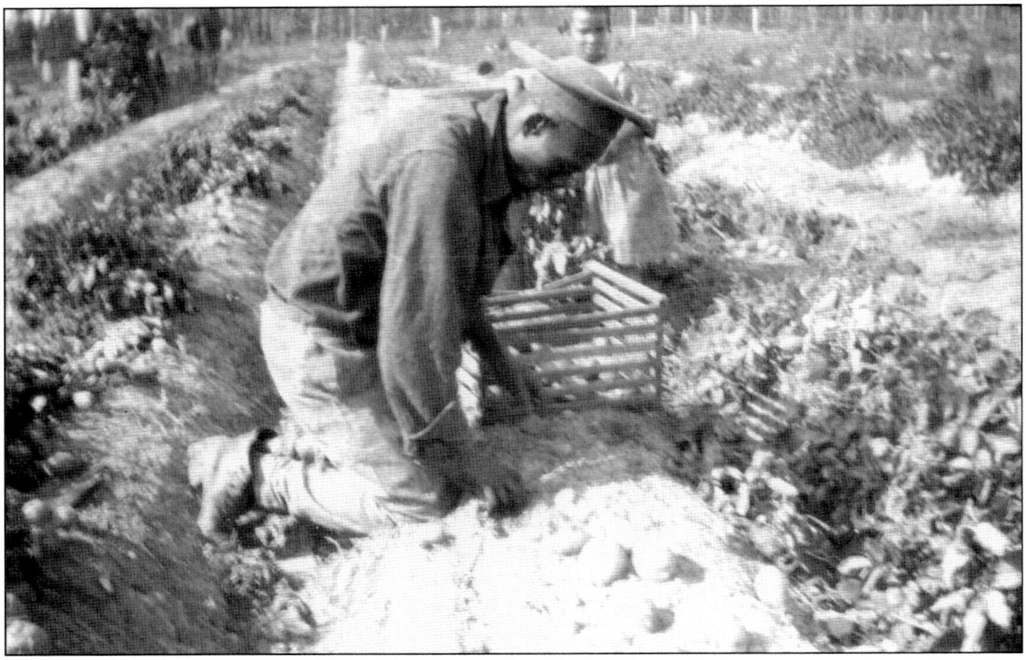

In this photograph taken in the early 1900s in Milledgeville, a man labors in the field with a young female at his side. These workers were most likely a family of sharecroppers. Sharecropping arose in the South for former slaves and poor whites striving to become self-sufficient. By 1910, about 37 percent of Georgia's farms were operated by sharecroppers in a system that proved to be unfair and did little or nothing to benefit those who worked the land.

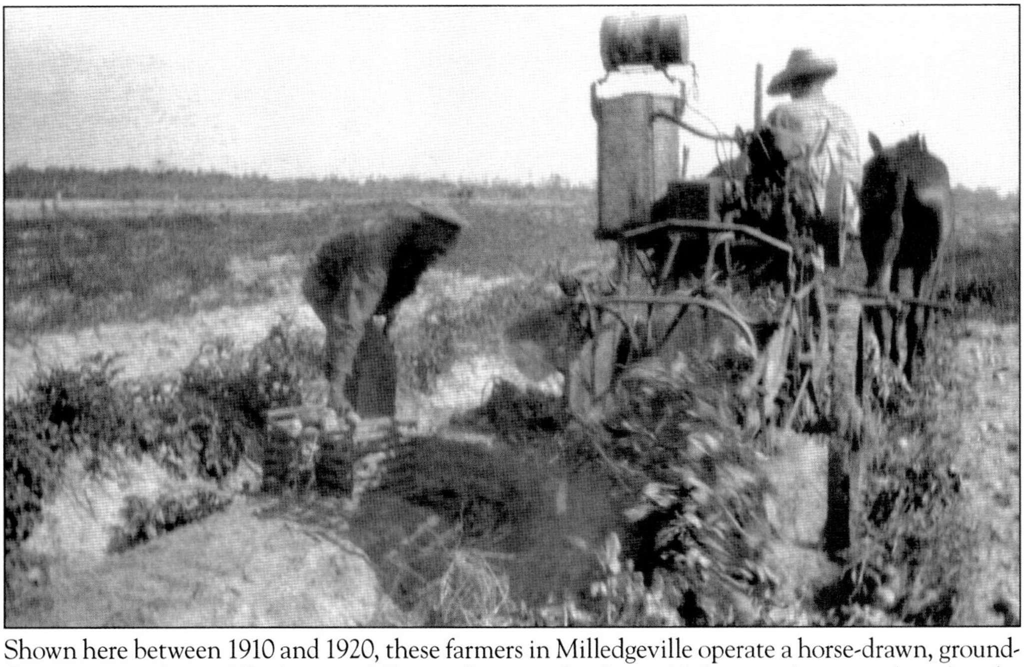

Shown here between 1910 and 1920, these farmers in Milledgeville operate a horse-drawn, ground-driven potato digger. The large paddles on the iron wheels would dig into the ground, and as the team pulled the digger down the row of potatoes, the paddles would turn the wheels that drove the belt lifting the potatoes out of the ground.

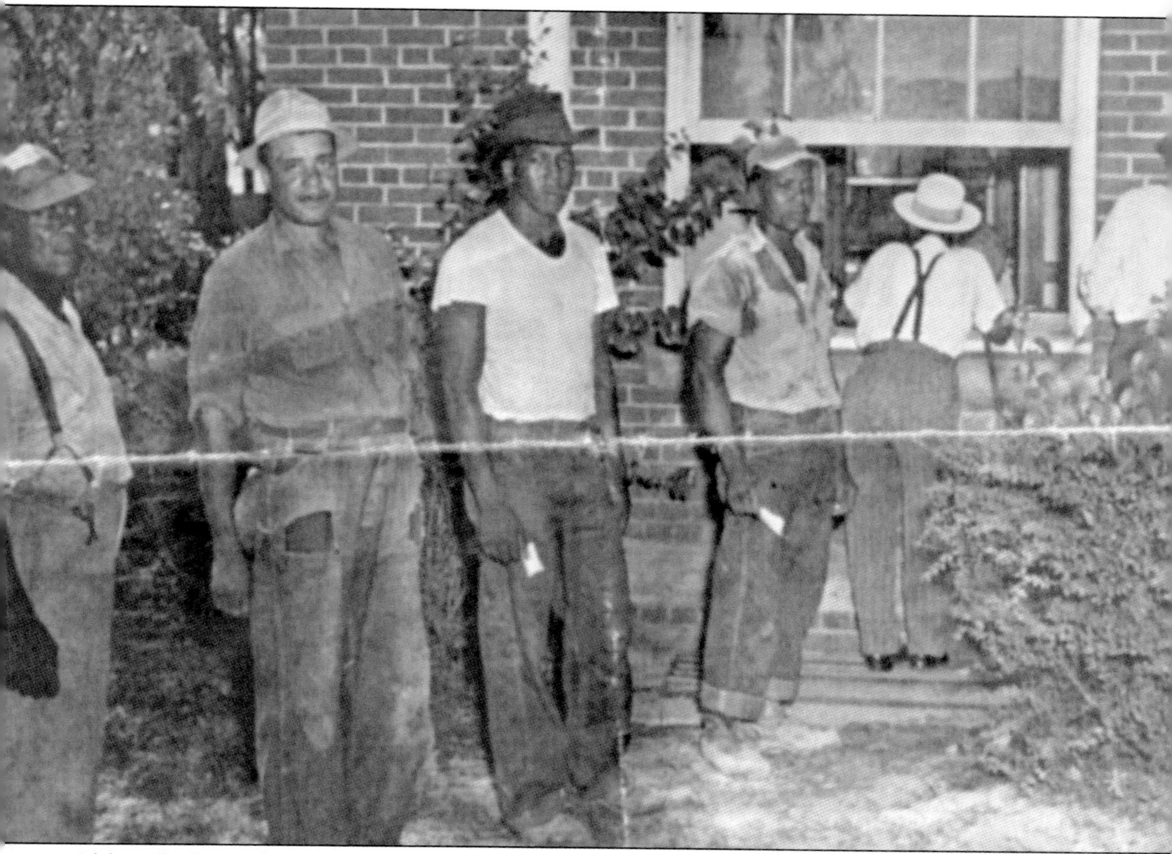

Although the 15th Amendment, ratified in 1870, gave men the right to vote regardless of race, color, or prior slave status, African American men were denied that right in some states. Between 1865 and 1869, states' enforcement of Black Codes, not to be confused with Jim Crow laws, were designed to revoke the right to vote by applying conditional criteria designed to deny civil rights. Examples of methods employed were literacy tests, suppressive election procedures, grandfather clauses, and violent intimidation. In the 1930s, interest by African Americans to vote was scant because primaries were still white only, denying the opportunity for fair representation. In this photograph, African American men wait in line to vote following the Civil Rights Act of 1957. Although these men are lined up exercising their right to vote, it is at the window of the old post office, as they were still not allowed inside of the building. (Courtesy of the University of Georgia, Richard B. Russell Library, Civil Rights, RBR-PF 736-3785.)